TRUE HUMANISM

JACQUES MARITAIN

TRUE HUMANISM

LONDON

GEOFFREY BLES

NEW YORK

CHARLES SCRIBNER'S SONS

TRANSLATED BY
M. R. ADAMSON

FIRST PUBLISHED 1938
FIFTH EDITION 1950

B
.821
.M34
(2)

PRINTED IN GREAT BRITAIN BY
BUTLER AND TANNER LTD., FROME AND LONDON

CONTENTS

CHAPTER   PAGE

FOREWORD - - - - - - - vii

INTRODUCTION: HEROISM AND HUMANISM - xi

I. THE TRAGEDY OF HUMANISM - - - - I

II. A NEW HUMANISM - - - - - 27

III. THE CHRISTIAN AND THE WORLD - - - 88

IV. THE HISTORICAL IDEAL OF A NEW CHRISTIAN ORDER - - - - - - - 121

V. THE HISTORICAL IDEAL OF A NEW CHRISTIAN ORDER (*continued*) - - - - - 156

VI. THE HISTORICAL POSSIBILITIES OF THE REALISATION OF A NEW CHRISTENDOM - - - 205

VII. THE MORE IMMEDIATE FUTURE - - - 251

APPENDIX: THE PLANES OF ACTION - - - 288

FOREWORD

This book represents the text of a series of six lectures delivered in August 1934 at the Summer School of the University of Santander; they have already appeared in Spanish under the title *Problemas espirituales y temporales de una nueva cristiandad*. I had hoped to recast them entirely in a much larger work; but time has been lacking; and, without abandoning all hope of proceeding one day to such a work, I have decided to publish the lectures in their original form, though revised and in several places enlarged. An introduction has been added, with one new chapter, and an appendix.

In the lectures I made use of various other essays,[1] where more detailed explanations will be found and deeper studies on the plane of philosophy that would be out of place here. I shall, I trust, be forgiven for quoting from these where the subject seems to require: all the more as this present work is primarily intended as a general study setting forth from a particular angle—that of the problems incident to a new realisation of Christendom—certain conclusions reached in the course of my previous studies in the philosophy of culture and society.

The questions dealt with here belong to that section of philosophy which Aristotle and St. Thomas called *Practical*, since in a general way it includes the whole philosophy of

[1] See J. Maritain, *Religion and Culture* (Eng. trans. 1931); *Freedom in the Modern World* (Eng. trans. of *Du Régime temporel et la liberté*, 1936); *Science et Sagesse*.

[vii]

human action. This is a branch of philosophy whose proper nature is nowadays commonly misunderstood: either because it is dissolved and lost to view in a philosophy that is purely speculative or because its scope and value are exaggerated in an effort to reduce the whole of philosophy to a system of knowledge in its essence directed to the transformation of the world and of our life.

Practical philosophy is still philosophy and remains a mode of speculative knowledge; but, unlike metaphysics or natural philosophy, it is from the outset directed to action as its object, and however large a part verification of fact may play in it, however much it must needs take historical necessities and conditions into account, it is above all a science of freedom.

I make no claim to speak with the authority of St. Thomas in dealing with questions whose major complexities belong to our own day: all I would claim is that I have striven to draw my inspiration and principles from the ever-living spring of his doctrine and spirit.

It is by no means easy to achieve impartiality and justice when dealing with problems that are orchestrated to the multitudinous sensibilities of human anguish and passion. At least I have tried to do my best, and can thus lay claim to the old formula, which it is the glory of French humanism to have made a commonplace, and present this book as one written 'in good faith', whose unique preoccupation is with the truth.

The world which issued from the Renaissance and the Reformation has since been torn by powerful and truly monstrous energies, where truth and error are strangely commingled and feed upon each other; by truths that lie and 'lies which speak the truth'. It is the duty of those who love wisdom to seek to purify these unnatural and destructive energies, and to rescue the truths that they have so distorted.

It would be folly indeed to try to conceal the fact that this is a peculiarly thankless task. Those who personify these energies in the world of to-day see no need for any purification; their adversaries see in them only the essence of evil. The philosopher attempts in vain to arm himself with the perfect instruments of purification and runs the risk of having everyone against him. If he is a Christian he will know that that is an old story and one to which he will pay little heed; being the disciple of a God who was hated alike by Pharisee and Sadducee, and condemned both by the chief priests and the civil power; an object of derision to the Roman soldiery.

25th April, 1936.

INTRODUCTION
HEROISM AND HUMANISM
The General Notion of Humanism

Some of us did not await the interest which has been aroused by the communist programme of *socialist humanism* to pose the problem that is inherent in the idea of humanism. Now this problem has become common talk and we may indeed be grateful for it, as matters of capital importance have been brought to the fore. Henceforward it will be impossible to speak as if the problem of Man would only begin to have significance *after* the collapse of the capitalist system.

But perhaps it has not been equally clearly seen that to adopt a definite position on this point of humanism is at once to raise many other problems.

Here, by way of introduction to the particular questions that are proposed in this book, I would like to draw attention to one of these problems. There is nothing man desires more than a heroic life: there is nothing less common to men than heroism. It is, it seems to me, a profound sense of this antinomy which gives at once its whole tragic and its whole spiritual force to the work of M. André Malraux. I imagine that this question of humanism, even in socialist terms, is not without its anxieties for M. Malraux.

Is it necessary to add that even to Aristotle it did not seem easy? To offer man, he pointed out, only what is human is to betray him and to wish him ill; for by the principal part of him which is the mind, man is called to something better than a purely human life. On this point (if not in their ways of applying it) Ramanuja and Epictetus, Nietzsche and St. John of the Cross are of one mind.

Is this comment of Aristotle's *humanist* or *anti-humanist*? The answer will depend on our conception of man. One sees immediately that the word *humanism* is ambiguous. It is clear that whoever uses the word brings into play at once an entire metaphysic, and that the idea we form of humanism will have wholly different implications according to whether we hold or do not hold that there is in the nature of man something which breathes an air outside of time and a personality whose profoundest needs surpass the order of the universe.

But since it is impossible to sever the tradition of humanism from the great wisdom of the pagans, we shall at least be on our guard against *defining* humanism by exclusion of all reference to the superhuman and by a denial of all transcendence. Leaving all these points of discussion open, let us say that humanism (and such a definition can itself be developed along very divergent lines) essentially tends to render man more truly human and to make his original greatness manifest by causing him to participate in all that can enrich him in nature and in history (by 'concentrating the world in man', as Scheler has almost said, and by 'dilating man to the world'). It at once demands that man make use of all the potentialities he holds within him, his creative powers and the life of the reason, and labour to make the powers of the physical world the instruments of his freedom.

Thus understood, humanism is inseparable from civilisation and culture, these two words being taken as themselves synonymous.

Is a heroic humanism possible?

It would seem difficult to contest the preceding remarks. Nevertheless, do not the *humanist* periods in the various cycles of culture in fact appear to be in opposition to the *heroic* periods, and show either as a decline of the latter into the human or as a turning of the human against the heroic, as a more or less general refusal of the superhuman? Is humanism only compatible with heroism, and with the creative, ascendant and truly organic moments of culture, when caught up in a historical movement where it remains hidden and unconscious; where even pain forgets itself and bears its burden in silence; where man remains unaware of himself as he offers sacrifice to something greater than he? Can humanism only become aware of itself and significant to itself, and significant also of its own postulates, in those moments of dissipation of energy, of disassociation and descent, when, to have recourse for once to the opposition between the two terms, 'culture' becomes 'civilisation', when pain opens its eyes and sees and finds its burden unendurable? Can man only come to know himself, on terms of renouncing the sacrifice of that self before something greater? Human, all too human, proliferating in that 'atomic anarchy' of which Nietzsche has spoken, is decadence in this sense a *humanist* phenomenon?

The answer is perhaps less easy than a certain facile aristocracy seems to believe. Certain forms of heroism would perhaps provide a solution of the apparent contradiction. Communist heroism claims to do so by the tension of revolution and the titanism of action, Buddhist heroism by pity and inaction. Another heroism claims to do so by love. The example of the humanist saints, the admirable Thomas More for instance, is from this point of view particularly significant. But does this example witness only to the fact that humanism and sanctity can co-exist, or also to the fact that it is possible to have a humanism fed from the heroic

[xiii]

springs of sanctity? Is there here a humanism free and conscious of itself, which leads man to sacrifice and to a greatness which is truly superhuman, because here human suffering opens its eyes and endures its pain in love,—not in the renunciation of joy, but in a greater thirst, a thirst which is already joy's exaltation? Is a heroic humanism possible?

For my part I answer, yes. And I ask myself whether it is not primarily on their answer to this question (and the grounds on which it is decided) that the various positions that men take up in face of the travail of history which is taking place before our eyes and the diverse practical decisions which they feel obliged to make, do not in fact depend.

Western Humanism and Religion

I am well aware that to some an authentic humanism can by definition only be one that is anti-religious. I hold the contrary opinion, as will be seen in the following chapters. For the moment I only wish to offer on this subject two observations.

Firstly, it is indeed true that since the dawn of the Renaissance the Western world has progressively passed from an order of dedicated and christian heroism to one of humanism. But Western humanism springs from religious and 'transcendental' sources, without which it would be incomprehensible even to itself,—(I call 'transcendental' all those forms of thought, however otherwise diverse, which find the principle of the world in a Spirit greater than man,—in man a soul whose destiny is outside time—in a natural or supernatural piety the centre of our moral life). The springs of Western humanism are classical and christian; it is not only in the mass of mediaeval antiquity, but also in the most authentic part of the heritage of pagan antiquity, that which is evoked by the names of Homer and Sophocles, of Socrates and Virgil, 'The Father of the West', that we see these characteristics of which I have spoken. Again, by the very fact that the order of mediaeval Christendom was one of a unity of soul and flesh or of incarnate Spirit, it held in its consecrated forms a virtual and implicit humanism. In the twelfth and thirteenth centuries this began to 'appear' and became manifest,—with the radiance of a premature and unstable beauty, for very soon the discord between the cultural styles of mediaevalism and classical humanism (not to mention the various disfigurations to which Christianity itself was to be subject, of which the principal ones have been Jansenism and Puritanism) was to cover and conceal for a time the profound accord between humanism and Christianity considered in their essence.

In the Middle Ages a communion in the same living faith of one individual with other real and concrete individuals and with the God they loved and the whole creation, made man amid a thousand misfortunes as fruitful in heroism as he was active in the pursuit of knowledge and the creative arts; and in the purest hearts a mighty love, exalting nature above itself, extended even to things the same fraternal piety. Thus a St. Francis understood that, before being exploited by our industry to our use, material nature demands in some way to be itself familiarised by our love: I mean that in loving things and the being in them man should rather draw things up to the human level than reduce humanity to their measure.

Again—and this is my second point—, in observing the contemporary forms of Western humanism which at the first glance seem to be at the farthest remove from any metaphysic of transcendence, it is easy to see that if a residue still subsists in common of the conceptions of human dignity, of freedom, of disinterested values, this residue is a heritage of ideas and of sentiments which once were Christian and are now no longer so. I fully appreciate that liberal-bourgeois humanism is now no more than barren wheat or than starchless bread. Against this materialised spirituality, the active materialism of atheism and paganism has the game in its hands. But, sundered from their natural roots and set in a climate of violence, it is still in part christian impulses gone astray which in fact, existentially, move the hearts of men and rouse them into action. Is it not a sign of the confusion of ideas which to-day extends over the whole world that we see such one-time christian impulses aiding the propaganda of cultural ideas which are diametrically opposed to Christianity? The time is ripe for Christians to bring things back to the fount of truth, reintegrating in the plenitude of their first origins those desires for justice and that nostalgia for communion (now so misdirected) in which the world finds comfort for its sorrow; thus raising a cultural and temporal force of christian inspiration able to act in history and come to the aid of men.

For this a sane social philosophy, a sound philosophy of modern history are necessary. Then they could work to substitute for the inhuman system which is in travail before our eyes a new form of civilisation which would be characterised by an *integral humanism*, and which would represent the outline of a new christian order no longer sacred but secular in its forms, on the lines which I have endeavoured to make clear in the studies which are collected in this volume.

This new humanism, which has in it nothing in common with bourgeois humanism, and is all the more human since it does not worship man, but has a real and effective respect for human dignity and for the rights of human personality, I see as directed towards a socio-temporal realisation of that evangelical concern for humanity which ought not to exist only in the spiritual order, but to become incarnate; and towards the ideal of a true brotherhood among men. It is not to the dynamism or the imperialism of a race, or of a class, or of a nation, that it asks men to sacrifice themselves: it is for the sake of a better life for their fellows and for the concrete good of the community of human individuals: so that the humble truth of brotherly love may advance—at the price of constant and difficult effort and of poverty—to the permeation of the social order and the structures of common life. In this way such a humanism can make man grow in communion: and in this way only can there be a humanism which is heroic.

CHAPTER I

THE TRAGEDY OF HUMANISM

The Problem before us

The problem of man will occupy our attention in this and in the following chapter.

What we are seeking to determine is, from the standpoint of a philosophy of modern history, the *practical and concrete* position of the human creature before God and his destiny, as these are characteristic of an age or a moment of culture. But this problem of the practical or ethical order is at once dominated and elucidated by a two-fold problem of the speculative order: the anthropological problem: What is man? and the theological problem of the relations between man and the supreme principle of his destiny, or, to speak in christian terms and to draw the problem to its keenest point, between grace and freedom.

I shall examine these three problems, first from the standpoint of mediaeval Christendom, then from that of modern humanism. We shall then see to what point the dialectic of humanism has brought the present age, and finally, we shall examine these same three problems from the point of view of a 'new Christendom' and a new humanism.

I

THE CHRISTENDOM OF THE MIDDLE AGES

The Problem of Man

Let us consider, then, from the standpoint of mediaeval Christendom, these three problems: the anthropological

[1]

problem, the problem of grace and freedom, and that of the concrete position of the creature before God.

For mediaeval thought (and in this it only showed that it was christian), man was not merely an animal endowed with reason, according to Aristotle's famous definition, which truly can be regarded as a 'naturally catholic' one,—and this commonplace concerning the nature of man already goes a very long way, for, in making man a spirit in his principal part it shows that he must have aspirations that go beyond our human life; and also, since this spirit is that of an animal, that man must needs be the feeblest of spirits, and that in fact he most often lives, not by his soul, but by his senses.

For mediaeval thought man was also a *person*; and one may observe that this notion of *person* carries a christian hall-mark, so to say, since it owes its evolution and its definition to theology. A person is a unity of a spiritual nature endowed with freedom of choice and so forming a whole which is independent of the world, for neither nature nor the State may invade this unity without permission. God himself, who is and who acts from within, acts there in a particular way and with a supremely exquisite delicacy, a delicacy which shows the value He sets on it: He respects this freedom, in the heart of which nevertheless He lives; He solicits it, but He never compels.

Moreover, in his actual historical existence man for mediaeval thought was never simply his natural self. He is a being out of joint and wounded,—wounded by the devil with the wound of concupiscence and by God's wound of love. On the one hand he carries the burden of original sin, he is born dispossessed of the gifts of grace, not indeed corrupted in the substance of his being, but wounded in his nature. On the other hand he is made for a supernatural end:

[2]

to see God as God beholds Himself, to reach even to the very life of God; he is traversed by the calls of actual grace, and if he does not turn against God his power of refusal, he bears within him even here below the truly divine life of sanctifying grace and of its gifts.

Hence, in point of existence, we may say that man is at once a natural and a supernatural being.

This is, in general terms, the christian conception of man; but what is important here is to note the special character which this conception took on in mediaeval thought, taken as that of a particular epoch in history. Let it be said that modes of thought which were first and foremost theological sufficed for the Middle Ages. These included a very sound psychology, but not in the modern sense of the word: for everything was regarded from the angle of the divine. The mysteries of man's nature were not studied for themselves, as a form of scientific and experimental knowledge. In short, the Middle Ages were the exact opposite of a subjective epoch: a sort of fear or metaphysical modesty, and also the predominant desire to see things and contemplate being and to take the measure of the world, kept the eyes of mediaeval man away from himself. It is a characteristic we shall find everywhere.

The Problem of Grace and Freedom

In the case, no longer of the anthropological problem, but now of the theological one of grace and freedom, it is again necessary to distinguish what belongs to general christian thought as such from what characterises in a particular way the thought of the Middle Ages.

Mediaeval theological thinking is dominated by St. Augustine, notably in the position taken up by Augustine in opposition to Pelagius. And in this the Middle Ages were purely and simply catholic and christian.

When they affirm at one and the same time the full gratuitousness, the sovereign liberty and efficacy of divine grace, *and* the reality of human free will; when they profess that God takes the first initiative in all good, that He gives both the will and the deed, that in crowning our merits He crowns His own gifts, that man alone cannot save himself, nor begin alone the work of his salvation, nor alone prepare himself for it, that by himself alone he can only fall into evil and into error,—and that nevertheless he is free when he acts under divine grace; and that, inwardly vivified by it, he freely performs good and meritorious acts; that he alone is responsible for the evil that he does and that his freedom gives him in this world a role and a power of initiative of unimaginable importance; and that God, who has created him by His independent act, does not save him without himself;—when the men of the Middle Ages professed this conception of the mystery of grace and freedom, they were professing purely and simply a conception which is christian, catholic and orthodox. At the apogee of mediaeval thought St. Thomas theologically elaborated the solutions discerned by the great contemplative intuition of St. Augustine.

Nevertheless it is not difficult to find here also that quality of which I spoke a moment ago, apropos the anthropological problem: the absence of a deliberately reflective attention turned on the creature as such.

The Middle Ages kept their eyes fixed on the luminous points revealed by St. Augustine in the mystery of grace and freedom, which is concerned with the divine depths of the mystery. The vast regions lying in shadow, concerned with its created and human depths, in particular with all that

[4]

relates to God's permission of evil acts and the production of evil by the creature, as also the whole significance and proper value, that is, in the orders of philosophy and of theology, of the temporal and secular activity of human beings: on the threshold of these regions the Middle Ages laid down boldly the principles of solution; but they advanced only a little way into that obscurity and these problems, and left much land in fallow and a whole field of complexities unexplored.

The result was that certain parasitic ideas, taking the place of the more elaborated solutions which were lacking, were able to come in and stamp a momentary and particular imprint on these eternally christian conceptions. I am thinking of a certain pessimistic imagery, a too simple dramatisation of fallen nature, and a certain too simple and also too summary image of the divine election and the bearing, if I may speak so, of the Divine personality with regard to created destinies. I am thinking also of a certain theological inhumanity in which mediaeval Catholicism,—while all the time keeping within the limits of orthodoxy these deficient elements, which (as we have seen in the sequel) tended of themselves to error,—was constantly and naturally tempted to find a justification for the weaker elements of the Augustinian synthesis. St. Thomas set all this in order, but too late for mediaeval thought to take profit from his principles and bring them to fruition.

It would be absurd to pretend that in the Middle Ages the act of self-awareness in the creature was not implicitly accomplished, in the very movement of metaphysical or theological thought towards being and towards God, and in the movement of artistic or poetic thought towards the work of creation. It was on the side of deliberate and express reflection that this self-consciousness was lacking. We find a

[5]

striking example among the mystics. The Middle Ages were rich in incomparable mystics, but if we only possessed the records which they have left, if we did not know the works of a St. Theresa, a St. John of the Cross, or a Marie de l'Incarnation, we should know little of the interior states, the trials, the night of the soul of those who entered upon that way: and we might come to the conclusion that the mediaeval mystics had no knowledge of these things. Ignorant indeed they were not; but they lived these things, they were not interested in them, and, except in the decline of the Middle Ages, in the time of Ruysbroeck and Tauler, held it of little use to speak of them.

Again the Middle Ages had a profound and eminently catholic sense of the role of the sinner, of his personal initiative, of his resistance, and of the mercy of God with regard to him, in the economy of providence. They had a profound sense of human nature, in its dignity and its weakness; they knew as no other epoch the worth of human pity and tears. But all this was rather *lived* than *known*, known in life more than in an act of reflective consciousness. And if we had regard only to the documents of their general theological tradition (I am not speaking of St. Thomas, who is much too great to be characteristic of any one period), we might conclude, and this would be an error, that mediaeval thought only knew the human creature in function of the problems of redemption and of the divine exigencies with regard to man and in function of the objective laws of morality, and not in the subjective resources of his greatness or the subjective determinism of his misery.

The practical attitude of the creature in face of his destiny

We have come to the third of the problems to be examined, that of the practical attitude of the creature with regard to his destiny. Our earlier observations will have made it clear that mediaeval man, in his response to the divine initiative, went forward in a direct and simple manner, without reflective self-consciousness, one may say (using the word in no contemptuous sense) naïvely, with only a passing glance upon himself.

The particular note of mediaeval Christendom is thus the *unconscious and unreflecting simplicity* of man's response to the effusion of Divine grace.[1]

There was in the midst of many relapses due to passion and to crime a simple movement of ascent: of the intellect towards its object, of the soul towards its perfection, of the world towards a social and juridical structure unified under the reign of Christ. With the absolute ambition, the ingenuous courage of childhood, Christendom set to work to raise an immense stronghold, at whose summit God should be enthroned. It prepared a throne for Him on earth because it loved Him. Thus all human things were stamped and ordered, protected and sealed by the sign of consecration, at least in the love that made them living. What mattered the losses, the many disasters? In the souls of the baptised a divine labour was being accomplished. Human nature was lacerated and in that fact exalted, losing itself in forgetfulness for the love of God.

The dissolution of the Middle Ages

When, however, the impulse of heroism which had borne it on was stayed, human nature, falling back upon itself, felt crushed by the weight of the world that it had built; it felt the horror of its own nothingness. Human nature can tolerate being despised, that is, accounted nothing before God, by the

[1]Cp. *Science et Sagesse*, Chap. III.

[7]

saints. It knows the saints are just. But it cannot bear to be despised by men of common clay, be they theologians or philosophers, men of the Church or of the State. And to this sense of contempt it was subject in the end of the Middle Ages, in the long agony of the fifteenth century, when the dance of death caracoled through men's minds and St. Vincent Ferrer announced the coming end of the world; while at the same time other vital formations, belonging to a wholly other and purely human type of culture, were striving to come to light. The catastrophe of the mediaeval order is thus the opening of the epoch of modern humanism. The radiating dissolution of the Middle Ages and of its *consecrated* forms represents at the same time the birth of a *secular* civilisation, one that is not indeed wholly secular, but which, as it advances, *severs itself* more and more from the Incarnation. It is still, if you like, the age of the Son of Man; but one in which men pass from the cult of the God-Man, of the Word made flesh, to that of Humanity, of man alone.

To characterise as briefly as possible the spirit of this epoch, that is of the epoch dominated by the Renaissance and the Reformation, we may say that it wished to produce an *anthropocentric rehabilitation* of the creature, whose external symbol, if we seek in religious architecture for a reflection of its soul, is the substitution of the Baroque style (beautiful as it is in itself) for Romanesque and Gothic.

II

CLASSICAL HUMANISM AND THE DUAL PROBLEM
OF MAN AND OF FREEDOM

The Protestant 'discovery'

We can see this at once in regard to the dual speculative problem; that of man, and that of grace and freedom.

[8]

Let us begin by looking at it from the angle of the 'discovery' of Protestantism. There this rehabilitation strikes us as travestied and turned exactly contrary to itself. What we see is a solution of despair. In this there lies an antinomy of rare dynamic violence, which it is most important to make clear.

If we interpret St. Augustine in material terms, by the pure light of a reason which is not truly theological but geometric, his teaching seems to annihilate the creature. As a result of original sin man is taken to be *essentially corrupt*: that is the doctrine of Luther, of Calvin, of Jansenius.

Is not this the purest pessimism? Nature is corrupted in its essence by original sin: and under grace it remains corrupt, grace being here not life, but a covering cloak. Yes, it is the purest pessimism: but there is a singular result. Human nature before sin possessed as its due all the privileges of Adam. Now this corrupt man, who can merit nothing for Heaven, and whom faith covers with Christ's grace as with a cloak, has nevertheless a value here on earth, even as he is and according to what he is, in the very corruption of his nature. Make way there for this sullied creature, since man must live in the hell which is this world!

Such is the dialectic, the tragedy of the protestant conscience, with its admirably vivid and aching sense, but too purely human, too darkly human sense of mortal misery and sin. The creature declares its nothingness. But this declaration is its own. Man is a walking corruption; but this irremediably corrupt nature cries out to God, and the initiative, do what one will, is thus man's by that cry.

The problem of grace and freedom finds a like and over simple solution. There is no free-will; it has been killed by original sin. This is the meaning, briefly stated, of the doctrines of predestination and reprobation as understood by the various schools of Protestantism: the theology of *grace without freedom.*

Calvinism gives us the best-known illustration. Everywhere we are faced with the same antinomy: man is bound down, annihilated under despotic degrees. But the predestined one is sure of salvation. Thus he is ready to outface anything here below and act as the elect of God on earth; his imperious demands (he who is soiled in his substance yet saved, forever fouled by the sin of Adam yet the elect of God) will be limitless; and material prosperity will seem to him a right due to his state.[1]

The humanist 'discovery' and the problem of freedom

Let us now examine these two problems from the standpoint of humanism.

In dealing with the problem of freedom and of grace we have need to distinguish between a modified and an absolute humanist theology.

What I have called a *modified humanist theology* is presented by Molinism. I hold myself that the celebrated Spanish theologian who, in the sixteenth century, invented a new theory of the divine prescience and of the relations between grace and the created will, has a very high significance in the history of culture. It is not my object here to examine that problem, nor to enter into the theological details of the quarrels *de auxiliis*; it is from a *cultural* point of view, from the standpoint of the philosophy of history and of civilisation, that I wish to say a word upon the matter.

[1]There are many qualifications, as has been shown, particularly by R. H. Tawney, to be made in Max Weber's theory of the origin of capitalism. But the fact remains that Calvinism (and Calvin's own doctrine of interest) played on its proper plane, and among other factors, a definite and important part.

From this point of view, whatever be the theological subtleties involved, one may say that Molinism amounts to a claim for the creature of a share, doubtless only a share, but certainly a share, in the *first* and absolute initiative in the order of goodness and salvation.

Till then the catholic Christian had thought that he had certainly the initiative and the free initiative in his good acts and in his *entirely* good acts, but an initiative that was secondary, not *primary*, God alone having the primary initiative: our good acts being *wholly* from God as their primary cause and wholly ours as their free secondary cause. Now, the Christian is to hold that there are two sides to be considered; these good and salutary acts are divided, duplicated, shared out between God and man. To each there are two sides, one belonging to God alone, one to man alone. Thus the Christian can hold that in one respect he also has a *primary* initiative in the good that he does.

Formerly, his mind was filled by a vital and spiritual idea of this mystery of the relations between his freedom and the divine freedom. God was the life of his life, not only in having given him life, but also as continually vivifying from the profoundest springs of being his created life and activity.

Now, his mind is illuminated by images of the mechanical order, by something like what will later be called the parallelogram of forces. God and man stand together at the wheel of the ship of his destiny, and so far as the direction is in his hands it is not in the hands of God.

This is then the typical man of the christian humanism of the anthropocentric epoch. He believes in God and in grace, but he disputes the ground with God; he claims his own share in the primary initiative with regard to salvation and to acts that merit eternal life; while he undertakes by himself and on his own account to look to his earthly life and happiness. Molinism may be called the theology of the christian gentleman of the classic age, as Jansenism is that of the christian magistrate of the same period. But as a sign of the times it has a quite special value. I do not know if Molina was a great theologian, but I hold that from a cultural point of view he is strongly representative of modern civilisation and the modern dissolution of Christendom.

Doctrinally considered, this modified humanist theology had in it an element of instability. Inevitably it had to give place before a purer form. So we come to what can be called *absolute humanist theology*: the theology of rationalism.

Here the formula is much more simple. Like Molinism this accepts the opposition, the so-called incompatibility, against which Protestantism had stumbled, between grace and freedom; and, like Molinism, it resolves this antinomy in a way opposite to the Protestant way: seeking to save human freedom at the expense of divine causality. But it follows this path to the end. As the pure protestant theology of grace is a theology of grace without freedom, so the pure theology or metaphysic of humanism concerning freedom is a theology or metaphysic of *freedom without grace*.

The great classical metaphysicians will none the less find great difficulty in justifying and saving by speculative means, with the principles of rationalism or absolute intellectualism, this very freedom of the human will. Leibniz and Spinoza will strive to furnish substitutes. For all of them, in the practical and ethical order, this freedom, to whatever substitute it may speculatively be reduced, is a demand and a privilege which man realises and brings to triumph by *himself alone*. Henceforth he alone is the maker of his destiny. Endowed by his science with the power to meet and subdue all necessity, he is able like a god to control the conduct of his own life and the operation of the great machine of a universe now given over to geometric determinism.

Finally, with the Hegelian conception of history, we have no longer two confronted freedoms, that of man and that of God, but a single freedom, which is man's: man in whom will come to Being the God that lies in Becoming in the world and in history.

The humanist 'discovery' and the problem of man

Let us pass on to the second speculative problem, that of man.

Here again it is necessary to distinguish between a modified and an absolute humanist theology.

The modified humanist theology is that humanism, or rather that christian naturalism, which regards grace as a simple ornament or crown of nature (of a nature which has need only of itself to be perfect in its order). Here grace renders meritorious, and colours with a sort of supernatural varnish, acts whose perfect rectitude is already sufficiently assured by the *reason* of the average honest man.

The Averroism of the Middle Ages, the Cartesian rationalism of the seventeenth century so claimed to furnish the world with a *perfect natural wisdom*, of which man considered existentially was supposed to be in fact capable, holding himself quite apart from the things of faith and of revelation, in an atmosphere remote from that of christian wisdom.

So in the practical and moral order we come to the conception, from which the political thought of Dante does not seem to have been exempt,[1] that man and human life are

[1]The good of 'civil life' or of civilisation is a final end *in a given order*, that of the temporal order or of the acquired virtues (cp. St. Thomas,

simultaneously directed to two different *absolutely final* ends, one a final end which is purely natural and is perfect prosperity here on earth, the other the supernatural final end which is perfect beatitude in heaven.

Thus, by a sagacious division of labour unforeseen by the Gospel, the Christian will be able to serve two masters at once, God for heaven and Mammon for this earth, and divide his soul between two obediences each alike ultimate and absolute, obedience to the Church for the things of heaven and to the State for the things of this world.

Here again we are face to face with a mechanical dichotomy which has taken the place of an organic subordination. The conception of man of mediaeval Christendom has been cut in twain: on one side there is the purely natural man, who has no other need than that of his reason to be perfect, wise and good and inherit the earth; and on the other, there is a celestial envelope, his *believing double*, who is assiduous at worship and who prays to the christian God, who surrounds and upholsters with the soft down of grace this purely natural man and renders him capable of gaining heaven.

When this double is stripped off, or rather, for the thing is not so simple, when it loses its identity in the subject that it covered, we are left with the purely natural man as the *theology of absolute humanism* conceives him.

Sum. theol., i-ii, q. 65, a. 2; *De Virtut. cardin.*, a. 4, ad. 3), but not *absolutely*; and by their subordination to an absolutely final end, i.e. to that of eternal life, this relatively final end and the temporal order itself are intrinsically raised to a higher level. Despite a reservation which is (very lightly) indicated in the very last lines of *De Monarchia*, it would certainly seem from the rest of its pages that Dante has treated the end of the temporal or political order as an absolutely final end (cp. Bk. III, c. 16); and the reproach of Averroism applied to him by M. Gilson would thereby seem justified.

[14]

What I have here called the theology of absolute humanism is most characteristically that of Jean-Jacques Rousseau:
the theology of natural goodness.

As we know, man according to Rousseau is not only free
of original sin and any defect of nature, he possesses in its
essence that pure goodness which renders him a participant
in the divine life and which was manifest in him in a state of
innocence. Here grace has been swallowed up by nature. The
true meaning of Rousseau's theory is that man is naturally
holy, much more holy indeed than virtuous. (Jean-Jacques at
the end of his life made no more pretence to be virtuous, but
as for goodness, he was more good than he had ever been.)
Man is holy if he is in divine union with the spirit of nature,
which will render good and right all his inclinations.

Evil comes from the constraints of education and civilisation, from reflection and artificiality. If we leave nature to
itself pure goodness will burst into flower in the radiant
epiphany of man.

The name of another great thinker must here be cited, that
of Auguste Comte. His theory of the great Being is full of
interest, in the sense that it exhibits the logical end of the
purely naturalistic idea of man. Clearly the God-Humanity
of Comte is at one and the same time the human race in its
natural and earthly reality and the Church, the mystical Body
of Christ, and Christ also and God.

Still more, Hegel, while he asks philosophy to save religion
and to this end dissolves the whole content of religion in the
supreme metaphysical enunciations of the pure reason, in
reality introduces the very movement of the Redemption
into the dialectic of history, and in fact makes of the State the
mystical body through which man attains to the liberty of
the sons of God.

Whether we turn to Rousseau, to Comte, or to Hegel, we find that, while for these great representatives of the modern age, on the one hand man is regarded in his existential condition as a *purely natural* being, who is exhibited as detached from any connection with a supernatural order introducing the ideas of original sin and of grace; nevertheless, he cannot be thought of as purely natural, so potent are these connections in his being. They claim to deal with a being in a condition or state of pure nature, and into this purely natural man are poured all the aspirations and all the appeals to a life truly divine,—*ego dixi: dii estis,*—which for the Christian spring from the grace of God.

The result is that man, separated from God, claims and demands everything for himself as if it were all due to him; as if he were (as indeed he is, but precisely on condition that he does *not* make himself his own centre), the heir of God.

III

CLASSICAL HUMANISM AND THE PRACTICAL ATTITUDE OF THE CREATURE IN FACE OF HIS DESTINY

The Flaw in Classical Humanism is not that it is humanist, but that it is anthropocentric

We have now come to our third problem, the problem of the practical attitude of the creature in face of his destiny.

What was this attitude in the epoch which followed the Renaissance and the Reformation? A remarkable confluence can be seen of the two pessimistic and optimistic attitudes which we have just observed, and the logical prevalence of the latter.

By an unforeseen turn of dialectic the ultra-pessimist conception of human nature held by Calvin and Jansenius resulted also in an anthropocentric position.

In effect this pessimism cut every connection between the

[16]

creature and a higher order. Then, *since the good life is a necessity*, the creature takes things easy and becomes himself the centre of his own lower world. This phenomenon becomes obvious even in the religious sphere in the liberal Protestantism of the nineteenth century.

As to the practical attitude of the men of the Renaissance, it was at first far from any conscious rupture with Christianity. As the pessimism of the Reformers unduly exaggerated the christian concept of original sin, so the optimism of the Renaissance unduly exaggerated an equally christian but opposite concept, that of the value of the human being who is the living image of God. The Renaissance sense of abounding life, that joy in the comprehension of the world and in freedom, the impetus towards scientific discovery, its creative rapture and delight in the beauty of sensible forms reveal an inextricable mingling of natural and christian sources. It was as though an ecstasy of well-being seized on men. They turned to the documents of pagan antiquity with a fever the pagans had never known: they believed themselves capable of grasping the very totality of their own being and of life, without any effort of interior renunciation. They desired joy without asceticism: as though they would bring forth fruits without pruning the tree, without their sap being vivified by the Spirit whose grace and whose gifts alone can render the life of man divine. Here again everything was to issue in the secession to anthropocentricism.

Thus, in general, the effort of this age of culture tended towards that rehabilitation of the creature of which I have spoken, but towards a rehabilitation of the creature turned back upon itself and cut off so to say from the transcendent principle of its life.

[17]

'In the Renaissance it was the cry of the creature's greatness and beauty, in the Reformation of its misery and distress, that went up to heaven. In every way, either in tears or in revolt, the creature cried out for rehabilitation. Now, considered in itself, apart from the erroneous forms it followed, what is the significance of this demand? The creature was claiming the right of being loved.

'Is it possible that God, whose love, in the words of St. Thomas, infuses and creates the goodness in all things, could have made the creature without making it worthy of being loved? I do not say, of being preferred. . . . Considered in this purely formal fashion, such a demand was in conformity with the laws of historical development.

'Thus a certain divine exigence torments the modern world. One may call it an awareness, a certain practical discovery of the proper dignity which is hidden in the mystery of human being.'[1]

Much progress has thus been made, above all in the world of reflection and self-consciousness, revealing often by lowly means, in science, in art, in poetry, in the very passions and even the vices of man, his proper spirituality. Science has undertaken the conquest of created nature, the human soul has made a universe of its subjectivity, the secular world has been differentiated according to its own proper law, the creature has come to know itself. And such progress taken in itself was entirely normal.

The misfortune of modern history has been that all this progress has been directed by a spirit of anthropocentricism, by a naturalistic conception of man, and a calvinist or molinist conception of grace and freedom. Finally it has been accomplished under the sign, not of unity, but of division.

[1]J. Maritain, *Science et Sagesse*, ch. iii.

And so we have been instructed by an experience of suffering and catastrophe; and the incontestable enrichments of civilisation have given entrance to the interior torture chamber of man become a prey unto himself.

Man, forgetting that in the order of being and of goodness it is God who has the first initiative and who gives life to our freedom, has sought to exalt his own proper movement as creature to the dignity of the first absolute movement and to attribute to his own created freedom the first initiative towards goodness. Thus his movement of ascension has necessarily been separated from that of grace, and this is why the age in question has been an age of dualism, of division, of disintegration, an age of humanism apart from the Incarnation, where the effort of progress must needs follow an inevitable course and itself contribute to the destruction of what is human.

In short, we may say that the radical fault of anthropocentric humanism has been its anthropocentric quality, not its humanism.

Theocentric and Anthropocentric Humanism

We are thus led to distinguish between two kinds of humanism: a humanism which is theocentric or truly christian; and one which is anthropocentric, for which the spirit of the Renaissance and that of the Reformation were primarily responsible, of which we have just been speaking.

The first kind of humanism recognises that the centre for man is God; it implies the christian conception of man as at once a sinner and redeemed, and the christian conception of grace and freedom, whose principles we have already called to mind. The second kind of humanism believes that man is his own centre, and therefore the centre of all things. It implies a naturalistic conception of man and of freedom.

[19]

If this conception is false, it is easy to see that anthropocentric humanism merits the name of inhuman humanism, and that its dialectic must needs be regarded as the *tragedy of humanism*. It is about this dialectic that I wish to say a few words in the last part of this chapter: considering it from three differing points of view; as it is concerned with man himself, with culture, and finally with the idea man fashions for himself of God.

IV

THE DIALECTIC OF ANTHROPOCENTRIC HUMANISM

The Tragedy of Man

In the case of man it is observable that in the beginnings of the modern age, first with Descartes, then with Rousseau and Kant, rationalism had set up a proud and splendid image of the *personality* of man, inviolable, jealous of his immanence and his autonomy, and, finally, good in essence. It is in the name of the rights and autonomy of this personality that the polemic of rationalism had condemned any intervention from outside in this perfect and sacred universe,— whether such intervention comes from revelation and grace or from the tradition of human wisdom, the authority of a law of which man is not the author, or of a sovereign good which solicits his will, or finally of an objective reality which would measure and regulate his intelligence.

Yet, in little more than a century, this proud anthropocentric personality has perished, and been involved in rapid ruin through the dispersion of its material elements.

We can mark a first significant moment in this process in the world of biology, with the triumph of the Darwinian ideas of man's simian origin. Man, in this view, is seen not only as emerging from a long-drawn evolution of animal

[20]

species (that is a purely historical and, after all, secondary question), but as issuing from this biological evolution *without any metaphysical discontinuity*, without at a given moment, with the coming of human being, anything absolutely new appearing in the series: spiritual subsistence implying that in each generation of a human being an individual soul is created by the Author of all things and cast into existence with an eternal destiny.

The christian idea of man and of human personality which is founded on revealed dogma was in no way imperilled by Darwinism; but the rationalist conception of human personality received a mortal blow.

The second blow, the *coup de grâce* so to speak, was delivered in the domain of psychology and by Freud (I am not referring to Freud's methods of psychological investigation, which include discoveries of genius, but to his metaphysic). The Christian knows that the heart of man, as Pascal said, is hollow and full of evil, but that does not prevent his recognising man's greatness and spiritual dignity. But, for the thought of rationalism and naturalism, what has man become in our day? The centre of gravity of the human being has sunk so low that we have, rightly speaking, no longer any personality, only the fatal to and fro of the polymorphic larvae of the subterranean world of instinct and desire,— *Acheronta movebo*, Freud himself says,—and the whole well-regulated dignity of our personal consciousness appears only as a lying mask. In fine, man is but the place of intersection and of conflict of a primarily sexual *libido* and a desire for death. That mystery of dolour and of divine life, which bears the stamp of the Creator's image, has become a despairing enigma of the complications of death. Man, who in the beginning was made at once a purely natural being and a

[21]

heroic, quasi-divine figure, has fallen, by the law which rules all paganism, into an unnatural mockery of his own nature, which he scourges all the more cruelly in the degree to which he cherishes it with complaisance and a sentimental pity. He has been thrown into disorder and become a monster, dear to himself.

After all the disassociation and dualism of the age of anthropocentric humanism,—the separation and opposition between nature and grace, between faith and reason, between love and knowledge, between the affective life of love and the senses,—we are now witnessing a dispersion, a decomposition which is final. It does not in the least prevent human being from claiming its own sovereignty more than ever. But this is no longer in the name of the single personality; that we know not where to find, it has vanished in disassociated, disintegrating fragments. It is ready to abdicate (yet what a renewal if it refuses and there where it will refuse to abdicate!), ready to abdicate in favour of the collective man, of that great historical image of humanity, for which Hegel built up the theology and which for him bears the name of the State with its perfected juridical structure, and for Karl Marx of the Communist Society with its immanent dynamism.

The Tragedy of Culture

Let us now look at these things from the point of view of *culture*. What, from this standpoint, has been the dialectic of anthropocentric humanism?

Three aspects or 'moments' which are inseparably linked can be distinguished in what might be called the dialectic of modern culture.

These three moments are in continuity one with another,

despite violent secondary oppositions; they have followed one another in time; but they also co-exist, mixing one with another in varying degrees. Elsewhere I have already endeavoured to characterise them.[1]

In the first (sixteenth-seventeenth centuries), when civilisation was prodigal of its fairest fruits, forgetful of the roots whence the vital sap is drawn, it was thought that civilisation should inaugurate solely by force of reason a certain human order, which was still conceived in the christian style inherited from previous ages; a style which became cramped and began to deteriorate. This may be called the *classical* moment of our culture, the time of christian naturalism.

In the second (eighteenth-nineteenth centuries), it was seen that a culture held apart from the supreme supernatural dimensions must needs take arms against these. Civilisation was called upon to liberate man from the superstitions of revealed religion, and to open out before his natural goodness perspectives of perfect security, due to the desire of riches accumulating all the goods of the earth. This is the moment of rationalist optimism, the *bourgeois* hour of our culture. Hardly yet are we clear of it.

The third moment (twentieth century) is that of the materialist reversal of all values, the *revolutionary* moment, where man, definitely setting his last end in himself, and unable longer to endure the machine of the world, engages in a desperate effort out of a radical atheism to bring a wholly new humanity.

Let us consider rather more closely the character of these three moments.

The first is seen to be a reversal of the order of ends. Instead of culture directing its proper good, i.e. earthly happi- .

[1] J. Maritain, *Religion et Culture; Du Régime temporel et de la liberté*

[23]

ness, towards eternal life, its supreme end is sought in itself, in the domination of man over matter. God becomes the guarantor of this domination.

The second moment is like a demiurgic imperialism with regard to the forces of matter. Failing to understand that the effort to perfect man's nature by a process in itself in conformity with the profoundest exigencies of his being, i.e. by the interior perfection of a wisdom which penetrates both knowledge and life, should always be man's prime endeavour, the chief aim of culture comes to be a mastery over external nature and an endeavour to rule it by means of technical processes,—an end in itself good, but which is here made primary and so expected to create, thanks to physico-mathematical science, a material world in which, according to the promises of Descartes, man will find a perfect felicity. God becomes an idea.

The third moment is the progressive forcing back of the human by the material. In order to rule over the natural order without taking into account the basic laws of *his* nature, man in his intellect and his life is in reality constrained to subordinate himself more and more to necessities which are no more human, but technical; to those material energies which he has himself set in action and which invade the very world of his own humanity. God dies, for man so materialised holds that he can only be in fact man or superman if God is not God.

Whatever may be the possible gains from other points of view, the condition of human life thus becomes increasingly inhuman. If things continue on these lines the world it seems, in the words of Aristotle, will become habitable only by beasts or by gods.

[24]

So we come to consider the dialectic of this anthropocentric humanism in relation to God, or rather the idea that men form of God. It is significant that this idea, in the exact degree to which it is not supported and purified by revelation, follows the same path as that of culture. I said that in the first moment of the dialectic of humanism God becomes the guarantor of man's domination over matter. This is the God of Cartesianism. The divine transcendence is still maintained, but in human terms, by a univocal, geometric reasoning, which is incapable of rising to analogical understanding. Hence this transcendence begins to be in jeopardy.

Though Jansenius, at the other extreme from rationalism, was already affirming the inscrutable transcendence of the divine Majesty, it was in the sense that this affirmation crushed and shattered reason. Reason could only acknowledge transcendence by sacrificing itself before it. Why? Because the reason of the theologians of the classic age had lost the sense of analogy and become the reason of Geometry, the enemy of all mystery, like the reason of the philosophers of the same age. Reason might recognise the existence of mystery and destroy itself, or it might refuse to destroy itself and so deny mystery.

For Descartes God is the guarantor of science and the geometric reason and his idea is the clear idea. Nevertheless the divine infinite is declared to be absolutely inscrutable, we are blind to it, so that a germ of agnosticism is already present in Cartesian rationalism. God acts by a pure plenitude of efficiency, without ordering things to an end, and His despotic Freedom rules good and evil as acts of His mere good pleasure, just as He can, if He will, create square circles and hills without valleys.

Despite his polemic against anthropomorphism, Malebranche will picture the glory of God (that most mysterious of all conceptions, which relates to the depths of uncreated love) as that of a monarch or an artist glorified by his works and causing his own very perfections to be admired in them. Leibniz also wants the perfections of the divine artisan to be judged according to the measure of the perfection of his work (which in that case ought also to be divine), and he will undertake to justify God in showing how the ways of God are in accord with the reason of the philosophers.

I have said that in the second moment of this dialectic God becomes an idea. This is the God of the great metaphysical idealists. Here the divine transcendence is rejected; a philosophy of immanence has taken its place. With Hegel God appears as the ideal limit set to the development of the world and of humanity.

Finally, at the third moment of the dialectic of humanism, it is the *death of God* that Nietzsche will feel it his terrible mission to announce. How indeed could God still live in a world from which his image, i.e. the free and spiritual personality of man, is fading away. The most representative expression of this third stage of the dialectic of anthropocentric humanism is to be seen in contemporary Russian atheism. At the end of this historic and secular evolution we thus find ourselves face to face with two absolute or *pure positions*: *pure atheism* and *pure Christianity*.

CHAPTER II

A NEW HUMANISM

I have said that at the end of the dialectic of anthropocentric humanism we find before us two pure positions: atheism and Christianity.

In the first part of this chapter I wish to speak of these two positions, and in particular to examine certain important problems which are bound up with the former. In the second part we come at length to those questions which concern not the Middle Ages and not the modern epoch, but the new age of Christendom whose character and features the typical changes which have taken place in the twentieth century call upon us to envisage.

I

THE ROOTS OF THE ATHEISM OF THE SOVIETS

The 'Religious' Significance of Communism

I wish to deal at some length with the problems concerned with atheism as a historical force, and shall consider it in its expressly atheistic form, of which recent years have in Russian communism furnished us a typical example (not that the pseudo-religious or pseudo-christian forms of atheism are any less perfidious: as a study of the doctrine of racialism will easily show). I wish, first of all, to inquire what are the deeper reasons for contemporary Russian atheism; then to examine the philosophical problem set by this atheism; finally, to consider its cultural significance.

[27]

It is often asked why the social solutions of communism, which are concerned with labour organisation and the secular community, cannot be taken apart from atheism, which has to do with religion and metaphysics.

The answer, I hold, is that, considered in its essence and its principles, communism as it exists,—above all the communism of the Soviet republics,—is a complete system of doctrine and life which claims to reveal to man the meaning of his existence, to answer all the fundamental questions which are set by life, and which manifests an unequalled power of totalitarian inclusiveness. It is a religion, and one of the most imperious quality: certain that it is called to replace all other religions; a religion of atheism, for which dialectic materialism supplies the dogma, and of which communism as a rule of life is the social and ethical expression. This atheism is not a necessary *consequence* of the social system (which would be incomprehensible), but on the contrary is presupposed as the very *principle* of the latter. It is the starting point.[1]

[1]Historically atheism is also at the starting point of Marx's own thought. Marx was an atheist before he was a communist. More, it was the *idée-mère* of the atheism of Feuerbach which, transferred from the sphere of religious to that of social criticism, determined Marx's adherence to communism. M. August Cornu has admirably shown (*Karl Marx, de l'hegelianisme au matérialisme historique*, Paris, Alcan, 1934) that the origin of Marx's communism was not economic, as it was in the case of Engels, but philosophical and metaphysical: man is alienated from himself and his work by private property as he is alienated from himself by the idea of God into which he projects his own essence, and by religion. At first Marx, following Feuerbach, conceived this alienation due to private property on the lines of the alienation due to religion; and next, in a second stage, he was led, in contradistinction to Feuerbach, to regard it as in fact primary and conditioning the former (historical materialism); it is from this alienation by private property that the alienation of man from himself by God takes its rise. It is necessary to bring this alienation from his work to an end (communism); after that follows as a corollary

[28]

This is why communist thought holds to it so ardently, as the principle which stabilises its practical conclusions and without which these would lose both their necessity and their value.[1]

the cessation of the other alienation (atheism). 'By the abolition of private property and the suppression of all such alienation, communism will mark the return of man to human life; and as this alienation exists at once in the spheres of consciousness and of concrete life, the social and economic emancipation of communism will have as its necessary corollary the religious emancipation of atheism.' (A. Cornu, *op. cit.*, p. 339, following the 1844 MS. of *Political Economy and Philosophy*.) In reality historical materialism and communism, in the sense that Marx conceived it in the very instant in which he devoted to it his thought and his heart, have themselves their roots in the atheism of Feuerbach.

[1]The objection has been raised on the communist side (by Georges Sadoul in *Commune*, Dec. 1935) that Marxism is no doubt 'entirely and totally atheistic', but that atheism is a consequence in it, not a starting point: the consequence, that is to say, of 'the recognition of the fact of the class-war'. It is not easy to see how from the recognition of the fact of the class-war one passes on to the conclusion that God does not exist. Doubtless hatred of the class-enemy can by association of ideas produce a detestation of his religion as of every other sign of his existence. But our inquiry is concerned with a sequence in the order of philosophy not in the nervous or digestive organs.

Does religion diminish the combative efficiency of the proletariat? Even if this were true (in the sense that true religion in effect produces obstacles to hatred, and may thus reduce combative efficiency), there is still a very considerable distance between that assertion and that of the non-existence of God. If they are bound up together in the mind of a thinker like Marx it is because he set out, as is indeed admitted, from 'the materialist conception of the world'. This certainly prevented him from making the struggle against religion the first article of his social programme (since on the contrary in his eyes the disappearance of the regime of private property brought in its train that of religion); but that is not the point of interest. Our question is whether atheism is not at the root of the very materialist conception of the world itself. And the answer to this seems to me to be clear, if only we take this conception as we find it in Marx (that it can be subjected to certain purifications is another matter) and if we understand the part played by metaphysics in

[29]

The particular point which I wish to examine is how this atheism is built up in principle and what is its logical connection with a particular social conception. A difficulty at once presents itself, which by its nature would seem to bar inquiry at the outset: regarded simply from a psychological standpoint and looking at the frame of mind of communists, particularly in France, at this actual moment (1935-1936) one has the impression that if many of them have received with satisfaction the new rulings of the party with regard to collaboration with believers it is, in precise contradiction to what I have been advancing, because communism has in their eyes no metaphysical or religious significance at all, but simply implies a form of economico-social ethics, that it is simply a technique for the transformation of the economic regime, which stands to them for their only faith. If then they can now draw to this faith those 'separated brethren' whom the discipline of their party hitherto had obliged them *a priori* to avoid, as Christians, it is natural that they should feel a kind of joy and exaltation; for they have there a promise of apostolic expansion and a release for the natural desire of human communication and comradeship.

Such is, I believe, the reality in the feelings, sincerely felt although bound under obedience, experienced to-day by a certain number of young communists. But when they interrogate themselves, do not these men find that at the same time, as if not to embarrass this enthusiasm, certain fundamental things are left in shadow, by a sort of involuntary censorship which retards or inhibits awareness? In particular it

the origin of systems which in the end decide against metaphysics. For the rest we shall be glad if this question is examined also on the communist side. It may perhaps lead some to ponder on the worth of their own atheism.

would seem that they do not elicit, in order to bring it into the full light of day, the problems of philosophy which underlie their revolutionary faith, and which that faith presumes resolved. The fact is that their atheism has become so total and so unconditioned, so detached from the conditions of its origin, that in their eyes it is a matter of course, like a truth *a per se nota* or a fact of experience. They are established on the ground of atheism as if it were the only one on which it is possible to build, and as if a certain philosophical journey were not required to reach that terrain itself. In short, neither in atheism nor in the materialist conception of the world do they find any problem: which is why they have no awareness of the metaphysical process which is logically implied in these positions.

This very fact confirms the assertion that faith in the communist revolution in reality presupposes a whole universe of faith and religious values in which that faith is set up. But this universe is so natural to them that they take no trouble to notice it for themselves. And more, this religion and this faith do not seem to them a religion, because they are atheists; nor a faith, because they regard it as an expression of science. Thus they have no sense that communism is for them a religion, and nevertheless in reality it is one. The perfect religious prays so well that he knows not that he prays. Communism is so profoundly, so substantially a religion,— an earthly one—that the communist does not know that it is a religion.

That this religion, although by nature as intolerant as all strongly dogmatic religions (to render tolerant a strongly dogmatic religion needs supernatural charity), should now appeal in terms of common social action to the faithful of other religions, whose final end is in heaven, and that it should contemplate the possibility of a real recognition of their freedom in the temporal city (in France, if not in Russia), is a paradoxical psychological fact which it is proper to take into account; one which, considered in itself, whatever one may think of the tactics and the political machiavellianism which have produced it, has an incontestable human significance. A precarious one, we may well fear; the precariousness of these good dispositions is all the greater in fact in the degree to which one has to do with a religion entirely and totally directed towards exclusively earthly ends, and the least deviation or opposition with regard to the 'general lines' defined in relation to its aim hurts it to the quick and moves its faithful followers to the defence of the things they hold sacred. It is in the logic of things that one day or another a hatred, a religious vindictiveness will be wakened against the faithful of other religions, as generally happens in the case of all political non-conformists, if only in the least degree they refuse to conform.

But it is not these questions of concrete psychology which are under examination here. It is the content and the texture of the doctrines themselves. It is from a view of the content of these doctrines, taken in themselves and in their inward structure, that I claim that communism springs, as from a first principle, from atheistic and antireligious thought: and it is the roots and the development of this atheism, of this opposition to religion, we have to consider.

A further definition is important. Among the original elements of communism there are some which are also christian. St. Thomas More held certain communist ideas. Communism in its earliest phases was not always atheist. The very idea of communion, which gives communism its spiritual drive, and which it seeks to realise in terms of our social and earthly life (as indeed it ought, but not exclusively there nor so as to ruin the life wherein it is realised in its perfection and in accord with the highest aspirations of human personality), the idea of communion is of christian origin. And it is the misdirected christian virtues, those 'virtues gone mad' of which G. K. Chesterton spoke, the spirit of faith and of sacrifice, it is these religious energies of the human soul, which communism seeks to divert to its own uses, it is of these things that it has need for its very existence.

The Sense of Resentment against the Christian World

But the essential and typical point is that communist thought, as it was built up in the latter half of the nineteenth century and as it is to-day, has turned these energies of Christian origin to the service of an atheist ideology whose whole intellectual structure is turned against christian beliefs. What is the cause of this? It is, I hold, because it originates, chiefly through the fault of a christian world unfaithful to its own principles, in a profound sense of resentment, not only against the christian world, but—and here lies the tragedy—against Christianity itself, which transcends the christian world and should not be confounded with it, and against every conception, even remotely savouring of what I may call the natural platonism of our minds. I hasten to add (since in all else I am no platonist) that this platonism is reducible to what Plato was able to bring forth from a universally human ground. If I speak here of a platonism which is native to our minds, it is only in the degree to which we are naturally inclined to admit the existence of eternal truths and transcendental values.

I have just said that the christian world is other than Christianity. It is essential to have a clear grasp of this distinction.

[33]

The word *Christianity*, like the words *the Church*, has a religious and spiritual significance; it denotes faith and supernatural life.[1] By the phrase *the christian world*, on the other hand, I mean something in time and belonging to this world, related to the order, not of religion itself, but of culture and civilisation. It is a particular grouping of political, cultural and social formations characteristic of a given age of history, whose typical spirit is principally due to the social elements which play in it a ruling and preponderant part, e.g. the clergy and nobility in the Middle Ages, royalty and aristocracy under the *ancien régime*, the bourgeoisie in modern times. A philosopher of culture who raises the question of the christian world is not raising the issue of the truth of *Christianity*, but of the *temporal responsibilities of Christians*.

The christian world has a temporal task, an earthly task to fulfil: an earthly task, since a civilisation, as civilisation, is directly ordered to a specific *temporal* end; an earthly *christian* task, since by hypothesis this civilisation is a christian one, since the world which is in question has received the light of the Gospel. This temporal task of the christian world is to work here on earth for a realisation in social and temporal terms of the truths of the Gospel: for if the Gospel is primarily concerned with the things of eternal life, and infinitely

[1]The words *the Church* denote 'the Mystical Body of Christ', at once visible in its social configuration and divine in its soul, whose proper life belongs to the supernatural order. The 'temporal christian world' may introduce, not indeed into the heart of the Church, but into the more or less extended parts of its human structure, impurities arising from the spirit of this world: the intoxication of magnificence and *virtu* in the time of the Renaissance, the spirit of bourgeoisie in the nineteenth century. Then, since the 'Gates of Hell' cannot prevail against her, there are purifications. The saints had been crying out in vain for a reform of the Church three centuries before the coming of the great tempest of Lutheranism.

[34]

transcends all sociology as it does all philosophy,nevertheless it gives us sovereign rules of conduct for our lives, and traces a very clear chart of moral behaviour, to which any christian civilisation, in so far as it is worthy of the name, should tend to conform, according to the diverse conditions of history, and its socio-temporal structure. A socio-temporal realisation of the truths of the Gospel; how mocking the words appear when we think of the temporal structures of modern centuries, particularly of the nineteenth century!

When we meditate on these things, we are driven to say that the christian world of modern times has failed in this duty of which we have been speaking. In general it has shut up the truth and its divine life in a limited section of its existence,—in the particular sphere of religious observance and, at least with the best men and women, in the interior life. The matters of social, of political and economic life it has abandoned to their own secular law; depriving them of the light of Christ;—Marx, for instance, 'is entirely right when he says that capitalist society is a state of anarchy,where life is entirely given over to the play of particular interests. Nothing could be more contrary to the spirit of Christianity.'[1]

Hence that *resentment* of which I spoke: resentment against those who have failed to realise the truth of which they were the bearers, a resentment which has reacted against that truth itself.

The First Stage of the Process of Substitution: The Rehabilitation of Material Causality

What has resulted in consequence is a process of *substitution*. This process has primarily been the work of Marxism: and in it several stages can be seen.

In the first place, the particular task of Marxism as a doc-

[1] N. Berdyaev.

[35]

trine of *resentment* has been, as it has been said, the denunciation of 'the lie of exalted ideas'. It claims to go on to a radical sentence on idealism,—as a metaphysical doctrine (which leaves us few regrets) and also as a simple affirmation (which is quite a different matter) of the value of the immaterial in general. In short, Marxism is an *absolute realist immanentism*; and this huge ideological proliferation of resentment and indignation could never have been but for Hegel.

In one sense Marx is the most consistent hegelian of them all; for if 'all that is rational is real' and if historical reality, in other words, existence in time, entirely and absolutely absorbs, because identical with it, the whole 'ideal' order which was hitherto regarded as extra-temporal, and is henceforth confused with the logical being of our thought and its characteristic movement, then the reversal to which Marx, following in the steps of Feuerbach, subjected the hegelian dialectic is justified. Again, just as philosophy must 'become practical,—not in Aristotle's meaning of the phrase, but in the sense that speculative philosophy must give way to a form of thought which is wholly occupied with *praxis*, and is by its very essence an activity that goes to the transformation of the world',[1] so also the movement of dialectic must henceforward be entirely absorbed in the 'material', i.e. in historical reality, entirely cut off from any transcendental elements,

[1]'The question of knowing whether human thought can attain to objective truth is not a theoretic, but a practical question. It is in *praxis* that a man should demonstrate the truth, i.e. the reality, the power, the precision of his thought. The controversy as to the reality or non-reality of thought isolated from *praxis* is a purely scholastic question. Hitherto philosophers have only given different interpretations of the world; what matters is to transform it' (*Second and Eleventh Theses on Feuerbach*). 'As soon as reality', i.e. practical activity, 'is properly explained, autonomous philosophy loses its means of existence' (*Die deutsche Ideologie*).

and considered above all in relation to its primordial concrete substructures.

Hence it is obvious that Marx's materialism is of no common kind, neither that of the eighteenth-century French materialists nor mechanist materialism. But, in the eyes of a metaphysician, its wholly hegelian quality and its blend of pure immanentism, only make it more real and more profound. To understand the bearing of this materialism we must have recourse, as I pointed out before with regard to Georges Sorel, to the aristotelian distinction between formal and material causality. The absurdity of the idealist or 'angel-minded'[1] misunderstanding of material causality led by reaction to a return to this, which was justified in its origin but was equally untenable in its result: for these two causalities must be taken *together* as a principle of explanation. Using aristotelian terms, we may say that Marxism springs from a perception, in some sense reactionary, of the importance of *material causality*, i.e. of the importance of the part played by material factors in the course of nature and of history. This material causality is brought to the forefront and integrated with the dialectic process and becomes the source of all activity.

What, then, represents this material causality in the social and historical orders? The processes of human activity in the economic order. No Aristotelian will contest the fact that these have an essential importance; but Marx makes them play the principal role and gives them a decisive influence.

Marx saw the essential importance of material causality, but he made it purely and simply primary.

[1] For an exposition of the theory that cartesian idealism postulates the mental attitude of an angel or 'angelicism', see J. Maritain's study of Descartes in his *Three Reformers* (Trans.).

[37]

I am well aware that there is ample scope for revision in the current interpretation of historical materialism, according to which everything—all 'ideologies', spiritual life, religious beliefs, philosophy, the arts, etc.—are mere epiphenomena of economics. This is the popular interpretation of Marxism and is far from negligible, for, having become the opinion of a large number of people, it is now one of the forces to be reckoned with in history. But Marx himself saw deeper into the matter; and just as one can speak of first 'spiritual' impulse in his thought (i.e. indignation at man's condition oppressed by the things born of his own work and himself degraded to the level of *a thing*) so one may say that, despite certain formulas, he always believed in a reciprocal action between economic and other factors[1]: economics taken alone were not for him the sole spring of history.

Yet, on deeper reflection and more careful examination, we see that the denial of the metaphysical primacy of act over potency, and of form over matter, and hence the denial of the proper autonomy of spiritual energies, that this double denial which is the distinguishing characteristic of metaphysical materialism is inevitably bound up, as I suggested above, with Marx's radical realist immanentism.[2]

On the one hand, if Marx had a profound intuition, an

[1] The following passage from Engel's letter (21st September, 1890) is frequently and rightly cited: 'Marx and I must bear the responsibility for the fact that so often the young attach more weight than its due to the economic aspect. In the face of our adversaries it was necessary to underline the essential principle which they denied, and since we have never found the time, the space or the occasion, to do justice to other factors which participate in a reciprocal action.'

[2] Hegel's immanentism is already a form of virtual materialism, which is only masked by his idealism.

intuition which is to my eyes the great lightning-flash of truth which traverses all his work, of the conditions of heteronomy and loss of freedom produced in a capitalist world by wage-slavery, and of the dehumanisation with which the possessing classes and the proletariat alike are thereby simultaneously stricken, in effect he immediately conceptualised this in an anthropocentric and monist metaphysic,[1] where hypostasised work becomes man's very essence and, in the recovery of that essence through the transformation of society, man is called to take on the attributes with which the 'illusion' of religion had endowed the Deity.[2] Thus, if economic servitude and the inhuman conditions of the proletariat are to cease, it is not in the name of human personality, —whose dignity is in reality at bottom spiritual, and has such imperious exigencies in relation to economic conditions only because it is grounded in transcendent rights and interests— it is in the name of the collective man, in order that in collective life and in the free disposition of his collective work, he may discover an absolute enfranchisement (strictly speaking, a state of *aseitas*)[3]: and in a word deify in himself the titanism of human nature.

[1]Cp. the study by Paul Vignaux, 'Retour à Marx' (*Politique*, November 1935). The task of a christian critique of Marx would be to divest this intuition of the philosophical errors which underlie Marx's conceptualisation. Such a task is all the more necessary, seeing that, whatever personal aversion Marx himself may have had for Christianity, this intuition is pregnant with judeo-christian values.

[2]There is a similar ambiguity, and for similar reasons, on the economic plane. Marx saw that the capitalist system in fact lived on the unnatural principle of the fecundity of money; he countered this view with an inexact and 'monist' theory of value and profit.

[3]'Communism, ... being an achieved naturalism, ... is the real end of the quarrel between man and nature and between man and man, the *true end of the quarrel between existence and essence*, between objective and

On the other hand, if the economic factor taken by itself is not for Marx the sole spring of history, the fact remains that, since the essential dynamism of evolution springs for him from economic contradictions and social antagonisms engendered by the system of production, it is the economic factor which plays the *significant* and primarily determining role[1] with regard to the various superstructures which come into reciprocal action with it.[2] How indeed could it be otherwise from the moment that, together with transcendence in

subjective, between liberty and necessity, between the individual and the species. It solves the riddle of history and it knows that it solves it.'

The 'veritable end of the quarrel between existence and essence' is *aseitas*, the perfection of an essence which is the very act of its existence. When I use this word, and when I say that in the marxian perspective the movement of history and the revolution tends to confer on the collective man and his dynamism the attributes, and particularly the aseity, with which religion endows God, it is obvious that this manner of speech implies the significance of Marx's ideas as they appear *to me*. No one need be surprised that in conducting a philosophical inquiry I have recourse to my own proper philosophical language and even when it is a case of a critique of Marxism, not to that of Karl Marx. It is in virtue of the same right that apropos of historical materialism I had recourse to the aristotelian concept of material causality. But, in addition, it is the genesis of Marx's ideas as springing from Feuerbach, i.e. as springing from a Christianity which is denied and turned against itself. That authorises the use here of the vocabulary of christian philosophy.

[1]I.e. primarily determining, not doubtless with regard to the intrinsic *content* of these superstructures,—Marx, unlike Freud, was not occupied with furnishing explanations of the content of art and religion (more or less orthodox Marxists, by a naturally inevitable descent, have proved themselves less discreet),—but in regard to their *existence* and their historic energies, and their real significance for human life.

For the rest, with regard to religion Marx presupposed that Feuerbach's criticism was decisive, as is clear in *Das Kapital* (see also p. 28, note 1 *supra*).

[2]As early as 1842 the young Marx declared that any philosophy, before acting on its epoch, is brought into being by its needs and tendencies(A.

[40]

general, the transcendence of the proper object which gives these their identity has been eliminated?[1] Hençe these super-structures lose their autonomy. In order to live and act in history they are not only *conditioned* by social and economic

Cornu, *op. cit.*, p. 175). This idea, which as such can be understood in an exact sense, progressively darkens till it results in the discovery of the theory of historical materialism, which consists precisely in the attribution to an economic dialectic of the prime determining rôle.

Let it not be said that by the very nature of dialectic progress itself, which is one of action and reaction, there cannot be a primary determination of the superstructure by the infrastructure. The dialectic process is above all concerned with *the antagonisms engendered by the system of production*; and if there is a reciprocal action between the infrastructure and the superstructure, the latter, from the moment that all transcendent value or reality which might endow it with an autonomous character is eliminated, finds its only just principle of existential determination in the infrastructure on which it reacts and in it finds its only real significance for human life.

'Thus morality, religion, metaphysics and the other ideologies, and the forms of conscience which correspond to these, cannot for long preserve the appearance of autonomy. They have no history, or process of development. Men, in the development of their material commerce and material production, modify at the same time their thought and the product of their thought. It is not conscience that determines life, but life that determines conscience' (*Die deutsche Ideologie*). 'On the diverse forms of property, the social conditions of existence, is reared a whole super-structure of impressions, illusions and ways of thinking, of various conceptions of life, each made up in a specific manner. These are class-creations, and result from the material and social foundations with which they correspond. The isolated individual, to whom these are transmitted by tradition and education, may imagine that these make the determining reason and point of departure of his actions' (*Der Achtzehnte Brumaire des Louis Bonaparte*). The *Communist Manifesto* restates summarily the same doctrine (pp. 92-4 of the Molitor edition, Paris, 1934).

[1] In the case of religion or metaphysics or the arts this transcendence is manifest; and even in science it also exists, inasmuch as even in science in the modern sense of the word we still find that ordination of the mind to Intelligibles whose necessity, according to that section of platonism that Aristotle saved, is as such above time.

[41]

factors, they are *determined* by these; and it is social and economic reasons which give them meaning and a real significance for human life.

It is indeed true that economic conditions—as in general all the conditions of the material order—have a profound bearing on the destiny of spiritual activities among men and that they have a constant tendency to bring these under their control, and that in the history of culture they are incorporate one with another: from this angle Marx's cynicism, like that of Freud, has brought many truths to light.[1] But it is a nonsense to take a material conditioning factor, however real it may be, for the prime determining reason—be it only in regard to its existence in history—of a spiritual activity, and as that which above all reveals that activity's significance for human life.[2]

It is of course necessary to take into account Marx's polemical position, which in itself led to a provocative exaggeration. Doubtless Marx, in his ardent polemic against idealism, called materialism what often merited rather the name of realism; but this is of small importance in regard to the doctrinal characteristics I have pointed out; or rather

[1]So we can say with M. Henri de Man that 'as applied to the social bearing of bourgeois capitalism the doctrine of "ideologies" formulated by Marx is indubitably true': but it is necessary to add with the same author that this is not the case 'if we cease to think of the bearing of a class and turn to "the spiritual superstructure" of an epoch, or again when from the ideologies of camouflage and flight which are part of the capitalist epoch the existence of similar or analogous phenomena in a previous period is deduced'.—H. de Man, *The Psychology of Socialism* (Eng. trans. 1930).

[2]'This mode of production (Capitalism) is in essence cosmopolitan, like Christianity. Christianity as a result is the special religion of Capitalism.' Such a sentence is a remarkable specimen of the absurdities included in historical materialism.

[42]

it is highly significant that the question of a possible distinction between realism and materialism never for a moment rose in Marx's mind: since his whole philosophy is in essence polemical, polemical exaggeration cannot be an accident in it.

Indeed the fact remains that, taken not in isolation, but, on the contrary, with all the superstructures which while acting upon it are originally determined by it, the economic factor (i.e. that nexus of human relations and energies which, with good reason, constituted for Marx the miscomprehended reality of the economic process) was raised by him into being the final reason of history. 'The materialist conception of history, according to which the forms and conditions of production determine the formation and evolution of human societies, represents the capital element in the doctrine of Karl Marx.'[1] The distinguishing feature of Marxism is not just that it assigns a preponderating rôle to the economic factor, other schools commit and have committed that error, but also that it reduces all the forms of life, with all their values and all their efficacy to dependence—they are not denied, they are subordinated—on this material absolute in dialectic movement. To return to our notional vocabulary of Aristotle, the material cause thus becomes in pure and simple speech the primary or first cause.

Second and Third Stages of this Process of Substitution: The Dynamism of Matter and the Redemptive Mission of the Proletariat

Again, in the second place, it is from this material causality that *salvation* is to be expected and the realisation, so to say, of the Kingdom of God. The dynamism of the Hegelian

---

[1] A. Cornu, *op. cit.*

dialectic being thrust back into matter, it is held that the economic process,—not automatically, but through the energies which it engenders and which react upon it, above all by the energy of revolutionary consciousness,—must needs lead to the empire of reason, to the elimination of man's slavery to irrational forces, to the victory of man over necessity, and his dominion over history. Socialised man, at the end of this development, will be the absolute master of history and the universe. The convergence of Marx's Messianism (at once Jewish and Hegelian) and the Messianism of Russia is from this angle of observation singularly significant.

Finally, and this is the third stage of the process, who will be the mediator of this redemption? The proletariat. If the theory of the class-war appeared to Marx as a revelation, it is because, as he conceived it, it essentially implies this element of Messianism. The proletariat is not only free of the original sin of the exploitation of man by man; precisely because it has been stripped of everything, because it is in the lowest place in history, it is the bearer of human liberation, the messianic victim whose triumph will be the final victory over all that oppresses humanity, a resurrection, as it were, from the dead. Berdyaev likes to point out the presence of this eschatological element in the thought of revolutionary communism, and it is a matter to which I wish to return. In the womb of history will take place the advent of a total and final deliverance, which will cut time into two. The step will be taken—from the kingdom of necessity to that of liberty.

That process of substitution of which I spoke is thus complete in three stages. Everything which had reference to a christian value (or even, in the sense I have specified, to any sign of the natural platonism of our minds) is henceforth *replaced*.

God is absolutely rejected on principle, in virtue of an absolute metaphysical dogmatism,—not, as was the case with rationalist or deist humanism, in the name of human personality, but along with the human person as a spiritual being made in the image of God,—and this in the name of the historical dynamism of the social collectivity, in the name of the collective or collectivised man, in whom and through whom human nature will find its fulfilment. And at the same time, and as a necessary consequence, a social conception imposes itself which can be no other (however multiform or diverse be the forms of the individual's integration into the group) than a monism of collective humanity. This is what gives to communism not the value of a relative economic solution, but rather that of an absolute historical exigency, necessary with a metaphysical necessity, by reason of which man raised to the fulness of his social and political life, the collective man who is the truth of man and in whom liberty will finally come to flower, will integrate in an absolute fashion into his being the individual human personality which was hitherto only a transient phase of its dialectic and subject to the play of heteronymous forces.

Thus the social implications of communism appear as the *conclusions* drawn from an original principle of atheism, or of a humanism conceived in terms of atheism. This marxist humanism must needs be regarded as the perfect fruit of hegelian immanentism, once the *reversed* hegelian dialectic has passed over from 'the ideal' to 'the real', i.e. to social and historical humanity. It ends in claiming for man—once he has been liberated by the abolition of private property—that sovereign independence in his control of nature and of the

[45]

direction of history which once, in the era of 'alienated consciousness', religion attributed to God.

A Denial of Historical Materialism?

There seems to be here an apparent contradiction of marxist
materialism, which regards every metaphysical or religious
idea as an expression (which is itself active) of the economic
factor: Marxist economy, marxist sociology, is itself subject to the primacy and determination of a metaphysic,—an
atheistic, dialectic-realist metaphysic of absolute immanentism.

I say an 'apparent' contradiction, for in reality *this* ideology,
this metaphysic, if we consider what is deepest in the doctrine
of Marxism, can never be 'made relative' by economics. Indeed
it is rather the setting aside, the contemptuous rejection of
any metaphysical ideology as the expression or transitory reflection of an economic moment which is, despite the insistence with which popular Marxism exploits the theme, a
theoretic and illusory appearance, or like the arguments of
the old Greek sceptics, is a drastic proposition intended to
purge the thought of their adversaries. It holds good, I
think, speaking in good marxist terms, with a certain metaphysic or ideology, i.e. bourgeois ideology. When the *bourgeois* invoke metaphysical values, *then* you have an unreal
superstructure. But the marxist metaphysic itself is no
momentary superstructure, since it is found immanent and
alive, incarnate in the proletariat and its action. Thus, after
the great day of universal revolution (and already in the
countries in which this has been inaugurated), we shall see
metaphysical and 'mystical' values, those for example which
are expressed by the words justice and liberty, and which were
heretofore regarded as belonging to the ideology of petit-

[46]

bourgeoisie, we shall see these values reappear with an almost infinite plenitude of reality and rectitude: for then they will not be *signified* in systems or philosophical opinions, but will be *lived* in a complete, an integral immanence through and by humanity, in the practical life of humanity liberated by the proletariat. Here again the keynote lies in the presupposition of an absolute metaphysic of immanentism.

The Kingdom of God in History

The preceding analysis has also made clear a contradiction which is often pointed out in Marxism: on the one hand the fundamental process which it recognises, the dialectic process, must needs be a movement which is endless; yet, on the other hand, revolutionary dynamism has its object and aim in a communist society which will mark the end of 'the quarrel between man and nature and between man and man'[1] and the *final* triumph of man over his destiny. In other words, to make use of a terminology more appropriate in its intrinsic significance and in its historical derivation, its aim is the Kingdom of God *in* history, as a part of history.

I hold myself that this second aspect corresponds in reality to an impulse anterior to Marxism itself and which is stronger than the logic of the hegelian Becoming (to which Hegel himself was indeed not always faithful),—to an impulse which springs from deep spiritual tendencies which are immanent in socialism in general.

Grant to a socialist every claim he makes for the régime of his future society, but add that even in the most perfectly justly and humanely organised socialist State man will still be subject to evil and misfortune because these are *in*

[1]See *supra*, p. 39, note 3.

man. The law of a conflict to be waged and of an agony of tension to be borne, the law that peace is the fruit of war, will still rend and stimulate man, because it is the law of creative life in man. The insatiable desire for beatitude and the pain of this earthly existence will still inhabit man's heart, because man is made to enter into the joy of our God: you will risk wounding the dearest feelings of your socialist friend without the least intention. He will listen with impatience to what you say. Indeed, I grant that he has good reason for his detestation of that tranquil pessimism and easy acceptance of the miseries of others which so often consoles the comfortable and appears to dispense them in their own eyes from any effort to transform the world!

In one sense he is right, he will always be right in his objection to the Christian, for the Christian will never be at the level of his Christianity, will always have a tendency to take his ease too soon—as if, poor fellow, he could ever rest anywhere save where his God is nailed upon a Cross. Human weakness is always trying to go to sleep: if it is not the doubt of the old Stoic humanism, it is the eternal truths of which it will make a pillow. If he is not kept awake in sorrowful communion with all the suffering and the outcasts of mortal life, the Christian is apt to make a sleeping-draught of the very love he has received.

But Christianity is the very opposite of such a sleep. Authentic Christianity has a horror of the pessimism of inertia. It is pessimist, profoundly pessimist in the sense that it knows that the creature comes from nothingness, and that all that issues from nothingness tends of itself to return to nothing: but its optimism is incomparably deeper than its pessimism; for it knows that the creature comes from God, and all that comes from God tends also to return to Him. A truly christian humanism does not, either for good or for evil, make man static at any one point in his evolution. It knows that not only in his social being, but in his inward and spiritual one, man is still but a sketch drawn by night of his true self, and that before he attains to his true lineaments—at the end of time—he must needs pass through many changes and renovations. For if there is a human nature which as such is unchanging, it is precisely a nature which is in motion, the nature of a being of flesh made in the image of God, i.e. astonishingly progressive both in good and in evil. And there are eternal truths immutable as such, yet which constrain history so that it ceaselessly changes its intellectual climate and enables these truths to realise under various forms their potentialities in time and in the things of time.

If it is true that evil and suffering will always be at grips with man, it is under new forms and in revealing new profundities; for death itself changes its aspect with time. And goodness and joy alike will go on revealing new depths to the end. If it is true that the law of creative conflict will always rule man, it is so that new and higher forms of active peace and transfiguring integration may be brought into being. If it is true that the heart of man will always suffer the anguish of beatitude, it is not that man is doomed always to stagnate here below in a narrow and miserable life, it is because the largest and most abounding life will always hold some element of contraction compared with the dimensions of his heart.

These explanations will perhaps seem reasonable to our socialist friend; they will not appease his inquietude: he will continue always to fear lest they may not conceal a betrayal of humanism or of the revolution. This is because (as the history of his philosophic origins indeed makes clear) his idea of humanism still includes, often, maybe, reduced to a

[49]

mere emotional connotation, a certain messianic claim, and his idea of the revolution a secularised transposition of the last Judgement and the Kingdom of God. It was so for socialism long before the discovery of historical materialism; even when it was fed by christian sentiments it mingled with its social and temporal claims a psychical instinct which was a practical ousting of Christianity, since it diverted to the things of time and history realities which for the christian faith are essentially *beyond* history and time.

In this socialist humanism follows in the steps of bourgeois humanism. For bourgeois humanism, as we saw in the previous chapter, God is no more than the guarantor of the demiurgic power of man working out his own prosperity. Finally, He becomes an idea and all the reality that was previously acknowledged as His passes to man. The accomplishment of this transmutation, not only in theory, but in fact, in terms not only of philosophical speculation, but of life, is the reversal of values which socialism had achieved long before the marxian reversal of the hegelian dialectic. That is why it has always held in suspicion the view of the temporal community which sees man as a pilgrim on the way to eternity.

Socialist humanism equally objects to christian asceticism. Doubtless this is the result of a misunderstanding, a mistaken belief as to the essence of that asceticism, which is regarded as proceeding from a manichaean hatred of nature: but it is also due to a double contradiction. On the one hand, socialist humanism is well aware in practice that nothing great is done without suffering and sacrifice; but it only recognises this law when it is a matter of major collective works; for, ignorant of the world of personality, it takes what is essentially the fruit of love and inner generosity for an egotistic search for personal perfection. On the other hand, what it knows very well in practice it rejects in theory, and here again it proves itself the heir of bourgeois humanism, not this time by way of reversal, but in simple continuity. Bourgeois humanism rejects the principle of asceticism, and claims to replace it by a technical or technological one, since it aims at peace, without conflict, at an indefinite progress in a perpetual harmony and satisfaction, made in the image of the non-existent man of rationalism. In the degree to which, in spite of everything, it remains,—at least for the age which will follow the revolution,—attached to a like optimism, socialist humanism holds a view of man that is equally light and shallow, rationalist and bourgeois.

By restoring, in contradiction to this idyllic utopianism, the values of conflict and warfare as an integral condition of the movement of history, the marxian dialectic has given socialism a grasp of existence and a drive which it lacked before, while at the same time endowing it with a sharp and simple conception of this conflict and this war, which are immanent in history.

But at the same time Marxism is itself subject to that utopian messianism which has been inherent since the beginning in the socialist tradition. And this is why, despite the theoretic exigencies of its dialectic, it sees as finally issuing from the conflicts of history a communist humanity which truly seems like the end of history, and in which all things will be reconciled as in the Word of God. Against what will man, delivered from all those things which oppress him to-day, still have to fight, except death? To conquer it also? The process of this dialectic ends in the Kingdom of God: because this dialectic obeys the inner law of the socialist *psyche*, not that of dialectic. But it is a secularised Kingdom of God, which while bringing history to an end, yet remains

[51]

in and a part of history, realised in terms of the *time of this world.*

This question of the Kingdom of God will be the principal theme of the next chapter. To my mind it is a betrayal at once of man and of God not to understand that history is a movement towards the Kingdom of God and not to wish for the coming of that Kingdom. But it is absurd to think that it will come *in and as a part* of history, where good and evil are inextricably intertwined. Prepared by the growth of history, and by the progressive mixing and refining of the human being that it involves, it will come *at the end* of history, at that hour of the resurrection of the dead to which all history leads.

II

THE PHILOSOPHICAL PROBLEM OF ATHEISM

Atheism cannot be lived

Let us now turn to the problem of atheism from a philosophical and doctrinal standpoint.

What do we learn from any authentic philosophical conception of the human will? That atheism *cannot be lived* in its metaphysical depth and absolute radicalism, if that is to say one can reach these limits.

In fact, the will by its nature aspires to the good as such, to pure goodness. From the moment it comes into action, it acts for a final end which can be no other than the good which will absolutely fulfil its aspiration. But where is this good in reality if not in the Being who is in himself the infinite plenitude of Goodness? Such, briefly, is the teaching of an authentic philosophy of the will. Thus every will, even the

[52]

most perverse, desires God without knowing it. They may choose other final ends, decide for other loves, but it is always and everywhere God that they desire under errant forms and despite their own choice.

Atheism, *if it could be lived down to its ultimate roots* in the will, would disorganise and kill the will metaphysically. It is not by accident, it is by a strictly necessary effect, written in the nature of things, that every absolute experience of atheism, if it is conscientiously and rigorously followed, ends by provoking its psychical dissolution, in suicide.

One may cite in witness the heroic and tragic experience of Nietzsche; or the profound intuition of Dostoevsky, as shown in the character of Kirilov. Kirilov precisely incarnates in Dostoevsky's eyes the effort of a man to live atheism down to its metaphysical roots, in its deepest ontological implications. Consider in *The Possessed* the conversation between Kirilov and Peter Stepanovitch, a few minutes before Kirilov's suicide, 'If God exists', says Kirilov, 'all things depend on Him and I can do nothing outside His will. If He does not exist, all depends on me and I am bound to display my independence. . . . For three years I have been seeking for the attribute of my divinity and I've found it; the attribute of my divinity is independence. That is all I can do to prove in the highest point my autonomy and my new and terrible freedom. For it is very terrible. I shall kill myself to prove my independence and my terrible new freedom.' Though he had not read St. Thomas Aquinas Dostoevsky was well aware that the profoundest metaphysical attribute of the Deity is *aseitas*. And it is this attribute which Kirilov, because he is an actual atheist, must manifest in himself:— subordinating his own existence to his own absolute independence.

[53]

Nevertheless the religious atheism of the communism of the Soviets is before us as a fact. Does this imply a contradiction of the law I have just enunciated; unless indeed Russian communism shall one day break before that law and awake —transfigured—as a man wakes from a nightmare in the morning?

Soviet communism has understood the gravity of the problem; and this is exactly the reason why it has undertaken to create a new humanity. As I pointed out above (I am speaking of the ideal exigencies of the system, whatever attenuations and accommodations it may or may have been necessary to introduce into it in concrete life), it is a question for it of changing man so as to oust the transcendent God of whom he is an image, of creating a human being who will be in himself the god, lacking no supra-temporal attribute, of history and his titanic dynamism, a human being who must first of all be de-individualised, whose joy will be in his devotion to all, in being an organ of the revolutionary community, in expectation of the day when he will find in the triumph of the collective man over nature a transfigured personality. [This need to transform man, which made a large part of the greatness of Lenin's revolution, seems to-day (1936) to have grown lukewarm. Though more or less thrust into the background, I hold, nevertheless, that it subsists, coming to terms in the concrete with the unforeseeable and spontaneous resurgences of human nature, which are themselves at once exploited by the literature of official propaganda.[1]]

For all that, it must be noted, there is no question and has

[1]Cp. Helene Isvolsky, *Soviet Man Now* (Sheed and Ward, 1935).

never been in this case of *living* atheism in all its *metaphysical radicalism*, at those depths which Dostoevsky saw in the case of Kirilov (although of men capable of divining these depths, such as poets, we see poets like the great Alexander Block dying of inanition in this spiritual atmosphere; and since then, at certain times, how many young suicides!).

More, in the degree to which the marxist theoreticians of the U.S.S.R. elaborate a metaphysic, it is to a form of hylozoism that they return; their general line in philosophy demanding that something resembling liberty and a soul be attributed to matter. They dare not yet declare, like the old Ionians, that everything is full of a universally-extended soul and divinity, *panta plêrê théôn*; but that certainly seems the direction in which they are going. How, indeed, could it be otherwise from the moment they make their dialectic one with matter? The metaphysical atheism which came out of the hegelian Left is thus returning little by little to its origins, to the old hegelian pantheism.

In reality, the question for marxist atheism, despite its pseudo-scientific appearance, remains much more ethical and moral than metaphysical: it is one of living out the *ethical translation* of atheism, i.e. the refusal of God as the final end and rule of human life. This refusal is in the eyes of Russian communists the first principle of a truly free and creative moral life which shall be worthy of the nature of man, since they are ignorant of God and do not know that He is the source both of man's humanity and his creative liberty. And more profoundly, in its most typical Russian (and human) subconscious connections, it signifies also a resentment and an attitude of revenge against God, to whom man refuses the headship of his moral life since he will not forgive Him the world and evil, I mean the existence of evil in the world,—in

[55]

other words, if we know indeed what we are saying, for the creation of the world. But this refusal of God in the ethical order, this choice of a final end for any reason other than God, is this anything else in christian eyes than the simple case of every sinner? That truly propounds no great metaphysical difficulty for the Christian, otherwise than as showing in action the mystery of the imperfections of our liberty.

The Resources of Grace

Meanwhile these interrelations of the speculative and the practical, particularly in the ethical order, must not be allowed to confuse our minds: the speculative refusal of God as a final end and as the supreme rule of human life does not necessarily imply, for a mind so blinded, a practical refusal to order one's life with regard to that same God, whose name is no longer known. The Christian knows that God has infinite resource; and that the possibilities of good faith stretch farther than men imagine. Under many names, names which are not that of God, in ways only known to God, the interior act of a soul's thought can be directed towards a reality which in fact truly may be God. For, as a result of our spiritual weakness, there can easily be a discordance between what in reality we believe and the ideas in which we express to ourselves what we believe, and take cognisance of our beliefs. To every soul, even to one ignorant of the name of God, even one reared in atheism, grace offers, at the moment when the soul deliberates with itself and chooses its final end, grace offers as an object, as something to be loved above all things, under whatever name the soul describes such an end to itself, —but it is then a case (and this is the whole question to which God alone knows the answer) of its thinking under that name of *something other* than it signifies, of going beyond the false

[56]

name,—offers that Reality of absolute goodness, which merits all our love and is able to save our life.

And if this grace is not rejected, the soul in question, in its choice of that reality, believes obscurely in the true God and really chooses Him, even where in good faith it is in error and adheres, not by its own fault, but by that of the education it has received, to a philosophical system of atheism, and conceptualises this faith in the true God under formulas which deny Him. An atheist of good faith would thus, against his own apparent choice, really choose God as the true end of his life.

Again, whatever be the forces of education and propaganda, a day will come when these fundamental problems will have to be posed anew. Are we to think that this day is already at hand? Following the black coat and the differences of military rank, the old style of marking examination papers and the christmas tree, the family homestead and the 'pleasures of life', is God also about to make His return in Soviet Russia? He is less easy to deal with in this way, though He is humble enough to take even that road. In any case, when these fundamental problems are posed anew, Russian communism will only be able to make a place for them—in order to keep in existence the regime and the social results already achieved—by the renunciation of an original spiritual error: it is the lesson of history. Criticising the so-called 'naturism' professed by some of his partisans in matters of sexual morals, Lenin said to Clara Zetkine: 'Sexual dissoluteness is something bourgeois; it is a phenomenon of decadence.'[1] A day will come, perhaps, when a suc-

[1]From Clara Zetkine's *Reminiscences* (1929) of Lenin.

With regard to atheism, we know that Lenin's was even more virulent, if possible, than that of Marx. 'Every religious idea is an abomina-

cessor of Lenin will proclaim, and with yet more justification, that atheism is a product of bourgeois decadence. But then Soviet Russia will have accomplished a new revolution, and to save the first will have transmuted all its values.

That original atheism, which conditions the communist conception of social life and politics, is in fact translated in the practical sphere by a particular scale of values. In actuality it is industrial production which seems to Soviet communism the most urgent value in civilisation. More generally, inasmuch as it will not recognise the presence in man of realities which are of a supra-temporal order and necessary to his happiness, it inevitably sees the communal work of earthly production as man's supreme means of happiness; and everything which puts a limit to this common work is a treason to man. Hence God can reserve no rights in man, and a totalitarian requisitioning of man's energies will be found at the end, as the fruit of an atheism affirmed at the beginning. If experience of human reality and the resistance of nature and a recognition of fundamental problems little by little eliminate that atheism, this scale of values founded on atheism will at the same time be eliminated and a system of personal values restored: and this will be accompanied, not by a return to the old order, but by a progressive renewal of the morals and the structure of civilisation.

tion,' he declared. The most definite anti-religious dogmatism, the assertion that all religion was nothing but superstition, and that any knowledge of what transcends the sphere of experience is impossible, were for him absolutely fundamental convictions. Cp. his *Materialism and Empirio-criticism*, 1909.

The Cultural Significance of Russian Atheism

A Resentment against God

We have now come to our third question: what is the significance of contemporary Russian atheism, no longer considered theoretically, but in historical and cultural terms?

It is not bound up in Russia (I am speaking in this of the people, not of the theories of the intellectuals) with a rationalist tradition, with the long-drawn conflicts of the *Aufklärung*, as is the case in the West. Rather its basis is in the very nature of the religious feeling of the people, which, like an immense, dynamic and irrational force, can be suddenly turned in one or other direction; moved by the same mystical vertigo either, under a sense of resentment against God, to plunge head foremost into the abyss of atheism or to mount upward in a new and more or less purified belief in God. On such historic and popular grounds can a 'scientific' atheism be built up? No doubt that is a somewhat disturbing question for the theoreticians of the anti-God campaign. It seems, however, at the moment that a large section of the young have arrived at a state of complete religious indifference,—due perhaps, in part, precisely to a transference of religious feeling to other ends.

A Purification by Fire

But what I would point out is that this brutal atheism of which I have been speaking (this anti-humanism) represents in a way the humanist phase of the history of the Russian people. We must not forget that, giving the words their full cultural significance, Russia has known neither a Middle Ages nor a Renaissance.

Without implying any insult to the Orthodox Church (it has had its saints; and many of its sons are to-day suffering heroically for their faith) it must be said that culturally and psychologically vast regions of the thought of the Russian people have been preoccupied by aberrant religious forms.

On the one hand, nature and reason have never been given their rightful and respective places. The natural order as such has never been rightly recognised; the rational has always been held in suspicion.

On the other, a religious feeling which is in origin earthly and pagan, a messianism holding in it many mixed elements, a cult of 'the holy Russian earth', a mysticism which developed especially in innumerable restless sects and which combined with its stuff all manner of impurities, all these invaded the notional and visible structures of the christian tradition, which was thus paganised from within. Christian concepts were thus left, as it were, in confusion on the field as a result of an inward and hidden process. Briefly, an extreme *supernaturalism*—whose tendency is to despise the reason and to regard nature, as even Soloviev himself said, as 'a process of corruption'—and a *paganism*, which was its inward parasite, formed an indissoluble complex which invited catastrophe.

As a result of a revolution which is itself at bottom the fruit of powerful and irrational forces, which lives by an irrational heroism and a mysticism *à rebours*, but whose aim is to rationalise all existence to the point of the elimination of the smallest element of mystery, reason and nature have perhaps a chance of recovering their place in the cultural structure of the Russian world, at the ultimate end of the most aberrant of all forms of anthropocentric humanism, and under the semblance of the most deceiving form of materialism and of pseudo-science.[1] But in the end there is here a cleansing, a purification, by fire: the dawn of a possibility for the Russian people of a full awareness of the proper values of nature and reason. And next a historical development which, being set in motion in an atmosphere of violent error and of the most perfectly simple-minded illusions—and (what is very

[1]It is notable that the most recent communist watchword is to-day that of humanism—a 'socialist humanism' for which there is sought a selection from the tradition of Western humanism of all that runs to the glorification of man as 'emancipated' from God. Communism thereby remains faithful to its atheistic postulate; but this new watchword, by its implication of that very choice, condemns it to an attitude which is truly rather 'sectarian' than 'humanist', and to a dogmatic misunderstanding of the profoundest historical sources of humanism and of an essential element in its riches. (In making his recent panegyric of Racine did Andre Gide realise the heretical position he was in with regard to 'socialist humanism'?).

More, in expressly tying up, as was the case with Marx himself, the proletarian conception of the world with a definitely bourgeois tradition (there is nothing in the world more bourgeois than rationalistic and atheistic humanism) this new watchword implies a denial, or in any case a considerable diminution, of the original claim of the communist revolution to engender a radically new type of man. When we see what have been the fruits of anthropocentric humanism for bourgeois civilisation we may well ask what are the advantages the proletariat will gain by absorbing its philosophy, and if it implies any honour to make it the heir of the stupidest thing the world has ever known, i.e. bourgeois freethought.

And yet, from another angle, it is possible to find in this desire for a socialist humanism the dim foreshadowing of a historical connection which will end perhaps very differently than they think. For the anthropocentic humanism of modern times is vitally bound up with a deeper and older tradition, springs from religious sources without which it is absolutely impossible to comprehend. And when one day men in Russia study these sources anew, they will take the risk of thereby recognising their value ... (July 1935)

Russian) after the experience of the most appalling catastrophes—will doubtless lead, if not for all at least for a section of the people, to a re-establishment of authentic cultural values.

The post-revolutionary point of view

We can thus comprehend the 'post-revolutionary' standpoint, which is in fact that of a number of Russian Christians. These start with the fact of the October revolution, and think that from its soil fruits very different and wholly new may spring. They even hope (it is good to be able to hope against hope) that having passed the halting places Russia may achieve before other nations the shaping of a new Christendom. At least, with more probability, we can believe that unknown possibilities of expansion and heroic spiritual effort will open there for a christian renaissance which is conscious of the integration of its divine and human elements, if only its protagonists are sufficiently enlightened and open-minded on all things except God.

IV
TWO CHRISTIAN POSITIONS
The Barthian Position

I have said that there was another pure position to which the dialectic of modern humanism led, that of pure Christianity: where it is not the God of the philosophers but the God of Abraham, of Isaac and of Jacob, that is acknowledged; where man is known as a sinner and in the light of the Incarnation, having his centre not in himself but in God; man as he is regenerated by grace.

Here again we can distinguish between two positions: one which is primarily a reaction, a will to purification by a re-

[62]

turn to what is past; and another, which is integralist and progressive.

The first, the 'archaic' position, we find in a certain school of modern Protestantism, marked by its return to primitive Calvinism. This position is primordially anti-humanist and in a word—despite all the involvements with which a highly intelligent and aware dialectic can decorate a doctrine—one which demands the annihilation of man before God. This, in brief summary, is the standpoint of the great Protestant theologian Karl Barth, who, partly under the influence of Kirkegaard, and partly in a violent renewal of the original Lutheran spirit armed with the sharp-drawn logic of Calvin, has completely reversed the standpoint of Protestantism in Germany. Schleiermacher, Harnack, the old liberalism and rationalism of the nineteenth century, all these are completely gone to dust: the modern objection to Catholicism is that it is too human. It is a return, in short, to the pure pessimism of primitive Protestantism. Hence what we can call the drama of Barth himself. He wishes to hearken only to God and he wishes only to hearken to God: he rejects and misconstrues the instrumental character of the human in the Church. Yet when he speaks, and most of all when he speaks in order to proclaim that man must only listen to God, it is he himself that speaks, he himself that is heard, and it is his personality which moves and stirs his listeners.

Finally, his error is that of Luther and of Calvin: it is to think that grace does not vivify. This is why, when he does justice to the past, he returns to the past as such, to a past that is static,—to a dead past, dead as for Calvinists human freedom remains dead under grace,—not to that substance at once eternal and progressive, the inner principle of activity by which the past lived and whereby we live also.

The other pure christian position, 'integralist' and 'progressive', is that of Catholicism, whose intellectual arms are supplied by St. Thomas. If it is true that there is a sort of blasphemy against God's government of history in the desire to *return* to a past condition, if it is true that there is an organic process of growth in both the Church and the world, then the obligation imposes itself on Christians of saving the 'humanist' truths which have been disfigured by four centuries of anthropocentric humanism, particularly at the moment when humanist culture is stricken and these truths are imperilled in the ruin of the errors which vitiated and oppressed them.

But this as obviously implies a total reconstruction of our cultural and temporal forms of life, forms which have been built up in an atmosphere of dualism and anthropocentric rationalism. We have to do with their substantial transformation and with a passage to a new age of civilisation.

V

A New Age of Christian Culture

The rehabilitation of the creature in God

In the first chapter I drew attention to three problems which are particularly significant for the philosophy of culture; and these were considered first from the standpoint of mediaeval Christendom, then from that of the classical period of humanism subsequent to the Reformation and the Renaissance.

Let us now turn to these three problems as seen from the standpoint of a new age of civilisation and of Christendom, and first to that of the practical attitude of the creature in face of his destiny.

For this new epoch in the history of christian culture the creature will neither be belittled nor annihilated before God; his rehabilitation will not be in contradistinction to God or without God, but *in* God. There is but one way of progress for the history of the world, that is, for a christian order, howsoever it may be otherwise: that the creature should be truly respected *in* his connection with God and *because* he is totally dependent on Him; humanism indeed, but a theocentric humanism, rooted in what is radical in man: integral humanism, the humanism of the Incarnation.[1]

Here it is necessary to comment for a moment on that 'contempt of creatures' shown by the saints, which is so often referred to in hagiographic literature. This phrase, which primarily exhibits the weakness of human language, must not be misunderstood. 'The saint sees in practical fact the nothingness of creatures with regard to the Being he loves and the End he has chosen. It is a loving contempt of all things other than the beloved. And the more he despises creatures in the degree to which they might be rivals of God, or objects of a possible choice to the exclusion of God, the more he cherishes them as loved by God, and made by Him as fair and worthy of our love. For to love a being in and for God is not to treat them as a mere means or a mere occasion for loving God, but to love and cherish their being as an end, because it *merits* love, in the degree to which that merit and their dignity spring from the sovereign love and the sovereign loving-kindness of God. So we understand the paradox whereby in the end the saint includes in a universal love of kinship and of piety—incomparably more free, but

[1] *Science et Sagesse*, ch. iii.

also more tender and more happy, than any selfish love of the voluptuary or the miser—all that passes in time, all the weakness and the beauty of things, all he had left behind him on his journey.'[1]

What I wish to put forward is that this attitude of the saint, which is truly one of no contempt for things, but rather the raising up, the transfiguration of things in a love which is higher than they, this standpoint taken as generalised, as become common, as become a commonplace of christian psychology, corresponds to that *rehabilitation of the creature in God* which I see as characterising a new age of Christendom and a new humanism,—essentially different from humanism in the ordinary interpretation of the term, from anthropocentric humanism, whose typical figures are the Renaissance hero or the 'honest gentleman' of the classic age, while the type of theocentric humanism is the saint: nor, indeed, can it be realised unless undertaken by saints. That is as much as to say that it can only be realised in the way christian spirituality calls the way of the Cross, not of the cross set as an exterior symbol on the crowns of kings or in the insignia of a nobleman's order, but the cross in the heart, the taking up of the cross of redemptive suffering into the very heart of our existence.

This attitude can only become general if it is bound up with a progress in the knowledge the creature has of itself, and at the same time of the mystery of the Cross as it is accomplished in us. In the actual conditions of our time and after the bitter yet real experiences we have endured, a sage reflectiveness would seem to be inherent in the attitude of a human being with regard to God and the mystery of his

[1]J. Maritain, *The Degrees of Knowledge* (Eng. trans. 1937).

destiny.[1] The injury caused by an unhappy and divided conscience can only be healed by a more perfect and more spiritual survey. Only a conscience rooted in the Gospel can cure the tragedy of a conscience rooted in naturalism.

In this way we understand that if the way towards God for a simple christian civilisation, for one, as I would say, which reckoned on the naïve and native unity of man, is primarily the building of a throne for Him on earth in accord with all the dues of his Majesty, on the other hand, for a christian civilisation which can no longer be simple, and where man must strive to win back the lost unity of his being under the guidance of grace, progress towards God will, it seems, before all be in the preparation of such conditions of earthly life for men that the sovereign love may rather be able to *come down* and make in man and with man a work that is divinely human.

Created Liberty

There will, without doubt, be in this new humanism a restatement of the speculative problems which dominate every great period of culture. Have I not said that to each age of civilisation there corresponds a certain typical interpretation of the relations between grace and freedom? In reference to this problem of grace and freedom the age of either modified or absolute humanist theology appears definitely to have come to an end. And as the Augustinian conception of grace and freedom dominated the Middle Ages, as that of Calvin and of Molina the modern age, so I hold the theology of St. Thomas will govern that of a new Christendom.

If it is true that this new Christendom will be completely

[1]Cp. *Science et Sagesse*, ch. iii.

free of any anthropocentric humanism, it will then be understood that, as St. Thomas teaches, it is not by disputing the ground with divine causality that the philosopher can affirm and recognise in face of God the existence of created freedom with the full measure it requires of being and of goodness. The new Christendom will recognise to the full the degree to which created liberty *receives* from God's causality: how it is invaded, traversed, saturated to the final limit of its actualisation by that creative causality.

This has been made abundantly clear by the dominican school of commentators, but in my opinion full utilisation has not yet been made of elements inherent in St. Thomas's principles, when it comes to dealing with the question of created freedom, not in relation to good or meritorious acts, but in relation to evil acts, in the order of evil-doing.

St. Thomas explains that 'the *first cause* of a lack of grace comes from ourselves', *defectus gratiae causa prima est ex nobis*,[1] and the implication of these words goes very far. In the line of evil-doing, it is the creature that is the first cause.

I hold that if the theology and the christian philosophy of the future apply themselves to finding the content of St. Thomas's principles on this theme important discoveries will be made, which will lead, in what is concerned with the failures of created freedom, to a deeper synthesis, a synthesis which will bring to light new aspects of the mystery of the divine knowledge and will with regard to man, and a fuller understanding of the degree of God's respect for that frail and free thing which is human freedom. If the creature has indeed the first initiative in the line of evil, it thereby—negatively—intervenes in the very moulding of the designs of providence. In that eternal moment, in which all the

---

[1] *Sum. theol.*, i-ii, 112, 3, ad. 2.

moments of time are held, God, if one may say so, in making and seeing in one single glance the whole of human history, waits on each one of us, on our refusal or acceptance of the gifts of that sovereign power from which all being and all action derive—all things, save the nothing we may bring.

And, precisely because this new age of Christendom of which I speak will be an age, not of a holy forgetfulness but of an evangelical attention to human things, of theocentric humanism, I hold that this new synthesis, these new aspects of the problem of grace and freedom, and also those aspects which concern the veritable and not only the instrumental value of human history and of our earthly and temporal activities, will be supremely expressive of that age.

A self-consciousness according to the Gospels

Finally, in what concerns the problem of man, it can be said that then the Christian's attention will not be, as it was in the Middle Ages, so to speak averted from the mystery of his created nature and its irrational depths; he will scrutinise this mystery, but in another mode of introspection from that of our modern naturalism: with what I called a moment ago a *self-consciousness according to the Gospels*, an evangelical self-consciousness. Such consciousness in my view implies two fundamental characteristics: it is a self-knowledge without search for it; the judgements of values which it posits are purely spiritual, free of any sociological preoccupation; that intervention of the social concept of man into our judgement of souls and of our own soul, to which Max Scheler has justly drawn attention, plays no part in it.

Hence it can attain to and scrutinise the human person in his value as a person without disassociating it, can discover his spiritual texture as the image of God, which no evil

[69]

can radically corrupt, and which by its nature cries out, not indeed for grace as such, which nature by itself does not know, but for that plenitude which in fact grace alone can give.

And this consciousness also attains to and scrutinises the obscure and secret places of the heart. It descends into that inward hell, it explores those lower regions, not as our modern naturalism does in a rejection of the distinction between good and evil, but transcending those purely sociological censures of which I spoke a moment ago, and as possessed of a truly christian knowledge of evil, in the application of that christian paradox: the sin which divides me from the just God is what calls the merciful God to my aid. Have pity on me, cries the christian soul, *because* I have sinned.

Finally, such self-consciousness implies an evangelical respect for both nature and the reason, for those natural formations which modern humanism has helped to discover and has not been able to preserve, and for the original greatness of man which can never be wholly effaced by evil.

The man of bourgeois liberalism

But another feature of this integral humanism must also be made clear. It is a taking cognisance of the exigencies of the Gospel with regard to our temporal and earthly life, the common life of day to day; exigencies which aim at the transfiguration of the temporal order, of our social life in itself (i.e. a transformation which is perpetually being renewed and deepened, until the hour of that final transfiguration when the body will rise again).

For too long—in these modern days—the christian world, stricken with dualism, has obeyed two opposing rhythms:

the rhythm of religion for Church services and occasions, the rhythm of naturalism in the affairs of the world and of secular life. The Middle Ages had the sense of unity. But by reason of too difficult historical conditions—because they had to work on barbarian and pagan ground, on a soil not yet purified by the terrible trials of history—the refraction of these evangelical exigencies in the socio-temporal sphere largely remained only symbolic and figurative.

Here again the Soviet State can furnish matter for most useful consideration. It is remarkable how its philosophical outlook turns back—in contradiction to the ideological heritage of Jean-Jacques Rousseau—to an element of pessimism.[1] For it also there is a sinful man, an 'old man' to destroy. That is why man must be changed. And who is this sinner? He is the *'petit-bourgeois'* man, the man of bourgeois liberalism.

How from our point of view is he to be characterised? He is seen to be the pharisaic and decadent product born of the spirit of Puritanism or Jansenism and that of rationalism. He prefers juridical fictions to love (as Sombart says, he is not 'erotic'); and he prefers psychological figments to being (which is why one can say that he has no ontological being).

A whole nominalist and idealist metaphysic is latent in him. Hence, in the world he has created, the pre-eminence of the *sign*: of opinion in political life, of money in the economic sphere.

This bourgeois man denies both evil and the irrational elements of his nature, so that he may be able to enjoy the witness of his good conscience, be content with himself, just in himself. He is thus firmly established among the illusions

[1]I say *an element of* pessimism. None the less, it continues to depend on its Rousseauian source and a philosophy of absolute optimism. Cp. *supra*, p. 50, and *infra*, pp. 220-221.

[71]

and deceptions of a false and nominalist conscience. Hence he makes great play with morality and a spiritual point of view; he can be animated by a devotion, which is often sincere and ardent, to the truths and virtues of the natural order; but he empties these of their most precious content and turns them in a way into myths, because he cuts them off from the living God and from love, for he is a deist and an atheist: it is he who has taught their atheism to his pupils and heirs, the communists.

Marx's endeavour (as later that of Freud) will be to expose the lie of this false conscience. This indeed covers over and conceals profound unconscious currents—not only economic or class interests, as Marx affirmed, but in general also a whole world of concupiscence and egoistic self-love, of the irrational and the demonic, which we wish to deny and which no man has ever characterised better than St. Paul.

This bourgeois man, who is as displeasing to the christian conscience as to that of the communists, communism hopes to change mechanically and from without, by technical and social means, and by the surgery and modelling of pedagogy and propaganda. And to this end it attacks not only bourgeois man, but the very nature and dignity of man himself, of man as the image of God, of man whose being in nature and in grace aspires to the supreme good of personality: God and eternal life, a freedom and a spiritual life centred in realities which though interior to man are superhuman; and attacks also the first social medium that is truly human, the family with its proper economic and spiritual life, and with its primordial claims springing from the Natural Law, claims of which the civil jurisdiction may fix the mode and limits but which it never creates.

Whatever be the corrections produced in it by the necessities of life, communist theory ends in making man simply one of the forces inherent in the life of the community: for, in marxist philosophy, every transcendental value whatsoever is bound up with the exploitation of man by man.

Marxism and Man

The tragedy of Marxism lies in the fact that, rightly desiring—but without taking any cognisance of the problems that are proper to personality—to find a way out of that despair and decomposition of human personality in which, as I said above, the dialectic of anthropocentric humanism ends, it is itself a tributary of bourgeois humanism at the most aberrant and inhuman point of its metaphysic, i.e. its atheism and anthropocentricism and immanentism, which it carries to the extreme point of exasperation. Lacking the indispensable metaphysical groundwork, its endeavour to give back the joy of life and the joy of work to human beings can thus only lead—I say, considered in terms of its own logic and the spirit of the system—to results even more deceptive than those of classical humanism. It is an excellent aim to wish to raise the mass of mankind to a real social and political life; but there is something essentially lacking in the aim itself if we refuse to understand that the social and political life of the human community on earth is, indubitably, a high and arduous one, but one which is directed towards something better; that it undoubtedly corresponds to the primary aspirations of human personality, of the person as person, but not to its deepest and highest aspirations, which seek to pass beyond to nobler forms of communion.[1]

It is highly probable in fact—less by virtue of Marxism

[1] Cp. *Du Régime Temporel et de la Liberté.*

than as a consequence of the violent destructions and purifications it has brought about, and the deep resources of human nature it has brought into play—that man, subject to an experience such as that of Russian communism, may rediscover some of the primary springs of his ontological reality and so (at a terrible price, from which only Christians, if they understood and they would, could dispense humanity) begin to surmount the final impossibilities and disassociations of the bourgeois phase of anthropocentricism. Thanks to the facilities of its dialectic, which always keeps, even in Marx himself, that ambiguity, that faculty for 'mystification' which he so excellently denounced in Hegel, which enable it at any moment, by a so-called development of the internal logic of its system, to open a door, no matter how, no matter where, though in fact it is opened by the irresistible pressure of an alien reality, thanks to this, Marxism will always be ready to integrate, or claim to integrate, all these human renewals in itself. The fact remains that in itself it only tends to restore the unity of human being by demanding that the latter abdicate all its most intimate exigencies for the benefit of the monism of collective life: and that in the very effort toward this integration it shows the profoundest inhumanity, for it claims for its accomplishment the right to bend man to its decrees. What matter their particular import: the important thing is to maintain this mastery. We can see the result in the strangest displays of obedient passivity, where human beings have become as supple as a glove. Some future successor to Stalin may command the faithful to adore electrons or to genuflect before ikons; in either case the grounds for a profound disquiet are alike. For whatever be the object of its good pleasure, caesaropapism is equally an insult to human personality and to God.

As I have said above, in my opinion a just critique of Marxism should first of all begin by distinguishing between certain true intuitions and the false principles and erroneous conceptualisations which have deformed these from the outset. Marx saw the essential importance of the system of production in evolution. Historical materialism contains an ill-formulated truth which a philosophy which applied the principles of hylemorphism to the movements of history could save: but in Marx's hands this is spoiled, as we have seen, by an atheistic monism of hegelian origin. Marx equally saw the usurious character which the spirit of capitalism has stamped on all modern economics; he conceptualised this intuition in an erroneous theory of surplus-value. He saw the class-war as the effective consequence of the capitalist system, and that the great historical effort of modern times must be the emancipation of the proletariat: but he invested this intuition with the messianism of an inexpiable social conflict and a false philosophy of man and of labour resulting in the socialisation of the entire man.

It is clear that we must, both now and still more in the future, separate the judgement we bring to bear on Marxism, which is a particular doctrinal form to be abstractly considered, and our judgement of developments in Soviet Russia, which are concerned with concrete human activities, set under the sign of Marxism (which is itself interpreted according to its most dynamic potentialities), but subject to the interference of the causalities which belong to existing realities, and affected constantly by the shocks of experience, the resistances and pressure of life, and the particular necessities of the actual historic state of Russia. And, if there is that ambiguity in Marxism as a doctrine of which I have spoken, we shall have no claim to be astonished at finding a similar ambiguity, considerably and in increasing measure augmented by the intervention of concrete historical factors, on the plane of existence, in Russian communism.[1]

We have no right to reject the witness of those honest inquirers who exhibit the way in which Soviet Russia has known, not without a diminishing in face of the real many theoretical claims, in the space of a few years, how to advance astonishingly a backward economic structure and cut for it new paths, and who tell us of the growth in Russia of a 'new form of civilisation' (the question remains, what is its value). This new form of civilisation, born into existence after the sacrifice of millions of lives and irreparable losses, can be summarised briefly, in my opinion, as to its positive content, in so far as it is possible to pronounce on what is only known at a distance and from books, in the liquidation of the 'profit system' and of the servitude of men's compulsory labour to the fecundity of money[2] (a liquidation which will be chiefly appreciable in its future forms, for at the moment its price is an oppressive

[1]Cp. Sidney and Beatrice Webb, *Soviet Communism: A new Civilisation?* (1936). The good faith of the authors and their desire for exact information does not exclude a certain naïveté which is fairly easily discernible; Ernest Mercier, *Réflexions sur l'U.S.S.R.*, January 1936, Centre polytechnicien d'Etudes économiques; Waldemar Gurian, *Der Bolshevismus, Einfuhrung in Geschichte und Lehre*, Freiburg, 1931 (Eng. trans. 1935); A. Rosenberg, *Histoire de Bolchevisme* (French trans. Grasset, 1936); Boris Souvarine, *Stalin*, Paris, 1935; and Mde. Helen Iswolsky's excellent little book, *Soviet Man Now*. See also Victor Serge's two letters to Magdaleine Paz and André Gide, *Esprit*, June 1936.

[2]One form of 'human exploitation' is thus abolished. For all that it is not sufficient to abolish the capitalist system (above all when it is replaced by communism) to finish off *all forms* of the exploitation of man by man:

[76]

domination by the State, but which largely explains the hopes roused in many sections of the world of labour by the Russian experiment); and in the perpetually renewed effort to inaugurate, at least in the sphere of legal morphology, a 'multiform democracy',[1] integrating the masses in the social, political and cultural life of the community. However hard the circumstances of life and the treatment of human beings, in this country where serfdom and its atmosphere have for so long endured there is at least the feeling that an age-long humiliation of social life has come to an end.[2]

No more can we reject the witness of others of equal good faith who insist above all on the errors and barbarous methods which vitiate the regime, and who also exhibit the complete contempt for human personality, the implacable harshness, the methods of terrorism (more intense than ever after eighteen years of revolution) and the bureaucratic despotism with which it works. This is an aspect which is at once inhuman and grim. Judging by testimonies in which it seems reasonable to have confidence, to my mind the profound evils of this 'new civilisation' are briefly summed up in the totalitarianism of communism itself, which brings to a maximum the fearful risks inherent in any strong collective organisation, destroying, as do other forms of totalitarianism, all liberty of thought, and wishing to socialise both the person and the mind; in the war against God, the work of

in particular, the exploitation of the individual man by the collectivites can attain vast proportions. The fact remains that the abolition of the form of capitalist servitude represented by wage-slavery is a necessity recognised as much by personalism as by socialism.

[1]'It is, more than anything else, this almost universal personal participation, through an amazing variety of channels, that justifies the designation of it as a multiform democracy' (S. and B. Webb, *op. cit.*, i, p. 427).

[2]Cp. H. Iswolsky, *op. cit.*

extermination of religion,[1] its idolatry of technical and phenomenal science, and in the activist dynamism and new

[1]The Webbs, while giving a highly objective documentation on the anti-God campaign, which is, however, limited to official information, very markedly reduce the scale and the significance of this anti-religious effort.

'It is very difficult to establish an exact figure with regard to the number of priests and religious who have been imprisoned or can still be found in the prisons and concentration-camps; for the servants of the Church have never been *directly* persecuted by Soviet law. This has been careful not to put them on trial on confessional charges, but rather to apply to them the articles of the penal code concerned with counter-revolutionary activities, spying, sabotage and 'the exploitation of the people's religious prejudices'. This voluntary confusion makes it exceedingly difficult, as I said, to evaluate the exact numbers of the victims of religious persecution. It is enough to say that not one of the 100,000 monasteries and convents which once existed in Russia remains: thus thousands of monks and nuns must have been decimated. Is it possible to talk of humanism while such a situation persists, while the terror continues to reign and the concentration-camps are packed? I have already cited the witness of the correspondent of the *Socialist Messenger* on the subject of a recrudescence of this terror. According to sources not less worthy of confidence, the number of those detained in prisons and concentration-camps and of those condemned to deportation has risen actually to seven millions. How is it possible to know how many among these unhappy beings are suffering on account of their religious convictions? Among the millions of the imprisoned there are orthodox and catholic priests, monks and nuns, pastors and rabbis, and the list of their martyrology is by no means closed' (H. Isvolsky, *op. cit.*). Meanwhile we can academically discuss the progress of religious persecution in Russia in comparison with the great persecutions of the past. Its distinguishing feature is that it is hidden. It is less persecution in the exact meaning of the word than a slow effort of spiritual destruction, whose aim is rather to annihilate the religious life than to execute believers, and one which seeks to avoid the public making of martyrs. The essential point is to imprison the word of God. Limiting ourselves to legal decisions, these latter, having proclaimed in theory liberty of conscience, have secularised all the schools, have forbidden the gathering together of children to teach them the catechism, and interdicted all religious instruction except in the child's own family and by it; they forbid the printing and publication (at

servitude—this time for the benefit of the collectivity—with which it menaces certain spheres of productive work.

Such, in the eyes of one who endeavours to judge objectively and impartially, is the ambiguity presented by the

least in Russian) or the importation of the Bible and religious books; they remove from priests the right of speech otherwise than in their churches, and from all religious organisations that of undertaking any work of education, recreation or charity. They have suppressed practically all the seminaries and they render a priest disqualified for social or political life, deprived of the right to vote in a system where the perpetual vote is a condition of existence. While they punish as a crime any public religious propaganda (with the exception of divine service and sermons delivered in church), they give, on the other hand, free scope to anti-religious endeavour and apply to that end all the powers of official instruction and practically the entire scheme of education: they allow and favour the direct atheistic propaganda of the Anti-God Society and its affiliated organisations; they make this propaganda (and how, then, can we be astonished that so many communes have voted en bloc for the suppression of their churches? Over the whole span of Russia almost a third of these are closed) one of the tasks of the spiritual authority which guides and animates the great body of Soviets, i.e. the Communist Party. It is to be observed that in Russia adhesion to the Communist Party depends on an explicit profession of atheism and a denial of any form of supernaturalism whatever. 'What the Communist Party maintains is a rigid law with regard to itself; no one may be admitted as a member (or put to the test as a candidate) if he does not declare himself a fervent and open atheist, and if he does not deny completely the existence of any and every form of supernaturalism' (S. and B. Webb, *op. cit.*, ii, p. 1012; cp. also i, p. 345). Does this clause operate outside the U.S.S.R.? The question is a specially interesting one from the fact that the Communist Party declares itself to be an entity transcending all national boundaries, and, in Russia itself, is not part of the Soviet constitution with its various legal powers. At the date at which I am writing (1936), the journal *Anti-God* has ceased to appear (perhaps because its readers have grown tired); there is a question of returning their bells to the churches; even one of the possibility of a synod. These forced concessions do not signify that the atheist and anti-religious zeal of the communist directorate will itself be relaxed. The new constitution announced by the newspapers seems even to include certain ameliorations in the conditions of the clergy.

actual realisations of Russian communism. Something of indubitable importance for the evolution of humanity's conditions of existence is there in process: and there a profound
evil rages against men. It is the load of errors embodied by
Marxism in captive truths which, combined with certain
characteristics of the Russian temperament, makes so potent
the negative aspect of the new civilisation which Soviet Russia is elaborating. By one of those ganglions of fortune and
misfortune which are customary in history, the social adjustments and new forms of life, of very varying value, which
are there coming into existence find themselves in fact
dominated to-day by intellectual and spiritual forms dark-
ened and rendered inhuman by the spirit of atheism. What
discoveries and agonies, what resurrections are called for,
whose time and season we cannot know!

Socialist Humanism and Integral Humanism

However preponderantly marxist may be the socialism of
to-day, the expression 'socialist humanism' is noticeably
wider than that of 'marxist humanism', which latter, despite
the ideas of the young Marx, seems, moreover, something of
a contradiction in terms. All socialism is not necessarily
atheistic, as is Marxism; but even in its non-marxist or earlier
than marxist forms, socialism is founded on a conception of
man, of labour and of society, encumbered with errors and
defects, which only the forms of a new synthesis can remedy.

There is in this socialist humanism a great urge towards
truths which cannot be neglected without grave detriment,
and which are highly relevant to the sense of human dignity.
To my mind the fundamental error of an atheistic philosophy,
or at least of those original deficiencies of which I have just
been speaking, spoil this impulse and deform and dehuman-

[80]

ise in a certain measure the various moral and social conceptions elaborated by it. Thus it would be highly illusory to hold that a mere juxtaposition of the ideas of God and of religious belief with those of socialist humanism would create a viable synthesis founded on the truth. No, what is required is a radical reconstruction. But it is also my belief that what I have called integral humanism is able to save and to promote, under the terms of a fundamentally different synthesis, all the truths affirmed or brought to light by socialist humanism, by uniting them in a way which is vital and organic with numerous other truths. This is what, to my mind, makes the very name, *integral humanism,* particularly appropriate.

The analyses contained in this chapter have, I hope, made obvious how much such a reconstruction is to be desired. However grave its errors and illusions have been, Socialism in the nineteenth century was a protest uttered by the human conscience, and of its most generous instincts, against evils which cry to heaven. It was a noble work to bring capitalist civilisation to trial and to waken against powers which know no pardon, the sense of justice and of the dignity of labour: and in this work it took the initiative. It has fought a hard and difficult battle at the cost of innumerable sacrifices, filled with the most moving of human qualities, the self-sacrifice of the poor. It has loved the poor. We can only criticise it effectively while remaining at many points in its debt. Yet the deception it has caused among men is for all that only the more bitter. It is pitiful to record how the errors in the metaphysic and the social philosophy on which it originally depends have spoiled such rich resources and how they have grown and aggravated with its growth and create, as long as they endure, so deep a separation between socialism and christian thought. Will these always endure? They are primordial; they all belong to that primary misunderstanding of what is eternal in man.

The social and political philosophy implied by integral humanism calls for radical changes in our actual system of culture; let us say, to make analogical use of the vocabulary of hylemorphism, a substantial transformation. And this transformation demands, not only the inauguration of new social structures and a new scheme of social life succeeding that of capitalism, but also (and consubstantially) a rousing of forces of faith, of intelligence and of love in the inner depths of the soul, an advance in the discovery of the world of spiritual realities. Only on these conditions can man truly enter more profoundly into the deep planes of his nature, without mutilating or disfiguring it.

'For the first time in history', wrote Maxim Gorky recently, apropos of Soviet communism, 'the truth of man's love has been brought into action (organised) as a creative force, having for its aim the emancipation of millions of workers.[1] I am deeply convinced of the profound sincerity of these words of Gorky, and of the sentiment that they express. And it strikes me as highly relevant that the theme of human love, which nothing can prevent from having, in the deepest springs of its historical beginning, a christian origin, should now rise up in a current of thought which, under materialist influences, has long wished only to give it a secondary and sentimental value.

But the force of love is a wild and dangerous one; and when it comes, in the object of its love, to doors which are barred against it and regions into which it cannot enter, it turns into a thing of terror, to a murderous hatred. The ques-

[1]*Pravda*, 23rd May, 1934 (quoted by H. Isvolsky, *op. cit.*).

tion is whether, in order to win the keys of these doors and to pass beyond, and for this love to be the true love of man, we do not also need to love in man what in man vivifies man, Love itself and the Spirit's gift of love.

And when we also read in *Pravda*[1] that 'the new man is not made by himself; it is the Party which directs the whole process of the socialist re-creation and re-education of the masses', we can well ask ourselves whether socialist humanism does not hope, in Gorky's words, to organise, i.e. *socialise*, love. Love is of the spirit; we know not whence it comes nor whither it goes. Once in history this veritable love, on one man's initiative and in the midst of the ignorance of the world, achieved the deliverance of man from lies and evil forces, in order to open to him the joy that does not pass away. And, since that hour, it is by the power of the love so known that any real emancipation of men, not only for the joy that is eternal but in this temporal life, has been and will be accomplished.

'It is easy', said Marx, 'to be a saint if you have no wish to be human'. Then, in fact, you are neither human nor a saint: it is the ancient lie of pharisaism. But did Marx think it was easy to be human without being a saint? This is the great lie of atheistic humanism: since we are born to tend to the perfection of love, of a love which really and universally surrounds mankind, which leaves no place for hatred towards anyone, and which really transforms our being, as can no social technique, no system of re-education, but only the Creator of our being: and the name of this is—sanctity. However generous the feelings of an atheist, atheism turns to stone certain deep inner fibres of his being: his love for his fellows is a violent demand for their well-being, which rises like a

[1]*Pravda*, 17th May, 1934.

destructive force and which, springing from the rock, hurls itself against the rock, against a universe of human beings who are impenetrable to it. The love of the saints is a unifying and vivifying force, a light which diffuses goodness, because they themselves are broken and consumed in a living flame which triumphs over the impenetrability of beings one to another.

True humanism is not manichean

One more point with regard to Marx's humanism. Bound up from the beginning, as I recalled a moment ago, with the conceptions of Feuerbach, and with those of atheism as the condition and means of ending the spiritual alienation of man (as communism is the condition and means for ending that still deeper alienation of men's work), Marx's humanism is pre-eminently of that *manichean* kind that I have studied at greater length in a previous book.[1] It is compelled to reject, to the extent to which it has been religious, a whole section of our human heritage.

Christian humanism, on the other hand, integral humanism, is able to accept all, since it knows that God has no opposite, and that all is borne on irresistibly by the tide of His providence.[2] It does not reject what springs from heresies and schisms in its human heritage, the works of the heart or of the reason gone astray; *oportet haereses esse*. It knows that these historical forces energised by error have served the work of God despite themselves, and that in their own despite throughout the whole modern period they have felt the surge not only of illusory, but also of christian energies in this temporal life. In the scheme of christian humanism

[1] J. Maritain, *Freedom in the Modern World*, pp. 68-88.
[2] Cp. St. Thomas, *Sum. theol.*, i, 103, 6 and 7.

[84]

there is a place, not for the errors of Luther or Voltaire, but for Luther and Voltaire to the extent to which, in despite of themselves, they contributed to human history a certain increase and growth (which belong to Christ, as does all the good we know). I am glad to be Voltaire's debtor in the matter of civil tolerance or Luther's in that of non-conformism, and for these things I honour them; they belong to my cultural universe, they have their part there and their office: there I can talk with them, and when I strive against them, even when there is war to the knife between us, they are still alive for me. But in the scheme of Marx's humanism there is no place for St. Augustine or St. Theresa of Avila, save as moments in the progress of a dialectic whose only advance is over the dead.

Integral Humanism and the liquidation of the bourgeois man

Let us return to that 'bourgeois man' whose portrait I have endeavoured to sketch. What is he and what is his future in the eyes of this integral humanism?

To this integral humanism it is clear that the bourgeois type of humanity is not only seriously compromised, but deserves condemnation. Other types of humanity will come to be, which may, indeed, be very different, for the human species, within the limits of its immutable characteristics, is capable of being modelled or deformed. The man of a new age may differ as much from the bourgeois man as the latter from a Renaissance hero or one of the faithful in the times of St. Louis or of Ferdinand of Castille, as much as a son of the civilisations of Europe or China differs from a primitive nomad. Of one thing we may be sure:—however different this new type may be, if it is formed apart from God and the climate of love, created by purely external and social or technical means, it will but end, after a certain expenditure of heroism (such as there is in all revolutionary periods and where part of the treasure of Christian mysticism is wasted), in a new pharisaism in place of the old: a pharisaic pride in the collectivity or the means of production in place of the old bourgeois honour and individual enterprise.

My new humanism certainly wishes to change the bourgeois man. To do so it is also necessary to change man himself. Indeed, at bottom, this is all that matters, i.e. in the christian sense of the words, that 'the old man' should die and give place to 'the new man' and the slow growth of this latter, in the life of the human race as in that of each one of us, to the fullness of our age, whereby the deepest impulses of our very being are fulfilled. But this transformation demands, on the one hand, a respect for the essential exigencies of human nature and of this *image of God*, for that primacy of transcendental values which exactly allows for and prepares such a renewal; on the other, that we appreciate that such change is not the work of man only but, first of all, of God and of man in union with Him; that it is not the result of extrinsic and mechanical means, but of vital and internal principles: it is the unchanging christian teaching.

Nevertheless, if it becomes possible to inaugurate a new Christendom, its distinctive character, I think, will be that this transfiguration—whereby man, consenting to be changed and knowing that he *is changed* by grace, strives to *become* and to realise the new man who *is* from God—that this transfiguration should extend really, and not only figuratively, to the social structures of humanity and so bring about—in the degree to which that is possible here on earth and in given historical circumstances—a veritable socio-temporal realisation of the Gospels. A new age of

[86]

christian culture will no doubt understand a little better than any of us can at present (and the world will never have done with that effort, with the endeavour to reject the 'old leaven of the pharisees') how necessary it is to give preference everywhere to the real and the substantial over the apparent and the decorative,—to the really and substantially christian, over the apparently and seemingly christian. It will also understand that it is vain to assert the dignity and vocation of human personality if we do not strive to transform the conditions that oppress these; strive to deal so that men can live worthily and gain their bread in honour.

CHAPTER III

THE CHRISTIAN AND THE WORLD

I wish, in the first place, in this chapter to recall to mind certain essential points connected with the distinction between the spiritual and temporal spheres. The second section will deal with the problem of the Kingdom of God; the third with the earthly mission of the individual Christian in the world.

I

THE SPIRITUAL AND THE TEMPORAL

Concerning Civilisation

The first question is to know what we mean by the words civilisation or culture. It is customary for Russian and German writers to make an opposition between them; but in this book the two terms can be treated as synonymous. Let us say that civilisation or culture is that flowering which gives space for a rightly human life; is concerned not only with the necessary material development which permits the leading of a proper life here below, but also and primarily with men's moral development, the development of those spiritual and practical (artistic and ethical) activities which rightly merit the name of human progress. Civilisation is thus seen to be a natural thing in the same sense as are the workings of reason and virtue, whose fruit and accomplishment it is. It answers to an essential impulse of human nature, but is in itself a work of our spirit and our freedom acting in co-operation with nature. Since this development is not only material, but also and principally moral, it goes without saying that the religious element plays a primary part in it, and that this development has two poles: one economic, on the side of the most urgent necessities of the ethico-biological order; the other religious, on the side of the most urgent necessities of the life of the soul.

Does this mean that religion is a *part* (be it a principal part), is one of the constituent elements, of the civilisation or culture of a people? It was so in the ancient world—that is to say, in all pagan antiquity, for the case of the religion of Israel is a case apart: this latter was, in one sense, a national religion, but the prophets were there to bring to mind the fact that it was in principle universal and that the God of Israel is also the God of all the earth.

If it is a question of the pagan religions, they are seen to be each a quality of one particular culture and so opposed to every other culture. They are divided like languages or social groups. Religion is then the soul of the city, as in aristotelian biology the vegetative soul is the substantial form of the plant: and in that case a differentiation between the spiritual and temporal orders as being specifically distinct is strictly speaking inconceivable, and the more the religion becomes earthly and socio-political the more this is so.

The militant atheism of our day in a way imitates the catholicity of the religion of Christ, but the universality to which it tends aims at imposing on the whole world a particular temporal order: this religion of atheism is not a purely private affair like that of liberalism, but is incorporated in the earthly development of certain social forces, and in a certain particular form of temporal community.

What, then, is the christian position? For the Christian the true religion is essentially supernatural and, because it is

[89]

supernatural, it is not a part of man, nor of the world, nor of a race, nor of a culture, nor of civilisation,—it belongs to the inner life of God. It transcends all civilisation and every culture; it is strictly universal.

It is, indeed, a sufficiently remarkable fact that while reason has failed to maintain among men the universality of what the philosophers call natural religion, the universality of a religion which claims a supernatural title, and to be above reason, has up till now withstood all and every assault.

Religion and Civilisation

But, if this is so, the distinction between religion and culture or civilisation takes on a new and potent meaning. In the eyes of a Christian, culture or civilisation, since they are directed towards an earthly end, must have reference and be subordinate to that eternal life which is the end of religion, and must procure the earthly good fortune and the development of the various natural activities of man in strict relation to his eternal interests and in a way which facilitates his access to his final supernatural end: thereby raising to a higher plane the proper order of civilisation itself. But culture and civilisation have a specific object (the earthly and perishable good of our life here below) whose proper order is the natural order (raised to a higher plane as I have said).[1] In themselves and in their own ends they belong to the things of time and suffer the vicissitudes of time. Thus none of them have clean hands. The order of culture or civilisation appears then as the order of the things of time, as the *temporal order*.

On the other hand, the order of faith and the gifts of grace, being concerned with an eternal life which is a participation in the intimate life of God himself, constitute an order to

[1] Cp. *Science et Sagesse*.

[90]

which the name *spiritual* most rightly belongs and which, as such, transcends the temporal sphere. And if for the Christian this spiritual order should vivify and elevate the temporal order, it is not because it is any part of the temporal order, but, on the contrary, because it transcends this and is absolutely free and independent of it. In a word, the spiritual order enjoys in relation to the temporal order something of the freedom that God has in relation to the world.

This distinction between these two orders is an intrinsically christian one. It was born at a crucial (indeed a crucial!) moment, and is a shifting of emphasis of capital importance for all temporal history and for civilisation as such. But it is an achievement which is essentially christian and only has its full force and meaning for a Christian, according to the words of the Gospel: 'Render unto Caesar the things that are Caesar's, and unto God the things that are God's.'

Yet, if this distinction represents a major gain in the world of spiritual freedom, it does not fail for this very reason to set before us redoubtable problems, in the order of theory and in the order of concrete and historical events.

II

THE PROBLEM OF THE KINGDOM OF GOD

The chief of these problems in the theoretical sphere is what may be called the problem of the Kingdom of God. We know of the need to realise this Kingdom from the second petition of the Lord's Prayer. What part is played in the realisation of this Kingdom by these temporal and spiritual orders which we have just distinguished? In order to make clear the setting of this problem it is necessary, first of all, to indicate three typical errors with regard to it, and then the christian solution.

'Politische Theologie' and the Theology of Politics

The theoretical elucidation of this problem has recently taken on new actuality in Germany, in the theological discussions concerned with the Holy Roman Empire and what is known as *politische Theologie*. Several books have dealt with this theme, in particular Aloys Dempf's *Sacrum Imperium, Geschichte und Staatsphilosophie des Mittelalters und der politischen Renaissance* (1929).

At this point I must briefly digress, in order to avoid ambiguity and to indicate that the meaning of the German phrase *politische Theologie* is other than that of the French expression *théologie politique*. The meaning of the latter phrase is that politics or political thought, like all things belonging to the domain of morals, is a subject for the theologian as it is for the philosopher, by reason of the primacy of the moral and spiritual values which are involved in the political order, and because these values, in a world at once fallen and redeemed, imply a reference to the supernatural order and to revelation, which is the proper object of the theologian. Thus there is a theology as there is a philosophy of politics, a science whose object is *secular and temporal* and which judges and knows that object by the light of revealed principles.

The meaning of the German phrase *politische Theologie*, on the contrary, is that this object in question is not in reality secular and temporal: it is itself *sacred or holy (heilig)*. Carl Schmitt, who was one of the intellectual inspirers and counsellors of the new German regime, once tried to show in the major political and juridical ideas of modern times a transposition of essentially theological themes. From this, regarded speculatively from a concrete and historical standpoint, without taking into account the distinction between

[92]

the formal objects of the sciences, it is very easy to arrive at the point of declaring that political realities, as such, belong to the order of the sacred and the divine. It is this sense that the contemporary German theologians of the 'Sacrum Imperium' school give to the words *politische Theologie*: referring it to the messianic and evangelical idea of the *Kingdom of God*, whose realisation they seek to find in time and in history. On these lines the protestant theologian Stapel has declared that the fulfilment of the redemption requires not only the unification of all men in the Church, but also in the empire,—which will be brought about by the Germans (that is, by the Prussians), because of the higher stage of humanity which they represented. Authors much more profound than Stapel, such as Eschmann, Hermann Keller, Robert Grosche and Erik Peterson, have touched on these questions: the first in studies which, to my mind, are as interesting as they are questionable; the others in criticising, in the most penetrating and remarkable way, the theology of the 'Sacrum Imperium'.

The Kingdom, the Church and the World

Leaving this digression let us return to our central subject, with, first of all, an attempt at a clear statement of the problem.

We find ourselves faced by three forms of thought: of which the first is that of the *Kingdom of God*, the city which is at once *earthly and heavenly*, where God is king and where He will be all in all. The Jews looked for the Kingdom in time. For the Christian it is outside time: it is an eternal Kingdom, whose place will be in the new world of the resurrection of the dead. Inasmuch, then, as it is the idea of a veritable Kingdom, of a polity where God is king, and is, as such, distinguished from the idea of the Church, as was shown by

Erik Petersen in a remarkable little book written before his conversion to Catholicism,[1] this idea of the Kingdom of God is eschatological, an idea concerned with the end of time. It does not belong to the things of earthly time, but to what will be thereafter.

But what comes after time is prepared in time: the Kingdom of God constitutes the ultimate end prepared for by the movement of all history and in which it concludes, towards which converge, on the one hand, the history of the Church and the spiritual world; and on the other, the history of the secular world and the political city[2]: with this difference, that the Church is already the commencement of the

---

[1] *Was ist die Kirche*, Munich, 1929. The distinction drawn by Petersen in this essay, in a way of which to-day he would certainly modify the light and shade (he pushed it then to the point of an opposition, which cannot be reconciled with the catholic theory of the direct establishment of the Church by Jesus), this distinction between the Church and the Kingdom, is obviously one which must not be overstressed. The Church *is* the Kingdom of God in its beginning, in a state which is 'on pilgrimage, militant, crucified' (C. Journet). But it is not the Kingdom of God in *full realisation*, and as this implies the entire life which (risen) humanity will lead in the 'new earth', i.e. the 'paradisal, triumphant, glorified' Kingdom. To simplify the course of my argument it is this wholly eschatological notion which is here implied by the phrase 'the Kingdom of God', taken in the fullest and strongest sense of its meaning.

This chapter was written and had already appeared in *La Revue Philosophique* when Fr. Charles Journet's very important theological studies, 'Les Destinées du Royaume de Dieu' and 'Le Royaume de Dieu sur terre' appeared in *Nova et Vetera* (January-March, and April-June, 1935). These studies throw precious light and give point to many lines of thought, including in a note the outline of an important discussion of the Barthian position.

[2] The reader is asked to bear in mind, in this characteristic French use of the word 'city', which has no direct English equivalent, the use of the word in St. Augustine's *De Civitate* and the etymological origin of our 'politics' and 'polity' in the Greek *polis*, a city (Trans.).

Kingdom of God in its beginning in time, the 'crucified Kingdom' which in the end shall be revealed; while the history of the secular world will only come to its ultimate end by means of a substantial 'mutation', described as the conflagration or burning up of the world, by which it will be born into the Kingdom.

The *second* notion is that of the Church, the chrysalis of the Kingdom; which latter it already substantially is, existent and living, but veiled and in a state of pilgrimage: its end is eternal life; it is in time but not of time. Inasmuch as it is the Church, the Christian can say of her as of her Master, that in her the prince of this world has no part.

The *third* notion is that of the World, of the secular city. Its end is the temporal life of mankind. The world is in time and belongs to time: and in it the devil has his part.

What are we to think of the world and of the earthly city in regard to the Kingdom of God? That is the problem.

The First Error

It is necessary, first of all, to point out three typical erroneous ideas. In the first place we may mention an error which existed in embryo among certain extremists of the first christian epoch: which consisted in regarding the world and the earthly city as purely and simply the Kingdom of Satan, as solely the dominion of the devil. Their whole history is thus directed in a sense exactly opposite to that of the Church and leads to the kingdom of perdition. This may be termed the *satanocratic* conception of the world and the political city.

This conception gained in doctrinal force at the time of the Protestant Reformation; it still tends to reappear, in a finely elaborated and sensitive theological form which as far as may be attenuates its excesses,[1] among the theologians of the school of Karl Barth: in fact it ends in the idea that the world is not saved, in the same way as man is not intrinsically justified; comes to the point of holding that nature and its exterior forms are abandoned by God into the hands of the devil, against whom we can only bear witness in the midst of perdition.

One form of catholic naturalism or rationalism (I am thinking of Machiavelli or of Descartes) reaches the same result by a different path, by the way of separatism, of a scission between nature and grace. Then nature is seen as shut in upon itself, and abandoned as a result to the interplay of its own forces.

In both cases there is a denial of the world's destination for grace and of the coming of the Kingdom of God. Redemption is limited to an invisible empire over souls and to the moral order. This represents the extreme point of error for Western Christendom (when it loses its sense of catholicity). It is condemned in the most fundamental and most simple of all the formulas which express the christian faith, that which speaks of Christ as the Saviour of the world, *Salvator mundi*.[2]

---

[1]Profound as this theological elaboration often is, it undoubtedly does attenuate in its conclusions with regard to nature and culture the excess of that radical pessimism held by Karl Barth as inherent in the christian faith: but I doubt if it can achieve this without dialectical artifice. Cp. K. Barth, *The Word of God and the Word of Man*; Denis de Rougemont, *Politique de la Personne*. M. de Rougemont considers, as I do, this absolute pessimism which 'abandons the world to itself' as a 'heresy.' But he also regards as a heresy ('the heresy of synthesis') the catholic solution, which he calls rationalist, and whose true sense he has not grasped.

[2]St. John iv, 42.

The Second Error

Another error, whose seeds are equally old in the West as in the East, may be called in the latter case *theophanic*, and in the former *theocratic*. This holds that not only is the world saved in hope, but that—in so far as the work of redemption is accomplished in it—it ought to show in its temporal existence as already really and fully so, i.e. as already the Kingdom of God: and either, in the one case, men wholly despair of it because this is not so; or, in the other, they hope too much of it since men strive by their own efforts to make it so.

In the East these ideas have largely taken on a mystical form (hence the appropriateness of the word *theophanic* I have suggested). Carried to its final point the thought of many heretical mystics leads to the claim that the divinisation of our life should bring about here and now our deliverance from any law, from that of reason as of natural conditions. I am certainly not imputing any such extreme error to Russian Orthodoxy, but I think that it illustrates the peculiar *temptation* of Eastern Christendom: the cry that here and now heaven should come down upon earth,—and meanwhile this earth is only able to receive one dewfall of redemption: that is, pity; cosmic, tender, distracted pity. By an excess of impatience and supernaturalism a point of view is reached singularly analogous to that of Calvinism. Here the world, in its present form, is surrendered to the devil; not that we may take possession of the world; but to rid ourselves of it, and (until the coming of the great day of God) to deliver it at least *within ourselves* by the tears we give its miseries and which transfigure them in us. Hence Dostoevsky will accuse the Catholic Church, 'theocratic' as he may otherwise be, of being too incarnate, or seeking overmuch to realise a Christian order here below to the point of being soiled with the soiled substance of time's corruption.

In the West this error has primarily taken on a political form, and has given rise to complex developments. This is what may be called *theocratic* utopianism, giving the word, theocratic, its most absolute sense. This asks of the world itself and of the political city an effective realisation of the Kingdom of God,—at least in appearance and in the formulae of social life. Hence the world and the Church occupy (and dispute) the same ground; secular history is in itself holy.

This is in contradiction to the words of the Gospel: 'My Kingdom is not of this world.' It runs contrary to the fact that Christ did not come to change the kingdoms of this world or accomplish an earthly revolution: *non eripit mortalia, qui regna dat caelestia.*[1] This theocratic error is exhibited in Dostoevsky's *Legend of the Grand Inquisitor*, who seeks to bring about absolute happiness in this world by political means and then, as this is to ask more of these means than they are normally capable of giving, by absolute constraint and universal servitude.

This error never formally imposed itself on mediaeval Christendom; the mediaeval ideal of the empire was never identified with this standpoint, and when it tended towards such a confusion Rome broke it at Canossa. The distinction between the two powers was always affirmed by mediaeval Catholicism. Indeed, the idea of making this world purely and simply the Kingdom of God is heresy for a Christian.

But it was the temptation, the evil spirit of mediaeval

[1]These words from the Hymn for the Epiphany are quoted by Pope Pius XI in his encyclical on Christ the King.

Christendom. Theoretically we find it professed by certain extremist theologians of the Middle Ages, particularly of the dying Middle Ages, who have never been followed by the Church, men in whose eyes all power, temporal as well as spiritual, belonged to the Pope, who delegated to the emperor, and through him to the other monarchs (*potestas directa in temporalibus*), temporal power for the perfect unification of the world in the reign of Christ. This is what may be called clerical theocratism or hierocratism.[1]

In the cultural order, Spain can witness whether an element of this theocratic temptation did not enter into the Castillian ideal at the time of Charles V and Philip II. In any case, in practice there were certain excesses in the use of political and human means, on the protestant side in Calvin's Geneva, on the catholic side at the time of the Counter Reformation and the *ancien régime* (the Church, as such, was not involved in these excesses, but they were produced within the Church), and men have long remembered the shadow and the shiver of this error.

But it is in becoming progressively more secular that the historical weight of this error has grown more and more heavy. The sacred mission which it implies passes, first of all, into the hands of the emperor (*imperial theocratism*); then, in a minor degree, to the kings (Henry VIII comes to mind, also Gallicanism and Josephism); then, with a return to the major degree, it passes to the State (e.g. in the philosophy of Hegel). A rudimentary hegelianism transferred it to the

[1]For the history of these 'hierocratic' ideas, see particularly the studies of M. Arquillière (*St. Grégoire VII*, Paris, 1934) and M. Jean Rivière (*Le Problème de l'Eglise et de l'Etat au temps de Philippe le Bel*) and Mgr. Grabmann (*Uber den Einfluss der aristot. Phil. auf die Mittelalt. Theorien über das Verhältnis von Kirche und Staat*).

nation or the race; or a deeper hegelianism to the class, and we are back at the messianism of Karl Marx. There the proletariat is regarded as having the sacred mission of the world's salvation. In this perspective the cultural character of contemporary communism must be regarded as that of an atheist theocratic imperialism.

The Third Error

The third error belongs to the modern age, which began with the Renaissance. It consists in seeing in the world and the earthly city purely and simply the domain of man and of nature, without any connection with the sacred or any supernatural destiny, with either God or the devil. This is what can be called detached or anthropocentric humanism, or liberalism (taking this latter in its theological sense, where it implies the doctrine that human freedom has no other measure or rule than itself). The history of the world is then taken as leading to the kingdom of pure *humanity*, which is, as can be easily seen in Auguste Comte, a secularisation of the Kingdom of God. This error is condemned by the text: man does not live by bread alone, but by every word that cometh from the mouth of God (*non in solo pane vivit homo, sed in omni verbo quod procedit ex ore Dei*). It is, moreover, in its very nature unstable, for its aim is at once abstract and fictitious. It belongs to the species of utopias in the true sense of the word (unrealisable utopias, if I may put it so, for in a sense there are utopias which can be realised). It had thus to end in that erroneous historical ideal, erroneous, but yet in a way realisable (for it appeals not to a fiction, but to force), of which I spoke under the second head,—in the error of atheistic theocratism.

The Double-meaning (*Ambivalence*) of the World

Let us now seek the christian solution. For Christianity, the truth about the world and the earthly city is that they are the kingdom at once of man, of God, and of the devil. This is the cause of the essential ambiguity of the world and history: it is the common ground of these three together. The world belongs to God by right of creation; to the devil by right of conquest, because of sin; to Christ by right of victory over the first conqueror, by his Passion. The task of the Christian in this world is to dispute his domain with the devil and wrench it from him. He must strive to this end, in which he will never wholly succeed while time endures. The world is saved indeed, it is delivered *in hope*, it is on the march towards the Kingdom of God; but it is not *holy*, it is the Church that is *holy*. It is on the march towards the Kingdom of God, and that is why it is treachery towards that Kingdom not to seek with all our power,—in relation and proportion to the conditions of earthly history, but as effectively as possible, *quantum potes, tantum aude*,—a realisation, or more truly, the refraction in this world of the exigencies of the Gospel. Nevertheless this realisation, even a relative one, will always, in one way or another, be deficient and disputed in this world. At one and the same time this world is on the march, —it is the growing of the wheat—towards the Kingdom of God; it is also on the march,—it is the growth of the tares, inextricably mingled with the wheat,—towards the kingdom of reprobation.

A Christian can thus put side by side contrasting texts which show this essential ambivalence of the world's history, as I have already shown elsewhere.[1] We read, for in-

[1]*Freedom in the Modern World.*

stance, that 'God so loved the world that He gave his only-begotten Son', that 'Christ has come to save the world', that He 'takes away the sin of the world'; and, on the other hand, that Jesus did not pray for the world, that 'this world cannot receive the spirit of truth', that 'the whole world lies in evil', and that the devil is the prince of this world and that the world is already judged.

These texts imply that the world is sanctified in the degree to which it is *not only* this world, but is assumed into the universe of the Incarnation; and that it is reprobate in so far as it shuts itself up into itself, in so far, in the words of Claudel, as it is entrenched in its essential difference, as it remains *only* this world, separate from the universe of the Incarnation.

While the history of the Church, which is, as Pascal said, the history of the truth, leads, as such, towards the final revelation of the Kingdom of God and has no other end than that Kingdom, the history of the temporal city, divided between two opposing final ends, leads, on the contrary, at one and the same time to the kingdom of perdition and the Kingdom of God.

Be it pointed out that it would be a complete misunderstanding and perversion of this idea of the ambivalence of the world and secular history, of the fact that the devil will always have his part *in this world* while time endures, to find there a motive for tranquilly accepting, particularly when it profits us, the iniquities of this world. It is in the same perverse fashion that some who believe themselves to be the defenders of order use the text: 'The poor you will have always with you.'[1]

[1]The text (Matt. xxvi, 11) does not say 'the poor (as a class)' (there will always be a poor class); it says 'the poor (i.e. the needy)' (*tous ptokhous*). The sense is clear: 'The needy, in whom I am, you will always find among

On the contrary, the significance of the text is that Christ himself will not always be among us, but that we can find Him and meet with Him in the poor, who are to be loved and served in Him and as His. This is not a question of any social class: they are those who have need of others to subsist, whatever be the nature, the cause, or the origin of their indigence. While there are oppressed castes or classes thither love will go to seek them first of all: and if on a day these are no more, it will seek and find them wheresoever they are. And because it loves, love looks for the day when there will be no more oppressed classes or castes.

In the same way, what I have said of this inevitable double-meaning (ambivalence) of secular history implies that the Christian must needs strive *as far as possible* to realise in this world (perfectly and absolutely in the case of himself as an individual; in a relative mode and according to the concrete ideal which belongs to each different age with regard to the world itself) the truths of the Gospel. We can never strive enough, never be sufficiently devoted to this endeavour to advance the conditions of our terrestrial life and to transfigure it. This state of tension and warfare is a necessary condition of the growth of history, the essential condition whereby the history of time enigmatically prepares its final consummation in the Kingdom of God.

But, if what I have said hitherto is correct, the aim the Christian sets himself in his temporal activity is not to make *this world in itself* the Kingdom of God, it is to make of this world, according to the historical ideal called for by the varying epochs and, if I may say so, as moulded by this latter,

you, to serve me in them; but I myself am going, and that is why Magdalene has done well in pouring on my head this perfume of great price. . . .'

the field of a truly and fully human life, i.e. one which is assuredly full of defects, but is also full of love, whose social forms are measured by justice, by the dignity of human personality, by brotherly love,[1] and which as much as it may prepares for the coming of the Kingdom of God, not slavishly, but in a spirit of sonship, of fraternity, where goodness is fruitful for good, not where evil, going in its own way to its own end, serves the work of goodness by a kind of violence.[2]

[1] By reason of the weakness of our species, evil is more frequent among men than good; and with the growth of history it grows and deepens at the same time as good and mingled with it: it is the statistical law of human behaviour. But social structures, institutions, laws and customs, political and economic organisations, are not men though they are human: in the very degree to which they are things, not men, they can be purified of certain particular miseries of human life; and like many of the works of men, they are made by man and are better than he, in their order and in certain aspects. They can be measured by justice or brotherly love, while the acts of men are rarely measured by that measure; they can be more just than the men who use and apply them. But they remain *things*, and are by that very fact realities essentially inferior in degree to that of the *persons* whose communications and life they serve to regulate.

[2] The criticism which M. Denis de Rougemont, in a book otherwise rich in true and penetrating comments (*Politique de la Personne*, Grasset, Paris, 1934), applies to all Christendom as such and the very notion (which, moreover, he has singularly misunderstood) of a christian order of the world, rests, it seems to me, on the principle (an erroneous one to the Catholic faith) that all human and natural activity being essentially corrupt in origin, and thus without any possible vital unity with inward grace, any effort to institute a 'christian temporal order' aims necessarily —in the name of Christianity—at doing the will of man without reference to the 'justice' of God, and is thus of necessity hypocritical. Moreover, to the Barthian view, the history of the secular world can in nowise prepare a positive growth of the Kingdom of God,—even enigmatically and on condition of that essential discontinuity which is marked by the final mutation and which separates the 'penultimate' from the ultimate.

III

THE CHRISTIAN'S TEMPORAL MISSION

The secular failure of a once christian world

We have thus come to a mighty question, one that is no longer theoretic but practical, that of the temporal mission of the Christian. I shall divide the study of this into three sections, endeavouring first of all to characterise what can be called the secular failure of a christian world which, in the course of the modern age and more particularly of the nineteenth century, has more and more become so only in appearance. I shall then try to indicate (referring the reader to what I have already written on the theme[1]) briefly the causes of this phenomenon, and shall next go on to a consideration of the temporal rôle of the Christian, treating this particularly in relation to the inauguration of a new christian life in this world.

It was pointed out at the beginning of this chapter that it is the office of spiritual things to vivify the things of time. Christianity should inform, or better, interpenetrate the world, not that this is its primary end (it is a secondary and indispensable one), and not that this world should become the Kingdom of God, but in order that the refraction of the world of grace should be more and more effective in it, and that man should live better his life in the things of time.

In large measure this was the case for mediaeval Christendom. Everyone knows the capital rôle played by the Church in the building up of the christian world of the Middle Ages: a world full of defects but livable.

[1] Cp. *Freedom in the Modern World.*

[105]

With the decadence of the mediaeval christian order and the coming of modern times, we see, on the one hand, a progressive detachment of the world from Christ; and, on the other, the Church still plays a very great part, endeavouring to maintain what has already been won with regard to the realisation of the principles of the natural law in the secular order and with regard to the subordination of this order to spiritual ends. It was a defensive position which though necessary was thankless, since it ran the risk in some degree of creating an apparent solidarity between Christianity and the forms of a world which meanwhile was becoming more and more inhuman.

Nevertheless the play of historic forces yet remained for long at a sufficiently normal level; and if the world of the *ancien régime* ended by becoming unlivable, its politico-social structure, with its three qualitative orders (the noblesse, the clergy, the third estate) for long continued to be an organic structure adapted to the needs of life.

This situation only became tragic after the fall of the *ancien régime* had become inevitable, after the French Revolution and Napoleon, with the coming of the industrial and mercantile world, when society found itself cut in two into two classes: the one living exclusively by its labour, the other which lives (or more truly lived) on the revenues of its capital, classes which have no other economic relation than the wage-system, whereby work itself has become a mere commodity. While all the time preserving an element of Christianity in its ethical and cultural foundations, and while making great use, among the conservative elements and for interested political ends, of the name of Christianity and its moral vocabulary, a civilisation which in the mass has turned away from Christianity under the pressure of adverse forces,

where the christian sap had itself grown weak, came, even in
its christian elements, to accept the inhuman position created
for the proletariat by an uncontrolled capitalism, and so became totally absorbed in the blind movement of a social
materialism which practically and in action proclaims by
what it is the ruin of the christian spirit.[1]

There is no need here to bring capitalism to book; its condemnation has become a commonplace that minds with an
objection to platitude fear to reiterate. I shall content myself
with the brief comment that if, taken in itself, the ideal
mechanism of the capitalist system is not essentially evil and
unjust as Marx held it to be,[2] yet, when we consider the
spirit which makes concrete use of that mechanism, and
which determines its concrete forms and particular realisations, it must be said that it hides a radical disorder. The
energy which stimulates and drives this economy has been
progressively soiled by a 'capital' sin: not certainly a sin

[1]'Compromise is as impossible between the Church of Christ and the
idolatry of wealth, which is the practical religion of capitalist societies, as
it was between the Church and the State idolatry of the Roman Empire.
It is that whole system of appetites and values, with its deification of the
life of snatching to hoard and hoarding to snatch, which now, in its hour
of triumph, while the plaudits of the crowd still ring in the ears of its
gladiators and the laurels are still unfaded on their brows, seems sometimes to leave a taste as of ashes on the lips of a civilisation which has
brought to the conquest of its material environment resources unknown
to earlier ages, but which has not yet learned to master itself' (R. H. Tawney, *Religion and the Rise of Capitalism*, 1926, pp. 286-7).

[2]I am primarily thinking of the mechanism, considered in itself, of the
law of partnership, with the remuneration for the capital involved which
it implies. In fact, by reason of the spirit of adventure for mercantile profit
and the accumulation of goods characteristic of the capitalist age, and by
reason of the special instruments which it has created (e.g. the limited
company), this contract has come in reality to play the part of a contract
by loan (*mutuum*), and its economy thus passed under the law of usury.
Cp. *Religion and Culture*, note 2.

which does to death the souls of the individuals compelled to live in such a world and utilise its machinery, but a sin which little by little brings about the temporal death of the social body: the cult of earthly riches which has become the form of civilisation. The objective spirit of capitalism is a spirit of the exaltation of men's active and inventive powers, of human dynamism and individual initiative; but it is a spirit of hatred of poverty and of contempt for the poor: the poor man only exists as an instrument of production, a 'hand', not as a person. The rich man, on the other hand, does not exist as a person, but as a consumer (for the benefit of the capital involved in this same production): and the tragedy of such a world is that the working and development of this frankenstein of a usurious economy should necessarily tend to make all men consumers or rich, while at the same time, if there are no poor, no instruments or 'hands', the whole economy stops and dies: and it equally dies, as we see to-day, if there are not enough consumers (in act)[1] to bring the 'hands' into work.

But is not the fact that such a system has been able to develop freely its most inhuman potentialities a singularly grave sign of decadence in the world that issued from the dissolution of Christendom, a world which long since has repudiated its own principles and denied its own God? And in this decadence of a world which sociologically and culturally, despite the power and variety of the forces of unbelief which it deploys, can still be called christian by reason of its historical foundations, is not there also a responsibility which

[1]The unemployed are potential consumers. In the face of this mass of humanity in a state of privation, the existence of a mass of products in *apparent* over-production, because no connection can be established between the two, stands as the condemnation of an economy based on the capitalist theory of profit.

falls on the Christians themselves? Does this not imply a bankruptcy of the 'christian world' in the strictest sense of that term, i.e. the social elements and formations gathered together under the names of religious and christian? I am well aware that it would be unjust to reproach Christians with not having prevented the development of the new forms of life and new economic structures which the errors and the evils proper to the capitalist age have deflected and deformed, but which in essence and abstractly considered are not evil and correspond to a normal progress. But in the purely ethical order of the personal use which they have made of these new economic structures (in other words, in the social order as envisaged from the standpoint of the private virtues) there is ample space for deploring the indifference shown by so many Christians, since the barbarous and victorious days of early capitalism, to the laws of christian conduct in their social bearing. A social system which, concretely taken, is in itself not good, has thus progressively worsened to the point of becoming intolerable. And we have equal need to deplore the fact that, in the social order as envisaged from the point of view of social life itself and the activities of earthly civilisation, the place which socialism found vacant, and took and planted with mighty errors, had not been taken and used by forces of christian inspiration, calling into play a social philosophy based on truth; and giving the signal for the movement of emancipation among the workers. We are faced by the question of explaining this double failure.

Some reasons for this failure

Many reasons could be suggested: first of all, the *dualism* of the modern age, whose extreme results are here seen in the form of that division of labour between God and Mammon, of which I have already spoken.

In the second place it may be pointed out that, generally speaking, it is natural that there should be more 'bad Christians' than 'good Christians' in a christian civilisation: and hence by a gradual decline a sociological *naturisation* of religion is too often achieved and a utilisation of Christianity for wholly secular ends.

There is yet a third cause, which belongs rather to the intellectual order, and which makes apparent to what an extent modern civilisation, even where it still calls itself christian, has suffered from the lack of a christian *philosophy*. In the christian world of the Middle Ages, despite enormous obstacles, civilisation was orientated, as though unconsciously and by the spontaneous instinct of faith, towards a realisation of Christianity not only in the life of souls but in the socio-temporal order as well.

'When with the "reflective age" the inner differentiation of culture became a leading feature of life, and art and science and philosophy and the State began each to be conscious (with what an awful conscience) of itself, it is perhaps not inaccurate to say that there was no similar study of the social order as such or of the essential nature of its being. How indeed could there in a world which was to grow up under the ascendency of Descartes? . . . It was not that the spirit of the Gospels was wanting in living and saintly members of the christian world, but an explicit and proper awareness was lacking of one of the areas of reality to which that spirit should be applied. And though the claim of August Comte to be the inventor of social science is largely inadmissible, it may fairly be argued that the "scientific" illusions of sociology—and likewise of socialism—have assisted the children of light by obliging them to explore by the aid of philosophic reflection these areas of human life and activity.'[1]

These considerations may contribute to an explanation of why the transformation which little by little substituted the system of lending at interest and of capitalism for the economic system of the Middle Ages, although it has, from the beginning and at various subsequent stages, as M. Groethuysen has reminded us,[2] roused the hostility of the Church and set many questions to the christian intellect concerned with the individual conscience and the confessional, has yet, for so long a time, not been thought out or measured by that intellect in terms of its veritable social significance and value: so that the capitalist system was able to establish itself in the world and encountered a passive resistance and dumb hostility in catholic social formations, but without provoking any efficacious efforts to redress the balance or an active and deliberate opposition in the heart of the christian world or of the 'christian temporal order', even in catholic circles.

'One ought, however, to observe that the catholic conscience did not fail to make its protest heard. In the nineteenth century in particular, at the very time when capitalism was reaching maturity and taking possession of the world, men like Ozanam and Vogelsang and Le Tour de Pin raised up their voices. And above all the Church itself made good the shortcomings of christian society by formulating the principles and essential truths that govern the whole field of economic affairs and that the established order of modern societies largely fails to recognise.'[3]

[1] *Freedom in the Modern World*, p. 123-4.

[2] Bernard Groethuysen, *Origines de l'esprit bourgeois en France, I: l'Eglise et la Bourgeoisie*, Paris, N.R.F., 1927.

[3] *Freedom in the Modern World*, p. 125.

The Christian's temporal part in the transformation of the social system

I wish here to bring forward certain considerations concerned with the temporal rôle to be played by the individual Christian in the work of transforming the social system. First of all let it be said that the *dualism* of the previous age is at least for christian thought now at an end. For a christian, separatism and dualism, whether of the school of Machiavelli or of Descartes, have had their day. An important process of integration is taking place, a return to a wisdom which is at once theological and philosophic, a return to a vital synthesis. There is much need for a similar integration to ethics of the things in the domain of politics and economics, due regard being had for their respective natures.

Again, that *social consciousness* which was more or less lacking in the christian world at the beginnings of the modern period is at long last coming into existence. This is a phenomenon of considerable importance, all the more so as this consciousness is informed and will be more and more informed by a just understanding of modern history and its normal processes which were vitiated yesterday by capitalist materialism and are vitiated to-day by the communist materialism which has succeeded it.

At the same time light has been thrown on the proper part to be played by christian activities in the things of time, with regard to the world and its culture. From this angle one may say that, while the Church itself, above all anxious not to become the adjunct of any one particular system, has been more and more freed, not from the necessity of judging things from above, but of administering and directing the temporal things of this world, the individual Christian finds himself more and more engaged in exactly these things, not so much as a member of the Church, but as a citizen of the earthly city, i.e. as a *christian citizen*, conscious of the task incumbent on him of working for the inauguration of a new secular order.

But as soon as things are looked on in this light at once a new series of problems arise.

It will be necessary to elaborate a social, political and economic philosophy, which will not rest content with universal principles, but which must be capable of coming down to the details of concrete realisation; a task which presupposes an immense amount of work, both vast and delicate. A beginning has already been made in the encyclicals of Leo XIII and Pius XI, which lay down the general principles. I may point out that this is a question of a work of the reason, of reason indeed illuminated by faith, but a work of the reason, in which, as soon as we quit the principles to come down to their particular application, it will be vain to look for a unanimous agreement. If there are diverse schools of dogmatic theology there will inevitably be a like diversity among the schools of christian sociology and of christian politics, divisions which will only increase the more with each approach to the concrete. Nevertheless a common doctrine can doubtless be formulated, at least in what is concerned with more general truths: and for the rest, what is important is that a general plan which is truly precise and practical should be elucidated for a sufficient number of minds.

But the Christian conscious of these things must also approach the point of political and social action, not only, as has always been the case, in devoting his professional gifts to the service of his country according to his capacities, but also and more particularly in order to work, as I have said, towards a transformation of the temporal order.

But, since it is clear that social Christianity is inseparable from spiritual Christianity, it is impossible that a vitally christian transformation of the temporal order can take place in the same way or by the same means as other temporal transformations and revolutions. If this is to be it will be a fruit of christian heroism.

'The social revolution will be moral or it will be nothing.' This famous saying of Charles Péguy can be entirely misunderstood. 'It does not mean that before a reform of the social order can be made effective all men must first be converted to virtuous living. Interpreted in that way, the saying would be merely a pharisaical pretext for avoiding any effort at social reform. Revolutions are the work of comparatively small groups of men who devote all their energies to the task: it is to these men that the words of Péguy are addressed. His meaning is: you can only transform the social order of the modern world by effecting at the same time and first of all within your own soul a renewal of moral and spiritual life: by digging down to the moral and spiritual foundations of human existence, and reviving the moral ideas that govern the life of the social body as such; and by awakening a new impulse in the secret sources of its being. . . .

'But has the true and perfect heroism, the heroism of love, no lesson to offer? Once the christian conscience comes to realise the essential character of social life, with its distinctive being and reality and technique, will not christian sanctity have to enter and labour in the same field in which the Hammer and the Sickle and the Fasces and the Swastika are severally pursuing their heroic task? Is it not high time that sanctity should descend from the heaven of cloistered life that four centuries of the baroque spirit had reserved for it, descend to the world of secular culture and labour in social and political affairs with a view to the reform of the temporal order of mankind? Yes, indeed; on condition that it retains its sanctity and does not lose its character on the way. There is the rub.

'The christian body has at such a time as ours two opposite dangers that it needs avoid: the danger of seeking sanctity only in the desert, and the danger of forgetting the need of the desert for sanctity; the danger of enclosing in the cloister of the interior life and of private virtue the heroism it ought to share among mankind, and the danger of conceiving this heroism, when it overflows into social life and endeavours to transform it, in the same manner as its materialist opponents: according to a purely external standard; which is to pervert and dissipate it. Christian heroism has not the same sources as heroism of other kinds. It has its source in the heart of a God scourged and turned to scorn and crucified outside the city gate.

'It is time for christian sanctity again as in the centuries of the Middle Ages to put its hand to the things of earth but with the consciousness that its strength and majesty are from elsewhere and of another order.'[1]

A vitally christian social renewal will thus be a work of sanctity or it will be nothing: a sanctity, that is, which has turned its energies on the things of time, of this world, of secular culture. Has the world not known heretofore leaders of the people who were saints? If a new Christendom is to arise in history it will be the work of such leaders and such sanctity.

[1] *Freedom in the Modern World*, pp. 142, 144-5.

A new style of sanctity

We have thus come to a new and final problem: if these observations are exact, we have the right to look for a new impulse of sanctity of a new kind.

Do not let us talk about a 'new type of sanctity'; the phrase is more than ambiguous: there is only one *type* of sanctity recognised by Christians, once and forever manifested in Christ. But the changing conditions of history allow of new ways, new styles of sanctity. The sanctity of St. Francis has a different physiognomy from that of St. Simeon Stylites. Jesuit spirituality, Dominican spirituality, Benedictine spirituality have each their different modes. We are thus justified in thinking that the Christian's awareness of his social and temporal office calls for a new way of sanctity, one which may be primarily characterised as a sanctity and sanctification of *secular* life.

But, indeed, this new way is new primarily in regard to certain erroneous and materialised preconceptions. This is so since—as often happened in the age of classical humanism —the well-known distinction between the two states of life (the religious and the secular), when subject to a form of sociological depression, is understood in a materialistic and inexact sense; the religious life, i.e. the life of those vowed to the search for perfection, is then regarded as the state of the perfect and the secular state as that of the imperfect, so that in a way it becomes the duty and metaphysical function of the imperfect to be imperfect and to stay so: to lead a good, not too pious, worldly life, solidly grounded on a social naturalism (above all in family ambition). On these terms it would be scandalous for lay folk to seek to live otherwise; their business is from their material resources to make prosperous,

[116]

by means of pious foundations, the religious who in exchange will win them a way into heaven, whereby all the claims of order will be satisfied.

This way of conceiving of lay humility seems to have been widely enough extended in the sixteenth and seventeenth centuries. It was for this reason that the explanatory catechism of the dominican Carranza, who was, moreover, Archbishop of Toledo, was condemned by the Spanish Inquisition at the direction of the celebrated theologian, Melchior Cano. This latter declared that 'it is entirely wrong to claim to give the faithful a form of religious instruction which is only suitable to priests. . . . He was equally in arms against the reading of the Gospel in the common tongue, against those who made it a duty all the day long to confess their faith. The zeal of spiritual directors for frequent confession and communion among the faithful was to him highly suspect, and the saying is attributed to him in a sermon that in his eyes one of the signs of the approach of Anti-christ was this general frequentation of the sacraments.'[1]

Going deeper into the matter, and thereby coming to a very important question for cultural philosophy, it can be said that there is a way of seeing this distinction between the sacred and the profane which is not christian, but pagan.

For pagan antiquity what was *holy* was synonymous with the *sacred*, i.e. with what physically, visibly, socially belonged to God. And it was only in the degree to which these sacred functions entered into human life that the latter had any value before God. The Gospel changed all this profoundly, by setting in the heart of man, in the secret and invisible relations between the Divine personality and the human, the

[1]Sandreau, 'Le mouvement antimystique en Espagne au XVIme siecle,' *Revue du Clergé français*, 1st August, 1917.

core of the moral life and the life of sanctity. Henceforth the secular is no longer opposed to the sacred as the impure to the pure, but as a certain order of human activities with a temporal specific end is in opposition to another order of human activities socially built up for a specific end which is spiritual. And the man who is engaged in this profane and temporal order can and should, like the man engaged in the sacred order, tend towards sanctity,—so as to himself attain to union with the divine, and also to bring about the fulfilment of the divine Will in the entire order to which he belongs. In fact this secular order, as a collective form, will always be deficient,[1] but we ought thereby to wish and to strive all the more that it be the best that may be. For the justice of the Gospels claims to penetrate all things, to be concerned with all things, to affect the lowest things as the highest. More, it can be pointed out that this evangelical principle is only progressively manifested and translated in concrete terms, and that the process of this realisation is by no means complete.

The foregoing remarks should have made clear the significance of this new kind of sanctity, that new stage in the sanctification of what is profane, of which I have been speaking. Let it be added that this new mode, which touches pure spirituality, will probably have the stamp of certain particular specifically spiritual characteristics—for example, an insistence on simplicity, on the value of ordinary means, on that specifically christian trait of perfection being the perfection, not of a stoic athleticism of virtue, but of the *love* between

---

[1]The order of sacred activities will also, in the degree to which it is a collective human form, be deficient here on earth. It is in so far as it is specially assisted by the Spirit of God, and in the degree to which it is governed by its invisible Head (and by its visible head when he acts by right of his universal authority), that the Church is indefectible.

two persons, created personality and the Person of God; finally, an insistence on that law of the descent of the un-created Love into the depths of the human, to transfigure without annihilating it, which was in question in the pre-ceding chapter,—characteristics of which certain contem-porary saints seemed charged to show us the importance. It is, moreover, in the order of things that it is not in the secular life, but in certain souls hidden from the world, some living in the world, some on the crest of the highest towers of Christendom, in other words in the supremely contemplative orders, that the first light of the dawn of this way of sanctity, of this new impulse of spirituality, is break-ing; to spread from thence into all our temporal and secular ways of life.

The mystery of this world

I shall reserve for a later page that question of the world and its significance which is a capital one for christian philo-sophy, and whose multiple problems call for deeper study. In this chapter I have only been able to touch on it from the outside, and to indicate certain general positions which strike me as of primary importance. To make a brief résumé of these: while yet in anticipation of that hour beyond history when the Kingdom of God will be fully manifest in glory, the Church is already the Kingdom of God in what we call the *spiritual* order and in a state of pilgrimage and crucifixion; and the world, the so-called *temporal* order, the world enclosed in history, is a divided and double-meaning domain, —belonging at one and the same time to God, to mankind and to 'the Prince of this world'.

The Church is holy, the world is not holy; but the world is saved in hope, and the blood of Christ, the vivifying prin-

[119]

ciple of the Redemption, acts already within it: a divine and hidden travail works in history, and in each age of civilisation, beneath each 'historic heaven', the Christian must strive for some proportionate realisation (in expectation of that final realisation which is beyond time), for some realisation of the claims of the Gospel and of practical christian wisdom in the socio-temporal order,—a realisation which is thwarted in fact and more or less masked and deformed by sin: but that is another matter.

Since men taken collectively live more often according to the senses than by reason, this work of which I speak (where the Christians to undertake it are not lacking,—otherwise it is adverse forces which take it in charge, under the banners of destruction) meets, in the ordinary course of things, stronger resistance and more frequent betrayal the more it succeeds in establishing itself in existence: hence the incessant necessity of beginning again, of starting once more at the lowest rung, of perpetually compelling history to rise always the same, from one fall after another, until the hour will strike that brings it to an end.

CHAPTER IV

THE HISTORICAL IDEAL OF A NEW CHRISTIAN ORDER

After certain preliminary remarks, this chapter is devoted in the first place to certain general aspects of the problem; in the second, to an endeavour to characterise the historical ideal of the christian order of the Middle Ages; and finally, to the question of what became of this ideal in a subsequent period, more particularly the results of the effort made by the *ancien régime* to carry on certain elements of that ideal into a world which had more and more turned against it

I

INTRODUCTORY

It will be necessary, first of all, to delimit our theme and make it more precise. What is in question is the *concrete historical ideal* of a new Christendom. What is meant by a 'concrete historical ideal' is that *prospective type*, that particular and specific (ideal) image of itself towards which a given concrete historical epoch tends.[1]

When Thomas More, or Fenelon, or Fourier, or Saint-Simon construct an *utopia*, they construct an *ens rationis* (i.e. a construction of the mind, not of reality), isolated from existence at any given date, from the atmosphere of any special period, expressing an *absolute* maximum of social and political

[1]Cp. *Freedom in the Modern World*, pp. 103-111.

[121]

fulfilment, developed to the highest point of imaginary detail, since what is in question is a fictitious model which is put forward *in the place of* reality. On the other hand, what I have called a *concrete historical ideal* is not an *ens rationis*, but an ideal *essence* which is realisable (with more or less difficulty, more or less imperfectly, but that is another affair; and not as a finished thing, but as a thing in process), an essence able to exist and called to exist in a given historical atmosphere, and as a result corresponding to a *relative* maximum (relative to that historical state) of social and political perfection, and only presenting,—precisely because it implies an order capable of concrete existence,—the lines of force and the rough outlines requiring further determination of a future reality.

In making this opposition between a *concrete historical ideal* and an *utopia* I intend no diminution of the value of the part utopias have played in history, and in particular of the importance of the so-called 'utopian phase' of Socialism in its subsequent development. This notion of a concrete historical ideal and the use that can justly be made of it seems to my mind to allow the preparation by a christian philosophy of culture of its future temporal realisations, and eliminates the need for any such utopian phases or for any recourse to the fictions of an utopia.

The historical ideal and liberty

Marx criticises this notion of an ideal and that of an utopia in the same terms, being unable to distinguish between them. This is a consequence of his inverted hegelianism.

Like every other man, and particularly all great men of action, Marx believed *in practice* in free will, i.e. in the will's mastery of its own motives, by which it dominates inwardly the whole conditioning of its acts[1]; *speculatively* his philosophy interdicted the belief in this 'spiritual' or 'christian' notion, and reduced human freedom to the spontaneous action of a vital energy which, by its awareness of the movement of history, becomes this latter's deepest and most effective force. But if the revolutionary thinker is thus like some historical prophet or titan it is in the degree to which he reveals the sense of history to itself, and lays bare the destined end of its action and directs human wills towards that end. This is the point of debate; not the question of knowing whether Marx was a partisan of fatalism or of mechanistic determinism, questions to which a negative answer must clearly be made.

Man, in Marx's eyes, is not a *passive* product of his surroundings: he is active, he acts on his surroundings to transform them,—but '*in a sense determined by* economic and social evolution'.[2] That is the important point here.

This assertion is indeed true and corresponds to the idea to which I have frequently referred in this book, of successive 'historical heavens', if it implies that history *has a meaning*—one that is *determined* in regard to certain fundamental characteristics by the immense dynamic mass of the past which drives it forward, but which is at the same time *indeterminate* in regard to the specific orientations which actualise themselves in the flow of the present and which translate the attractions exercised upon it by one or another form of the concrete future, according as these find a more or less effective

[1]It should be remembered here and elsewhere that the English 'free will' corresponds to the more exact French '*libre arbitre*' or 'free choice' (*liberum arbitrium*), and the theological implications must be taken as applying to the latter, not the former. 'Free will' is not exact, but it is consecrated by the habit of general use (trans. note).

[2]Cp. A. Cornu, *op. cit.*, p. 392.

welcome in the actual thoughts and desires of men. Marxist formulae often give it a very different sound; and Marx, by his lack of any clear idea of the virtual or of freedom, seems to have failed to appreciate the meaning of that sphere of *indeterminateness* to which I have just referred.

He was deeply, almost tragically, aware of the way in which history shapes men instead of being shaped by them. But if he had had a just metaphysical idea of human freedom, had understood that man is endowed with a liberty whereby, in the degree to which he is a person, he can, with more or less difficulty indeed, yet really, triumph over necessity within himself, he would have understood that, without thereby being able arbitrarily to twist the course of history to his fancy or his tastes, man can yet raise new currents in the flood of circumstance, which make one with other forces and trends and pre-existent conditions, to determine the movement of history, which is not *fixed in advance* by evolution: rather it depends on an enormous mass of accumulated necessities and fatalities, but one in which the interventions of that freedom can take effect; it is only fixed in advance in the degree (too high a one, it is true) to which man renounces his own freedom.

If in fact this freedom plays so small a part in the history of the world, it is because men collectively considered live so little the true life of reason and of freedom; hence it is not surprising that they are so largely in fact 'subject to the stars'. Nevertheless we can escape from that subjection. And when we view the perspectives of history from a great enough distance, we see that one of the primary exigencies of human history is exactly a greater and greater deliverance from fate (*fatum*). While human nature pursues the normal progressive path of its manifestation and realisation, in the midst of

[124]

the falls and disasters periodically evoked by the growing extension of the fields of consciousness and reason (which are too weak not first of all to confuse what they essay to rule), history shakes off the yoke of fatality, and in the same moment feels it weigh more heavily and seems to be in severe subjection to it. Nevertheless it advances mysteriously towards deliverance. Yes, to its deliverance from fate! But this can only be real in the degree to which the life of reason grows truly and effectively, and in so far as it is nourished in secret by grace and the influx of the creative freedom. Marx's terrible mistake was in having thought that to escape from fate it is necessary also to escape from God.

In the place of that real though impeded freedom which I have tried to characterise, he sought for an illusory freedom which is infinitely more ambitious; for, to him, the human will is indeed the unique *spirit* of history, of a history no transcendent God governs from on high; and when the human will is delivered from a condition of 'alienation' the whole of history will go as that will pleases; it will become the God of history, exercising an absolute sovereignty.

Marxism only rejects the notion of the ideal at the price of a contradiction (and, in fact, its propaganda evades neither the idea nor the term, 'Communist ideal'). It claims expressly to be a philosophy of action, of action that will transform the world: and how can man act upon the world without having an end which is not only fixed by economic and social evolution, but also by his own choice, and by his chosen love: an end in which is not only included the movement of the real, but also in his own creative freedom which strives to direct these? Such an end is what we mean by a concrete historical ideal.

This notion of an ideal rightly understood has no smack of idealism (in the philosophical sense), no more than that of reason implies a savour of rationalism, nor that of matter of materialism. The notion of a concrete historical ideal corresponds to a realist philosophy, which understands that the human mind presupposes things and works on things, but that it only knows them in laying hold of them to transfer them into its own proper life and immaterial activity, and that it transcends them to disengage from them either those intelligible natures which are the objects of speculative knowledge or the intelligible and practical themes which direct action, to which category belongs what I have called a concrete historical ideal.

The notion of Christendom

Furthermore, it is the historical ideal of a *new Christendom* which will be in question in this chapter. Let it be called to mind that this word, Christendom (as I understand it), describes a certain *temporal* regime whose formations, in very varying degrees and in very varying ways, bear the stamp of the christian conception of life. There is only one integral religious truth; there is only one catholic Church; there can be diverse christian civilisations, diverse forms of Christendom. In speaking of a new Christendom, I am therefore speaking of a temporal system or age of civilisation whose animating form will be christian and which will correspond to the historical climate of the epoch on whose threshold we are.

II

THIS TEMPORAL POLITY CONSIDERED IN THE ABSTRACT

Its communal and personalist aspects

Let me at once make clear, as an essential preliminary, what to my mind should be the general idea, in sufficiently abstract and theoretical terms, of such a temporal order, taken in its typical lines in whatsoever historical setting it may be.

The conception of a regime of civilisation or of the temporal order which appears to me to be founded on reason has three typical characteristics: first, it is *communal*, i.e. the rightful and specifying end of its polity and culture is a common good other than a simple sum of individual goods and which is superior to individual interests in as much as each individual is a *part* of the social whole. Essentially this common good is the proper earthly life of the assembled multitude, of a *whole* made up of human persons: that is to say, it is at once material and moral. But, and exactly because of this, this temporal common good is not its final end. It is ordered to something better, i.e. the extra-temporal good of the person, the achievement of perfection and of spiritual freedom.

This is why this just conception of the temporal regime has a second characteristic, it is *personalist*: i.e. it is essential to the common good that it respect and serve the supra-temporal ends of the human person. In other words, the temporal common good is its *intermediate or infravalent end*.[1] It

[1]Yet more precisely one may say that 'the good of civil life' is a final end in a given order (*finis ultimus secundum quid*) in itself relative and subordinate (and so, intermediate or infravalent) to an absolute final end (*finis ultimus simpliciter*). Cp. St. Thomas, *de Virt. card.*, a. 4, ad. 3; *Sum. theol.*, i-ii, 65, 2; see also *Science et Sagesse*, pp. 245, 299-304, 346-56.

has a specific character which distinguishes it from the final end and the eternal interests of the human person: but this specific character includes its subordination to those interests and that end from which it receives its ruling principles. It has its own proper consistency and goodness, but precisely *on condition* that it recognises this subordination and does not claim to make itself an absolute good *per se*.

The absolute and fixed centre to which it has reference is not in itself but without: and it is therefore essential that it suffer the attraction of a higher order of life, which it prepares in greater or lesser measure according as it belongs to one or other of the diverse formations of political society and that it should bear within itself the beginnings of something that goes beyond its bound.

It is not the business of the social polity to lead human persons to a state of spiritual perfection and full freedom of autonomy (i.e. to sanctity, to that state of liberation which is indeed godlike, for then it is the very life of God that lives in man's heart).[1] But the social polity is essentially directed, by reason of its own temporal end, towards such a development of social conditions as will lead the generality to a level of material, moral and intellectual life in accord with the good and peace of all, such as will positively assist each person in the progressive conquest of the fullness of personal life and spiritual liberty.

I would here recall two sayings of St. Thomas which by the very nature of their contrasting and complementary qualities seem to me to include the whole substance of the matter: the one directed against any excess of individualism, the other against any totalitarian conception of the State.[2]

[1]Cp. *Freedom in the Modern World*, chap. i.

[2]We may call 'totalitarian' any conception in which the politic community,—whether it be the State in the strict sense of the word or the

[128]

Every single person, says St. Thomas, is in regard to the community as a part is in regard to the whole and is thereby subordinate to the whole: *quaelibet persona singularis comparatur ad totam communitatem sicut pars ad totum.*[1] This is so because man is not a pure person, a divine person, but stands in the lowest order of personality as of intellectuality. Man is not only a person, i.e. spiritually subsistent, he is also individual, i.e. an individual specimen of a species. This is why he is a member of society as a *part* of it, and has need of the constraints of social life to be led to and sustained in his own life as a person.

But the point of this is only and indispensably completed by St. Thomas's other saying: that man has in him a life and goods which surpass the ordering of the social polity; *homo non ordinatur ad communitatem politicam secundum se totum et secundum omnia sua.*[2] Why? Because he is a person. The human person is a member of society as a *part* of a greater whole,—but *not to the whole extent* of his being or of all that belongs to him! The core of his life as a person takes him beyond the temporal city, of which, nevertheless, it has need.

Here we see that antinomy which creates that state of tension which is native to the temporal life of human being.

organised collectivity,—claims the entire man for itself, either to shape or to be the end of all his activities, or indeed to be in itself the essence of his personality and his dignity. Thus, according to Signor Mussolini, the State is 'the veritable reality of the individual': the Fascist State is 'the highest and most potent form of personality'; 'nothing human or spiritual, in so far as it has any value, exists outside the State'; 'its principle, the directing inspiration of human personality joined in one society, penetrates into the soul . . . the soul of the soul'. B. Mussolini, *The Doctrine of Fascism.*

[1] *Sum. theol.*, i-ii, 64, 2.   [2] *Ibid.*, i-ii, 21, 4, ad. 3.

[129]

There is a common work to be accomplished by the social whole as such, by that whole of which human persons are part: and thus these persons are subordinate to this common work. And meanwhile what is deepest in the person, his eternal vocation and the goods which belong to that vocation, are superior to this common work and give it direction. I shall return hereafter to this paradox to which, for the moment, I have only wished to draw attention, before coming to the third typical characteristic of my conception of the temporal regime.

The peregrinal aspect

This orientation, which directs the mind of the temporal city above itself and takes from it the character of a final end, which makes it a *moment*, the earthly moment, in our destiny, not the term, must also be stressed as another essential characteristic: this city is a society, not of men and women who are settled in their permanent habitations, but of those who are *en route*. This is what can be called the '*peregrinal*' conception of the city. The necessary paradox of a being called out of nothingness to progress to the superhuman causes man to have no static equilibrium, but only one of tension and of movement: and causes his socio-political life, which must tend to raise as high as possible in relation to the given conditions the general level of existence, to lead also to a certain heroism, asking much of men to whom much will be given.

It follows from this that the conditions of life of the members of the temporal city must not be confounded with an earthly beatitude, nor with any restful felicity or ease. But it certainly does not follow that temporal civilisation is nothing but a pure means on the way to eternal life and has not in itself the dignity of an (infravalent) end; nor, on the pretext that this life is a vale of tears, that the Christian should be resigned to injustice or to the servile condition and misery of his brothers. The Christian, indeed, is never *resigned*. His conception of the city holds in it of its very nature the wish to adjust the conditions of this vale of tears so as to procure a relative but very real earthly happiness for the assembled multitude; a polity in which all can find a good and decent living, a state of justice, of amity and prosperity making possible for each the fulfilment of his destiny. He claims that the terrestrial city should be so directed as effectively to recognise the right of each of its members to live, to work and to grow in their life as persons. And the condemnation which he pronounces on modern civilisation is indeed more grave and more reasoned than that of the socialist or the communist, since it is not only the terrestrial happiness of the community, it is also the life of the soul and the person's spiritual destiny that are menaced by this civilisation.

The analogous nature of this conception

This conception of the earthly city was that of mediaeval Christendom. But the Christendom of the Middle Ages was only one of its possible forms of realisation.

In other words, this conception is or can be realised at different epochs of the world's history not *univocally*, but *analogically*. We see here the essential importance of the idea of the analogy for a sane philosophy of culture. It is this principle of the analogy, which dominates all thomist metaphysics and according to which the highest ideas are realised in existence in a way which is essentially diverse, while all the while keeping their proper formality, which must be our guiding star. St. Thomas and Aristotle made use of it in their political philosophy, and that in the most far-reaching way, apropos of the various political systems and specifically different types of *common good* which correspond to each of these. 'The diversity of cities', writes St. Thomas in his commentary on the *Politics*, 'comes from a diversity of ends or of different manners of reaching the same end. By the fact that they choose differing ends or different ways of reaching the same end, men create varying forms of common life and in consequence differing cities, *diversas vitas faciunt, et per consequens diversas respublicas.*'[1]

It is a like analogical diversity which it seems to me valuable to bring to light with regard, not to political systems, but to types of culture or of christian civilisation.

The philosophy of culture ought, to my mind, to avoid two opposite errors, one which binds all things in a *univocal* rigidity, the other which dissipates everything in equivocation. The latter form of philosophy holds that historical conditions become so different with time that their very governing principles must be heterogeneous: as though truth, right, the supreme laws of human action were mutable factors. A *univocal* philosophy, on the other hand, leads to the belief that these supreme rules and principles must be everywhere applied in the same way, and, in particular, that the way in which christian principles are to be applied and realised in the varying epochs of time and history ought not to vary.

The true solution springs from the philosophy of *analogy*. The principles do not vary, neither do the supreme practical laws of human life: but they are applied in ways which are essentially diverse, corresponding to one and the same concept only by a similitude of proportion. But this pre-

[1] L. vii, lect. 3; cp. *Sum. theol.*, i-ii, 61, 2.

supposes that one has a notion which is not only empiric and in a manner blind, but also one that is truly rational and philosophic, of the diverse phases of history. For a simple empiric cataloguing of factual circumstances can only make for a certain *opportunism* in the application of these principles, and this is poles apart from the standpoint of wisdom. That is not the way in which the atmosphere or 'heaven' of a historic epoch is brought about: but by the bearing of rational judgements of *value*, by the discernment of the form and significance of the intelligible constellations which govern the diverse phases of human history.

Statement of the problem: Mediaeval Christendom and a new Christendom

Hence the particular problem now before us, which can be formulated as follows: should a new Christendom, in the conditions of the historic age on which we are entering, while incarnating the *same* (analogical) principles, be conceived as belonging to an *essentially* (specifically) distinct type from that of the mediaeval world? To this question I answer, Yes. I hold that a new age of the world allows the principles of all vitally christian civilisation to be realised in terms of a new concrete *analogue*.

Not only indeed do I recognise the fundamental irreversibility of the movement of history (in contradistinction to the pagan concept of eternal recurrence), but I believe it the stage of a drama at once human and divine, of which visible events are only the symbols; and that, borne on by this irresistible movement, humanity passes beneath varying historic skies, heterogeneous in type, which create specifically differing conditions of realisation for the principles of culture, and that the moral physiognomy of these skies differs much more profoundly than is generally assumed. Why, generally speaking, is this so?

First of all, by reason a law which dominates the temporal as such, and which concerns, if I may put it so, the junction of Man and Time. This law is that a *too complete* experience cannot be recommenced. By the simple fact that man has lived, has lived to the full a certain form of life, has experienced to the full the good and the evil that the pursuit of a certain historic ideal has stamped upon his way of life, those things have come to an end; it is impossible to return to them: it is a law of the temporal, of the things of history, as such. Those things alone escape it which belong to a supra-historic, supra-temporal order, the things of life eternal. The Church does not die, civilisations die.

'Suffering', said Leon Bloy, 'passes away; *to have suffered* never passes away.' All the past which man has suffered remains, it has its place,—but as past, as having lived, as defunct: it lacks the capacity for once more coming into action, of being suffered anew. In the phraseology of the grand style do we not say 'he has lived', meaning 'he is dead'? That is how it is with the civilisation of the Middle Ages; it has borne its fruit.

More, it is impossible,—it would be contrary to the mental structure of humanity, for every great experience, even accomplished in error, is orientated by the attraction of a certain good, however evilly sought for, and in consequence reveals new regions and new riches for our exploitation,—it is impossible to conceive that the sufferings and experiences of the modern age have been useless. This age, as I have said, sought to rehabilitate the creature; it has pursued that end along evil roads, but it is our duty to recognise and save the truth which is hidden, is held prisoner, in that aim.

[134]

Finally, if it is true and no Christian can think otherwise, that history is governed by God and that, despite all obstacles, He pursues in it a certain divine design, so that in time and through time a divine work and divine preparations are accomplished, it would be to go against God himself and to fight against the supreme government of history to claim to make immobile in a form that is past, in a univocal form, the ideal of a culture worthy of being the aim of all our action.

Two preliminary comments

I shall therefore endeavour first of all to characterise the historic ideal of mediaeval Christendom, and then, in relation to the points of comparison thus determined, what I called a moment ago the *prospective image* of a new Christendom.

With reference to this prospective image or historical ideal of a new Christendom, I must make two preliminary comments:

The first is that it goes without saying—apart from those more particular indications which I shall try to give in the last chapter,—that it relates to a concrete and individualised future to the future of *our* time, but that it matters little whether this future be near at hand or far. In contradistinction to the ideals of immediate application invoked by the practicians of either politics or the revolution, it is a universe of possibilities envisaged by the philosopher on the level of a (practical) form of knowledge which is still speculative in its mode. Moreover, given the particular conditions in which today the problem is set, given that in the whole period of anthropocentric humanism which we are leaving behind, the note of civilisation has been finally tragic, where the truths and new values engendered by history were congenitally vitiated

[135]

by a false metaphysic, by the instinct of anarchic disassociation which stimulated the impulse of research, our first task must be, in the act of trying to draw out this prospective image of a new Christendom, to strive to save these values and these truths which have been at once acquired and compromised by the modern age, at the very moment when the errors which have been their parasites have brought them into peril. From this point of view the immediate future, though it touch us more nearly, is less interesting to our philosophical researches,—given over as it is in too large a degree to the fatal consequences of a choice which has already *been made*, and the antinomies of a dialectic long ago started on its course. On the other hand, what interests us is the distant future, since the span of duration which divides us from it is sufficiently great to allow for these necessary processes of assimilation and redistribution, and affords to human freedom the opportunities of delay of which it has need when striving to turn the heavy mass of our social life in a new direction.

My second point is that in taking up, not the standpoint of marxist hegelianism and historical materialism, from which many of their critics often borrow their *way of posing the problem*, but that of a christian philosophy of culture, I shall envisage from another angle than that of most socialist or anti-socialist theorists this matter of our socio-temporal relations. The very posing of the problem, the nature of my questions is hence different. Great as is the part (which I in no wise seek to diminish) played by the economic factor in history, it is not primarily from economics but from more human and deeper aspects of culture, and above all from the implications of the spiritual and the temporal in civilisation, that I shall seek my guiding light.

[136]

Thus the perspective from which I view things is irreducible to any other, and is typically different from that of the greater number of marxist and anti-marxist controversialists, who, on the one hand, put the economic factor first (when it does not occupy the whole field), and, on the other, however strong the eschatological element in Marx, in reality look to the immediate future, to a zone of the future, if I may put it so, utilisable for immediate tactical ends. For marxist ideology, indeed, the essential is doubtless what will come later (*after* the dictatorship of the proletariat, *after* the necessary and transitory stage of state-socialism, *after* humanity's leap to freedom and the control of history), but nothing is ever said about this; nor, indeed, can it be, for to say anything would be to fall into the ideal.

III

THE HISTORICAL IDEAL OF MEDIAEVAL CHRISTENDOM
The idea of the Holy Empire or the temporal conceived in christian consecrational terms

Very generally speaking, we may say that the historical ideal of the Middle Ages was dominated by two notes: on the one hand, the idea or myth (in Georges Sorel's meaning of the word) of force in the service of God; on the other, of the concrete fact that temporal civilisation was in some way itself a function of consecrated activity and thus imperatively demanded religious unity.

In a word, we may say that the historical ideal of the Middle Ages could be summed up in the idea of the Holy Empire. I am not here referring to the Holy Roman Empire as a historical fact; strictly speaking one might say that this latter never achieved real existence. The idea of the *sacrum imperium* was preceded by an event: the empire of Charlemagne (which was itself, it seems, not exempt from a strain of caesaro-papism): and the idea which arose after this event was only capable of precarious, partial and antithetic realisations: impeded and contradicted as it was, on the one hand, by the opposition in fact between the Emperor and the Pope, 'those two parts of God,' in Victor Hugo's phrase; and, on the other, by the opposition between the Empire and the French monarchy, which would never admit its dependence on any temporal superior.

Neither am I speaking of the Holy Empire as a *theocratic utopia* (that question has been dealt with in the last chapter): but of the Holy Empire as a concrete historical ideal or historic myth, i.e. as the lyrical image which orientated and raised a whole civilisation. On this view of the matter we must say that the Middle Ages lived by the ideal of the Empire (and died of it). If we understand the myth in a large sense, in its whole symbolic and representative value, this idea dominated ideally all temporal mediaeval forms and the very conflicts, those antithetic realisations which prevented the establishment of the *sacrum imperium* as a fact.

It is in this sense of a concrete historical ideal that the Holy Empire still saturates our imaginations, and from this angle it is most necessary to subject our more or less unconscious mental images to a drastic revision. In the Latin countries it exercises a secret influence (under various cultural aspects, such as that of the quarrels between clericalism and anti-clericalism) on the conceptions of certain Catholics—and still more perhaps of their opponents—of the meaning of a christian restoration. In the Germanic countries this image survives under its directly imperial colours. In a most interesting study a benedictine theologian, Fr. Hermann Keller of Beuron, calls the *sacrum imperium* the secular dream of the German nations and points out how 'the political distresses of these last years in Germany have revived the old nostalgia for the Holy Roman Empire of the German nations'. Fr. Keller remains himself a determined adversary of the theological theories to which this old dream has given rise, which seek to find in the Holy Empire the *unity* of the political city and the Church. He condemns these theories and almost seems indeed to sympathise with the barthian position. I have already, in the previous chapter, given some indications on the state of the question in contemporary German thought. It should be added that the extreme partisans of racism in Germany, those who wish to return to a national and racial (Nordic) religion anterior to Christianity, cherish a like aversion to the Holy Empire as for Christianity itself. At the same time, it is undoubtedly by means of this very notion of the Holy Empire, materialised and become the privilege of a naturally chosen people, that the political ideal of Germanic racism has to-day been able to penetrate sections of the German population which otherwise remain attached to christian culture.

Just before I revised these pages, I received a copy of a magazine published by a group of young German Catholics, disciples of Carl Schmitt and partisans of the new regime, the *Kreuzfeuer*: it contained a study of one of my books and the only criticism made was of my having said that the Holy Empire was an out-of-date ideal which it was important to expel from our imaginations (not certainly because it was evil in itself but, on the contrary, because it was one that has *come to an end*). 'Is it because Maritain is a Frenchman', it was asked, 'that he thinks this, or for some other reason?'

If I speak in this way it is because I know the dangers of a univocal conception of the christian temporal order, which

[139]

would tie it up in dead forms, instead of making fast to the living tradition of the past.

The tendency to a maximal organic unity

The object of this digression was to show the reader that the problem of the Holy Empire has a living significance for us to-day. Let us return to our theme, to the historical ideal of the Middle Ages. This concrete historical ideal, this myth or symbol of the Holy Empire, corresponds to what may be called a *christian consecrational conception of the temporal.* Let us try to disengage its typical, organically connected features. To my mind it is characterised by five points.

In the first place, there is a tendency towards an organic unity at the maximum in point of quality: a unity which excludes neither diversity nor pluralism, else it would not be organic; and which seeks to adjust the unity of the temporal city at the highest possible level in the life of the person, in other words, to put its foundation in the fact of spiritual unity.

This tendency towards unity is clearly marked at the heart of each of the political unities which built up the order of Christendom. A typical example is furnished by what was accomplished by the French people and its monarchy, or by the king and people of Castille. And, when this impulse towards national unity was no longer held in check by the more spiritual and religious impulse towards a united Christendom, when it carried all before it in the decline of the Middle Ages, it then changed into absolutism, and a type of unity which was mechanical rather than organic, where in reality policy held the primacy, not religion.

Again, is there anything more characteristic in the whole order of the Middle Ages than their effort to attain an organic unity in civilisation itself, in the community of christian peoples? The endeavour to unify the whole temporal world under one emperor as the whole spiritual world, the Church, is unified in the Pope.

No doubt this historic ideal failed of its highest ambitions, primarily on account of the pride and cupidity of the princes. Nevertheless, in however precarious a fashion, but one of which nowadays we can be terribly envious, there was at any rate a christian order, a christian temporal community, where national quarrels were quarrels within one family and did not break the unity of culture: there was a christian Europe.

Whether it is a question of each christian nation or of the higher unity of Christianity itself, the temporal unity envisaged by the Middle Ages was a *maximal* one, a unity of the most exigent and monarchical type: the core which gave it consistency was set very high in the order of personal life, above the temporal plane, in that spiritual order to which the whole temporal order and its common good are subordinate: its source was thus in the hearts of men, and the unity of the national or imperial formations only made manifest this primordial unity.

But this temporal unity of christian Europe did not only spring from the religious sense of unity. It included also, as was indispensable when it was a question of a maximal temporal unity, the puissant unity (however general it might be and compatible with the sharpest divisions and rivalries) of a certain common basis of thought and of doctrinal principles (in all the various philosophical schools the human intellect spoke with one tongue), and a highly remarkable and extraordinarily vigorous effort (it never attained its end) towards a high and perfect unification of the intellectual and political structures. This was the mighty and sublime, too great and too sublime, conception of the mediaeval Papacy in the days of its plenitude. In order to shape a christian Europe in conformity with the perfect image of the unity of a christian world, that figurative but so powerful and energetic refraction of the Kingdom of God in the socio-temporal order of which I have spoken, the Popes knew that it needed—and they wished—a high doctrinal, theological and philosophical unity, a unity of the wisdom of minds enlightened by faith. From this point of view the centre of Christendom—its supranational, scientific centre—was the University of Paris.

And they knew also that it needed—and they wished—a high political unity among the peoples, an imperial unity set above the various kingdoms as the unity of wisdom reigns over the other sciences: the political, supranational centre of Christendom was the holy Roman emperor of the Germanic nations.

The effective predominance of the ministerial idea in the temporal order

Unity of such a high degree was only conceivable in con-secrational terms. To say that its centre stood at a high point in the life of the person is to say that the principle ruling the temporal order was its subordination to the spiritual one.

We thus come to the second typical feature of the his-torical ideal of the Middle Ages: the predominance of the *ministerial* rôle of the temporal order in relation to the spiritual.

The scholastics, as we know, distinguish between the *infravalent end*—for example, the professional activity of a philosopher or of an artisan, which has a proper value as an end (although subordinate to a higher end, e.g. the rectitude of the moral life),—and the *means* which exist purely *ad finem*, are specified by that end, as reasoning is for science. Again, they distinguish in the line of efficient causality between the *principal secondary cause* (for example, the plant's vegetative energies), which, though inferior to a higher cause (e.g. solar energy), nevertheless produces an effect proportionate to its degree of specific being, and the *instrumental cause*,—for example, the brush in the hand of an artist,—which, only exercising its own causality in the degree to which a superior agent makes use of it for its own end, produces an effect higher than its degree of specific being.

In the line of these ideas, it is notable how in the mediaeval order the things that are Caesar's, while being clearly distinguished from the things that are God's, filled to a large extent a *ministerial function* with regard to them: to this extent they were *instrumental causes* with regard to the sacred, and their proper end ranked as a means, a simple means, in relation to eternal life. Is there any need to give examples: to recall the rôle of the secular arm, the title of 'exterior bishop' often given to the king: to instance typical happenings such as the Crusades? This is not in any way a question of any theocracy: the proper finalities of the temporal order were clearly recognised, and the proper domain of civil society. Nevertheless, this avowed ministerial function of socio-political action in relation to the spiritual order, accidental as it might remain in itself and be regarded in relation to the political sphere, was exercised in a normal, frequent and highly characteristic fashion.

The use of secular means for spiritual ends

The third characteristic feature of the mediaeval historical ideal lies in the use made of secular and political means, correlative to this ministerial function of the polity (external and visible means in which social constraints played a large part, the constraint of opinion, coercion, etc.), the use of the institutional forces of the State for men's spiritual good and the spiritual unity of the social body itself,—for that spiritual unity whereby the heretic was not only a heretic, but one who attacked the lifespring of the socio-temporal community as such.

I have no desire to condemn such a system in theory. In one sense an earthly order capable of putting to death for the crime of heresy showed a greater care for men's souls and held a higher ideal of the dignity of the human community centred in this way on truth than one which only looks to punish crimes against the body. But it is the point where human nature must most fatally lead to abuses; abuses which became more and more intolerable (and later, in very truth, the condition became monstrous), when, after the ruin of mediaeval Christendom, the State, ceasing to act as the instrument of a higher and legitimate spiritual authority, arrogated to itself and in its own name rights of spiritual interference. The absolutism of a Henry VIII or of a Philip II, Gallicanism, Josephism, the enlightened despotism of the eighteenth century, Jacobinism represent in this regard a highly significant line of progress which is continued in the totalitarian States of to-day.

The diversity of 'social races'

I find the fourth characteristic of the mediaeval historical ideal in the fact that a certain as though essential disparity (between the leaders and the led), a certain disparity of essentials between the hereditary social categories, or again, to use those amplifications of meaning of which the word 'race'

[144]

is susceptible, a diversity of *social races*, was then recognised as the foundation of the hierarchy of social functions and relations of authority, whether it were a question of political authority in the State or of those other forms of authority which intervene in a country's social and economic life. It may be said that in the Middle Ages temporal authority was primarily conceived on the lines of a father's authority in accord with a *consecrational* conception of the family, conceptions of which we have an example in the Roman idea of the *paterfamilias*, an idea which Christianity was able to sublimate in attaching it to that of the universal fatherhood of God.

I spoke of a disparity 'as though of essence', despite the fact that a father and his children are obviously of the same kind and the same race: but the child is as such in a position of *natural* inferiority to his father, who seems to the child to possess a superior essence: a position which is reinforced in a conception of the family where the father's authority is a sacred function, invested, so to speak, with the personality of God.

The consecration of a king makes him the father of his people, confirms in the order of grace his natural authority as head of the social polity, and attests that he governs in the temporal order in the name of the Supreme King. It was the whole political thought of the Middle Ages which blazed up in a final light in Joan of Arc, when Joan put such energy and such obstinacy in her demand for the king's consecration, and when she persuaded Charles VII that he should abandon his '*sainte royaume*' to Christ, and then solemnly returned it to him on His behalf, in order that he should hold it henceforward '*in commendam*'. The king who has received the unction of consecration is not only the vicar of his people but also of

[145]

God. (In the era of monarchical absolutism he was no longer the people's vicar, but only God's.)

To the Middle Ages the fellowship of workers was an extension of domestic society; the workers were the parts and organs of this fellowship, and the corporations or guilds were regarded as an extension of the family, a family of workers, whose unity included masters and men (so that though there were indubitably rich and poor, and heaven knows how much misery, yet the existence of a *class* reduced to a state of wage-slavery, of mere hands, of a proletariat in the true sense of the word, was inconceivable). A rigidly hierarchical conception formed the base of the relations of authority in this paternal or semi-paternal organisation and in the economic system of feudalism.

Such a 'heterogeneity' in the social structure was, moreover, compensated for in the Middle Ages—precisely because of this family-like conception of authority—by the organic suppleness and the *familiarity* (brutal enough as it could be, but anything is better than indifference and contempt) of the relations of authority, and by a progressive and spontaneous growth, which was lived rather than consciously known, yet was very real and effective, of popular liberties and enfranchisements.

Let it be added in parenthesis that, like the first and the third characteristics which I have pointed out (the tendency towards organic unity, the use of temporal means for spiritual ends), this fourth characteristic had to give way in the immediately subsequent epoch, i.e. under the *ancien régime*, to its opposite, not by defect, but by excess and progressive petrifaction.

We find a very representative example of this mediaeval conception of authority in the religious Order which, founded as it was before the date of the true Middle Ages, played so large a part in the formation of its culture and, so to say, opened the door to it: in the Benedictine Order and the benedictine conception of authority: a father, the abbot, the *paterfamilias* clothed with a consecrated and evangelical character; and the other monks are as children, his children.

The common work: the building up of an empire for Christ

The fifth characteristic of this historical ideal is concerned with the common aim of the city's labour: the establishment of a social and juridical structure devoted to the Redeemer's service by the power of baptised men and a baptised polity. As I said in the first chapter, with the absolute ambition and simple courage of children, Christendom built up an immense stronghold, where God should be enthroned. Without misunderstanding the limits, the misfortunes, the conflicts proper to the temporal order, without falling into any theocratic utopianism, the faithful strove to build a figurative and symbolic image here on earth of the Kingdom of God.

IV

THE DISSOLUTION AND PSEUDOMORPHOSIS OF THE MEDIAEVAL IDEAL IN THE WORLD OF ANTHROPO-CENTRIC HUMANISM

The regime of the baroque age

All this came to an end, little by little wore itself out. A long historical analysis would be necessary to elucidate this; let me here only recall that the development of national aspirations, the growth of new forms of social and economic life, and their conflicts with feudalism, as well as the corresponding changes in the order of thought, necessarily led

[147]

to a breakaway from the consecrational ideal of mediaeval Christendom. The break-up of spiritual and intellectual unity began with the Renaissance and the Reformation. From this point of view the reign of Alexander VI is no less significant than the campaigns and violences of Luther and Calvin. One saw an absolutist reaction striving to save the intellectual and spiritual unity on which any culture must be based, and with it political unity which thus became the primary aim of States more and more jealous of their sovereignty.

> A single flock, a single pastor on earth:
> One monarch, one empire and one sword,

exclaims Hernando de Acuna, the poet of Charles V. In fact this unity was becoming less and less that of Europe; it was more and more shut up inside the frontiers of the various States.

Indeed this absolutist effort suffered from a vice which too often gives an air of majestic hypocrisy to an age in general characterised, as we have seen, by dualism and sub-division. The primacy of the spiritual order continued to be affirmed in theory, and practically what was everywhere affirmed was the primacy of policy: policy tended to become in fact a technique to which nothing came amiss,—even virtue or its semblances, even international law and the respect man showed to it by shaping it to suit their end,—in securing the final triumph of the Prince or the State. The age of the king-saints is indeed over. For Protestants and Catholics alike the temporal order was effectively dominated by the thought of Machiavelli, the most general and most generally *accepted* heresy in the practical order of modern times.

The old conviction that religious unity conditioned *from*

above the unity of civilisation, turned upside down for the benefit of policy, gave birth to the cynical adage: *cujus regio ejus religio.* The Treaties of Westphalia marked the political ruin of the Christendom that had been.

Grave as these evils may have been, the general character of this absolutist reaction was the use, doubtless not exclusively, but in a predominant manner, of human means, of public and political means in the endeavour to save the spiritual and political unity of the social body. This characteristic is everywhere apparent in the epoch of the Counter Reformation. Faced by a furious assault from without, what remained of Christendom sought to defend itself by measures of the sharpest constraint (which kept, nevertheless, a certain element of moderation and, being unable to equal the fierceness of the assault, could only delay the moment of collapse). To a potent loosening of passionate and wilful forces there responded a supreme tension of the combative energies of the human will roused in defence of its good. This is clear even in the orders of the spiritual life and of sanctity. The society of Jesus is the type-form of the spiritual forces of the period. In a recent book René Fülöp-Miller has suggested that there stand at the commencement and the decline of the modern age two corresponding figures, two giants of comparable psychic tension, St. Ignatius and Lenin.[1] Whatever the difference in the ends that they pursued, and consequently in their methods, there is in both cases a highly significant exaltation of the heroic will.

No doubt it was necessary to find out by experience how much man can do in defence of the Christian order by using as his principal weapons human energies and human means of action, with his human initiative used (by the saints) in

[1] R. Fülöp-Miller, *The Power and Spirit of the Jesuits* (Eng. trans. 1930).

[149]

the endeavour to make charity triumph in themselves and in others and to make more brilliant, to *augment* the glory of God,—His accidental glory (God's essential glory is Himself and cannot be augmented). To pray as if everything depended on God alone and to act as if everything depended on man alone, is a maxim which is equally very significant. He who truly were to act as if everything depended on man alone would, it is clear, use, if he is logical, only human means even for the cause of God.

In any case, the regime of the period of the Counter Reformation, or, to take a definition from the world of art, of the baroque age, shows itself as in general markedly more severe—for this reason precisely that human force turns back upon itself in the defence of the divine order,—than that of the Middle Ages. It is sufficient to compare from this point of view certain typical figures: Philip II and St. Louis, or St. Pius V and St. Gregory VII.

At the same time a human, too human deformation of the spirit of grandeur and ambition attacked those social formations which the Middle Ages had kept in a spirit of poverty and humility. A certain absolutism, which was sometimes fierce and often excessively proud, developed in the family (when we see to-day a deplorable weakening of this family we may perhaps think that we are witnesses to the action of a blind 'judgement of history' against such secular abuses). The monarch is no longer the *vices gerens multitudinis*, and no longer possesses merely the power to rule and to govern[1]; he holds directly from God the right of subjecting to his will this multitude which has been given to him, which is his, and to which all constituent power

[1] Let me here recall the thomist notion of royalty: 'Unlike the Sovereign Pontiff who is not the Church's vicar but Christ's, the king is the

(exercised at least in the beginning) is thereby found to be denied. The guilds, become too rich, and grow oppressive, despotic and reactionary.

Yet, inasmuch as spiritual unity had not been completely done away with as the primary foundation of the social body, and in so far as spiritual goods, in despite of all survived, and the transcendental value of these goods was recognised, there remained an incontestable greatness in, and a justification for, this absolutist effort for the defence by all too human means of those spiritual goods and of that unity. And the epoch of which I am speaking, above all in the era of the Renaissance, remains one which is humanly great, rich in beauty, in intelligence, in veritable force, in virtue, and one whose glaring faults should not make us forget its admirably generous spiritual *undertow*. It was the flower of classical civilisation, and even though it will sink—so soon—in decomposition, the eighteenth century keeps its charm and beauties which exhale a certain sweetness beneath a dark and tragic sky.

The vanishing victory of liberalism

The barricade of absolutism which I have been endeavouring to characterise could not last for long. With the triumph of rationalism and liberalism, i.e. of a philosophy of freedom which makes of each abstract individual and his opinions the source of all right and truth, spiritual unity has 'gone west'; we have ourselves been able to experience the benefits of this dispersion.

vicar of the multitude, *vices gerens multitudinis*. The *constituent* power remains the appanage of the multitude. The king only possesses the power of a regent (cp. *Sum. theol.*, i-ii, 90, 3, with the commentary given by R. P. Billot in his *De Ecclesia Christi*, q. 12, n. iii. Rome, 1921, p. 493).'
C. Journet, Preface to the French translation of *De Regimine principum, Gouvernement Royal* (Paris, 1931).

But this individualistic liberalism was palpably a purely negative energy; it lived by its opposite and because of it. Once the obstacle has fallen it lacks any support. And we become aware of the manifestations of a much deeper force, due to the internal conflicts of the capitalist and industrial system, whose claim to greatness is that it is concerned with no mere change of ownership, but with a 'substantial transformation' of social life.

Contemporary anti-liberal reactions

At such a moment it is natural that there should be not only revolutionary explosions which menace the very essence of this individualistic and liberal civilisation, but also reflex actions of defence, anti-liberal reactions, so to speak, of a biological order. It is the final stage of that process of descent of which I have spoken. For these reactions have no other interior source in the life of souls than physical and moral distress and too great suffering. And if they are indubitably capable of rousing heroism, faith and an almost religious devotion, it is by the expenditure of an inherited spiritual capital; they have no power to recreate it. Thus the political unity of the commonwealth can only be sought for by external adjustments, by compulsion and political pedagogy, by a use of the State highly resembling in technical character those employed by Soviet communism for its own dictatorship. And since it is well understood that an inner accord of thought and feeling is necessary for the solidarity of the political unity, intellectual and spiritual pseudo-unity will be sought and imposed by the same means. The whole machinery of ruse and violence of political machiavellianism is so brought to bear on the universe of the conscience itself and claims to storm this spiritual stronghold to extort the assent and the love of which there is such imperious need. This is a highly characteristic form of violation of invisible sanctuaries. And, if my reading of the evidence is accurate, these anti-liberal reactions are much less likely to prove durable than the much nobler endeavours, nobler because much more rich in humanity, of the epoch of the Counter Reformation and political absolutism.

But a period which is brief enough in the eyes of history may seem of fearfully long duration to those who must bear its weight. The world will not soon have done with this ultimate phase of materialistic imperialism, which invokes the dictatorship of the proletariat or reacts against it, and we shall perhaps see upheavals of world dimensions if what is indeed in question is the liquidation of a whole age of civilisation.

Howsoever this may be, by a singular process of dialectic the christian absolutism (or one which was at least christian in appearance) which followed on the mediaeval world has been ejected by anti-christian liberalism, and the latter having itself been overthrown by the very fact of its success the space is open for a new absolutism, this time a materialist one (either avowedly so or in disguise) and more inimical to Christianity than ever. Along the whole path of this evolution, even and above all in the liberal-democratic and individualist period, one thing has consistently grown and enlarged its pretensions: the State, that sovereign machine which gives a body to political power, and which stamps its anonymous imprint on the social community and the obedient multitude.

Rationalism, as it awaits the results of this promising growth, taking no account of its own responsibility, laments that the youth of the entire world should show at the moment such a lively appetite for collective forms and spiritual standardisation, in despair of the unity which is lost. It sees with astonishment a romantic distress which could find no reason for living succeeded by a joy in command and the fascinations of a bravado which satisfy themselves with the most superficial justifications of life. It sees too late that only a faith superior to reason, which vivifies at once intellectual and affective activities, can assure the existence among men of a unity which is not founded on compulsion but on interior assent, and make of that joy in existence, which is indubitably natural but which nature alone cannot safeguard (pagan wisdom held that the best fortune were never to have been born), an intelligent delight.

It is highly notable that in fact Christianity alone seems able to defend at various vital points of Western civilisation the freedom of the individual and also, in the degree to which it illumines the temporal order, those positive liberties which correspond on the social and political plane to that spiritual freedom. We have thus come back to the most logical historical position: to the old combat of the christian faith against the despotism of the powers of this world.

A great deal of misunderstanding was produced in the time of Gregory XVI and Pius IX on the theme of the attitude of the Catholic Church. It was then in a paradoxical historical situation, compelled to defend against a number of fundamental errors which claimed to represent the modern mind and which were primarily the fruits of naturalism and liberalism, truths which the decadence of a temporal order, where the remains of the epoch of christian absolutism were in dissolution, sought to treat as a shield for its defence. To-day we can clearly see that what the Church was then defending were the essential truths of a christian conception of the world and of life, not that perishing and perishable order.

Recently men have recalled Charles Péguy's words: 'Christendom will come back in the hour of distress.' It is coming back: but how, in what way, to what tune, and in the terms of what historic labour and on what lines, that is what is so difficult to know.

Whether it be a question simply of an ideal perspective or of partial preparations, or the outline of something much greater and more hidden, the considerations which we have brought to the fore in this chapter show in any case what a real interest there is for us in the *suggested image* of a type of Christendom specifically distinct from that of the Middle Ages and directed by another ideal than that of the Holy Empire. We have thus come to what will be the object of the next chapter, in which I shall endeavour to characterise, in its very contrast with the mediaeval cultural ideal, the ideal of a new Christendom conceivable in terms of to-day.

CHAPTER V

THE HISTORICAL IDEAL OF A NEW CHRISTENDOM (*continued*)

I

PLURALISM

A christianly secular conception of the temporal order

For myself I hold that the historical ideal of a new Christendom, of a new christian temporal order, while founded on the same principles (analogically applied) as that of the Middle Ages, will imply a *secular christian*, not a consecrational, conception of the temporal order. Its characteristic features will thus be at once opposed to those of liberalism and the inhuman humanism of the anthropocentric age, and inverse to those which sprang from the mediaeval ideal of the *sacrum imperium*: they will be the fruits of what I may call an integral or theocentric humanism in full autonomy of action. The guiding star in the supernatural world of this new humanism, the idea at its heart,—not that it will claim to bring it down to earth, as if it were a product of this world and could be built up in this world as a basis for men's common life, but that it may be refracted through the whole sinful and earthly substance of socio-temporal things, and orientate them on high,—will not be that of God's *holy empire* over all things, but rather that of the *holy freedom* of the creature whom grace unites to God. Of this freedom liberalism is but a caricature, and even at times a mockery.

The pluralist structure of the commonweal

The first characteristic feature will be that instead of the predominance of that tendency towards unity which we saw as so typical of the Middle Ages,—and from whence has been derived, in the course of a progressive spiritual dispersion, a more and more mechanical and quantitative conception of political unity,—there will be a return to an organic structure which implies a much more developed element of pluralism than that of the Middle Ages.[1]

In the mediaeval order this pluralism was manifested primarily by the multiplicity of sometimes overlapping jurisdictions and of customary laws. To-day, I am convinced, it must be expressed in other ways. I am not only thinking of that just degree of administrative and political autonomy which should be possessed by regional units, without at the same time sacrificing higher political ideals and wellbeing to the claims of regionalism or nationalism; it is plain that the problems concerned with national minorities call in themselves for a pluralist solution. I am above all thinking of an organic heterogeneity in the very structure of civil society, whether, for example, it be a question of economic or certain juridical and institutional structures.

In opposition to the various totalitarian conceptions of the State which are to-day in vogue, this is a question of the conception of a *pluralist commonweal*, which will gather together in its organic unity a diversity of social groupings and structures which embody positive liberties. 'It is an injustice, a grave evil and a disturbance of right order for a larger and higher organisation to arrogate to itself functions which can be performed efficiently by smaller and lower bodies.'[2] Civil

[1] See *Freedom in the Modern World*, pp. 60–61.
[2] Pius XI, encycl. *Quadragesimo Anno*.

[157]

society is not only made up of individuals, but of social groupings formed of these; and a pluralist commonweal would give the fullest possible measure of autonomy to these groupings and diversify its own internal structure in accord with the typical claims of their nature.

Economic Pluralism

Thus, in my opinion, in a society in conformity with the concrete historical ideal with which we are dealing, and if we take cognisance of the conditions created by economic evolution and modern technical achievements, the regulation of industrial economy, which the advent of machinery has extended beyond the limits of the family-type, and of agricultural economy, which is much more closely bound up with that form, would be fundamentally different. In the first case the interests of the person in themselves demand a certain collectivisation of ownership. Under the capitalist system is not an industrial enterprise a hive composed of, on the one side, salaried workers and, on the other, of capital united in a company,—a grouping not of men but of paper and of money, of symbols of wealth, whose soul is the desire to create new rights of possession? The perfecting of technical means, the rationalisation of industry and methods of financial mobilisation, only accentuate this tendency to collectivisation. If we imagine in the place of the capitalist system a future system whose spirit and economic structure would be in conformity with the communal and personalist conception of society, this collectivisation would not be suppressed by its economic regulation, it would be organised on entirely other lines and for the benefit of the human person. I shall shortly return to this point.

On the contrary, it is towards a renewal and revivification

of the family-type of economy and ownership, under modern forms and utilising the resources of mechanisation and co-operation, that the regulation of rural economy would tend, an economy which is besides more fundamental than that of industry and whose wellbeing should, in a normal society, be first assured. Co-operative services, however generally developed they might be, and a trade-union type of organisation, whatever new methods it might imply, would have to respect this fundamental direction in agriculture. I would recall the peasant's saying reported by Proudhon: *when I turn my furrows I feel like a king.* The primary relation between ownership and personal work and the affective tone of personal property show here with an elemental simplicity that an industrial economy, once it has passed under the dominion of the machine, cannot know.

Juridical Pluralism

But it is in the sphere of the relations between the temporal and spiritual orders that the pluralist principle which I hold will characterise a new Christendom will find its most significant application. The prime and central fact, the concrete fact which characterises modern civilisations as distinct from that of the Middle Ages, is surely the existence in modern times of a civilisation and a temporal system which admit within themselves of a religious diversity? To the Middle Ages unbelievers were outside the walls of the city. In the modern city believers and unbelievers are mingled. Doubtless the totalitarian city claims to impose anew a single rule of faith on all, in the name, however, of the State and the temporal power: such a solution is unacceptable to a Christian. So that a christian commonweal under modern conditions could not be other than a christian city within whose walls believers and unbelievers live alike and share together in the same temporal commonwealth. This is as much as to say that, unless we limit ourselves to simple empiric expedients, we must invoke that pluralist principle of which I have spoken and apply it to the city's institutional structure.

In those cases where the civil law is most typically related to a conception of the world and of life, the legislature would hence recognise the differing juridical status of the diverse spiritual groups included in one commonweal. Clearly for a sane philosophy the only morality is the true morality. But for the legislator, who must look to the common good and peace of a given people, is it not necessary that he should take into account their state and the more or less defective, yet actually existing, moral ideals of the various spiritual groups which make up the community, and in consequence make use of the principle of the lesser evil?

There is a way of understanding this pluralist solution which falls into the error of theological liberalism, of which perhaps we have an example in the legislation of the Hindus: then it is thought that because all human opinions of whatsoever kind have a right to be taught and propagated the commonweal should be obliged to recognise as licit for each spiritual group the law worked out for that group according to its own principles. This is not my meaning. To me this principle signifies that in order to avoid greater evils (which would be the ruin of the community's peace and lead to the petrifaction—or the disintegration—of consciences) the commonweal could and should tolerate (to tolerate is not to approve) ways of worship more or less distant from the truth: *ritus infidelium sunt tolerandi* was the teaching of St. Thomas[1]; ways of worship and thus also ways of conceiving

[1] *Sum. theol.*, i-ii, 10, 11.

the meaning of life and modes of behaviour; and that in consequence the commonwealth would decide to accord to the various spiritual groups which live within it the juridical status which the city *itself in its political wisdom* adapts on the one hand to their condition and, on the other, to the general line of legislation leading towards the virtuous life, and to the prescriptions of the moral law, towards whose fulfilment in the fullest obtainable degree it should endeavour to direct this diversity of forms. Thus it is towards the perfection of the natural law and of christian rectitude that the pluriform juridical structure of the city would be *orientated*, even in its most imperfect stages and those which are farthest from the ideal of christian ethics. The positive pole of its direction would be integral Christianity, the various degrees which are more or less remote or diverted from this end being ordered according to its political wisdom. Thus, the commonwealth would be vitally christian,[1] and the various non-christian spiritual groups included in it would enjoy a just liberty.

[1]This phrase, 'the christian city', must be rightly understood. *In the absolute sense of the words*, the true christian commonweal or city is the Church and no temporal body. In this case, however, we are speaking of a temporal city.

Like philosophy, the political order has its own proper specification. But, like philosophy, it can come under the influence of Christianity and thus be in a *christian state*; and, moreover, just as there is, in my opinion, a practical philosophy, an 'adequately comprehended ethic' which is subordinate to theology, and which thereby implies in its very specification a christian colouring (see *Science et Sagesse*), in the same way the political order, by the fact that it is intrinsically an outcome of ethics, can and should also, while all the time remaining in its own order, bear in its proper political specification an impregnation of Christianity. A christian city or commonwealth is a temporal city intrinsically vivified and impregnated with Christianity.

Is it necessary to add that the 'christian State' which Prussia claimed to be in the time of Hegel and the young hegelians, and which certain

The unity of such a civilisation would no longer be a unity of essence or of a constitution assured from above by the profession of the same faith and the same dogmas. Less perfect, and more material than formal yet nevertheless real, it is rather, as I have just suggested, a unity of orientation, which proceeds from a common aspiration (traversing various levels of heterogeneous culture, some of which are perhaps decidedly imperfect) for a form of common life in better accord with the supra-temporal interests of the person; and the part of the agent of unity and formation which was played by the christian king in regard to the city of yesterday belongs— whatsoever otherwise be the form of the regime—to the most politically evolved and the most devoted section of the christian laity and the popular elite in the new temporal order here in question.

For a moment a parenthesis. What St. Thomas said of the prince, i.e. that he must be purely and simply *bonus vir*, so that he should direct as he ought the multitude towards its common temporal good, it is necessary, it seems, to say also of these *cives praeclari*, that enlightened political element who will play this animating and formative part of which I have been speaking. But to be purely and simply a good and virtuous man firmly set in a state of moral rectitude, implies, in fact, the gifts of grace and of charity,[1] those 'infused virtues' which rightly merit, since they come from

contemporary political conceptions seem also to claim to be on the strength of man knows not what 'positive' or nationalised Christianity, is nothing but a bitter derision of this ideal?

[1] See *Science et Sagesse.*

Christ and in union with Him, the name of christian virtues, even when in consequence of some obstacle for which he is not responsible the subject of them is ignorant of or alien to the profession of Christianity. It follows from this that a city animated and guided by such elements will in reality be to an extent (and in that wholly relative sense in which these things must be understood in the temporal order) under the reign of Christ. The universal principle of Christ's royalty, the axiom that without Christ nothing firm or excellent can be built, even in the political order, has here its application in very truth, not in the externally manifested and symbolised fashion of the Middle Ages, nor in the apparent and decorative way of the classic age, but in a way which is real and vital, though less openly announced in the structures and symbols of social life.

Another question presents itself apropos of these political elements, to which I have attributed, to borrow a word from Mr. and Mrs. Webb, the *vocation of leadership*.[1] How can they fulfil it effectively unless organised?

Each from their own standpoint, Communism, Fascism and National Socialism have already given their answer to such a question. After explaining that political unity implies the triple essence of the State, the Movement and the People, M. Carl Schmitt declares that the proper organ of the Movement is the National Socialist Party (*der Staat = und volktragende Führungskörper*) and that the connection between the Party and the State consists in a personal union, primarily realised in the man who is at once *Führer* and Reich Chancellor.[2] Similarly the Fascist Party is, according to the law of

[1] In English in the original (trans.).

[2] Cp. Carl Schmitt, *Staat, Bewegung und Volk, die Dreigliederung der politischen Einheit*, Hamburg, 1933.

[163]

29th December, 1929, an 'organ of the State' (*un organo dello Stato*), without being at the same time a part of the State (*organo statale*) or a part of the structure of the constitution; but an organ of the Party, the Fascist Grand Council, is and thus assures the connection. Unlike the Italian or the German conceptions, the Soviet idea is more radical and more significant. The Communist Party occupies no place in the constitutional structure of the Soviet republics, and the connection between the Party and the State comes neither from a unity under one supreme individual head[1] nor from a particular disposition, but solely from the political, moral and intellectual influence which the Party exercises in every way, and by the continuous penetration of its trusted servants into the workings of the State; the Communist Party is a sort of secular and atheistic order, comparable to an inverted image of the Society of Jesus. Considered as a world-organisation (the Communist International) it is international or supra-national. And in a country which has a communist State, it claims to use its powerful directing influence all the more effectively in the degree to which it animates the State by way of *spiritualis auctoritas*.[2]

It is in none of these three ways that I envisage the organisation of those animating elements we are considering. I hold that the idea of an organised political fraternity or a political order holds the indubitable promise of important historic destinies. But in a pluralist and personalist city it would be realised in a novel way. Not only will the spirit and methods of its political formations be entirely different from those of the Communist or similar parties, but these forma-

[1]Stalin is secretary of the Communist Party; he has only a secondary function in the hierarchical structure of the State.

[2]Cp. S. and B. Webb, *Soviet Communism*, i, ch. 5.

tions will be founded on *freedom*: and they will be *multiple*, that is the capital point. They will likewise differ from the parliamentary political 'parties' of to-day in their essential structure and their moral discipline, as by the personal and spiritual effort they will ask of their members (and because, in another way, in a healthily conceived representative system, where the legislative and the executive will be rendered sufficingly independent of the deliberative assemblies, even the possibility of using power to satisfy coalitions of cupidities and interests would have disappeared). Finally, these civic fraternities will, in the secular sphere, be to the State and its constitutional structure as in the sacred sphere the various regular orders are to the Church and its hierarchical structure: with this difference, that in the latter case it is a case of a 'mixed system' which is in principle monarchic, in which the religious orders are linked to the hierarchy (or at least its Head) in strict dependence, while in the former it will be a case of a 'mixed system' which is principally democratic, where the political fraternities will constitute formations that are independent of the State and only subject to its general dispositions touching the right of free association.

Minimal Unity and Civil Tolerance

But let us return to this question of the unity of the pluralist city. Such a temporal unity will not be, as was the consecrational unity of mediaeval Christendom, a maximal one: it will be, on the contrary, *minimal*,[1] its core of formation and organisation in the life of the person not being on the

[1]This unity which I have called *minimal* is none the less organic, and is much superior to that of the liberal-individualistic order, which is in fact *not in the least* organic and only exists as a mechanical unity assured by the dominance of the State.

highest level of the latter's supra-temporal interests, but on the plane of the temporal itself. It is for this reason that this temporal or cultural unity does not *in itself* require a unity of faith and religion, and that it can be christian while including non-Christians in its circle.

Even supposing that one day religious divisions should come to an end, this more perfect differentiation in the temporal order would endure as an achieved gain,—the distinction between *dogmatic tolerance*, which regards the liberty of error as in itself good, and *civil tolerance*, which insists that the commonwealth respect the rights of conscience, will remain stamped in the substance of the city.

En passant, it is interesting enough to observe how, in a matter such as this of *civil tolerance* for example, having served as a mask or pretext for the energies of error which set up captive truths in opposition to christian belief, when a growth in historic progress has been achieved, it is then Christianity which strives to maintain this progress, which it is claimed has been won against its will, while those false energies, now turned to the right about, seek to destroy the very progress which was before their glory.

The unity of the pluralist city

It is important to insist on the bearing of this pluralist solution: it is as distant from the liberal conception in favour in the nineteenth century,—since it recognises the necessity for a definitely religious and ethical specification of the temporal city,[1]—as from the mediaeval one, since it allows of a heterogeneity of internal elements and is only based on a

[1]Inasmuch as the religious element impregnates the political specification as such. Cp. *supra*, p. 16, n. 1.

general sense or direction, a common orientation. The pluralist city multiplies liberties, whose measure is not uniform, which vary according to a principle of proportionality. Again, this solution gathers the whole unification of the temporal community into one essential and natural point: a simple unity of friendship.

In the period of the consecrational concept of Christendom this unity of the temporal community was raised to a higher plane, and participated in a sense in the perfect unity of the Mystical Body of Christ. Its source was in the unity of faith.

When it lost its organic and vital quality, the Europe of the baroque age, as I said in the preceding chapter, strove to preserve it in an absolutist fashion. And here again, throughout the whole modern period, we can see philosophy making a most significant effort to fill the same cultural function as religion did in the Middle Ages: philosophers, haunted by the memory of the unity of the Middle Ages, be it Descartes or Leibniz, Hegel or Auguste Comte, have called on reason to furnish temporal civilisation with that supratemporal principle of perfect unity which it no longer finds in the faith. Their failure has been resounding.

The lesson of this experience seems obvious: nothing is more vain than to seek to unite men by a philosophic minimum. However small, however modest, however tentative this may be, it will perpetually give rise to contests and divisions. And this quest of a common denominator in contrasting convictions can develop nothing but intellectual cowardice and mediocrity, a weakening of minds and a betrayal of the rights of truth.

Hence we must renounce the search for a common profession of faith, whether it be the mediaeval one of the

[167]

Apostles' Creed, or the natural religion of Leibniz, or the positive philosophy of Auguste Comte, or that minimum of kantian morality invoked in France by the first theorists of laicism; we must give up seeking in a common profession of faith the source and principle of unity in the social body.

But the simple unity of friendship of which I spoke does not suffice to give a form to the social body,—that ethical specification without which the common good of the city cannot be veritably human; rather the existence of a common unity of friendship itself presupposes such a form and specification. If this form is christian it is then because the christian conception will have prevailed—as I have said, in a secular and pluralist way.

But how? Because the bearers of this christian conception will have had enough spiritual energy, enough force and political prudence to practically exhibit to men capable of comprehension that such a conception is in conformity with good reason and the common good; and also,—for the number of men capable of comprehension is small,—to rouse and merit the confidence of others, to lead them with the authority of veritable leaders, and to exercise power in a commonwealth which it is permissible to imagine as possessed of an organically constituted political structure; a political structure where the concrete interests and political thought of human persons and social and regional bodies in mutual subordination will be represented (it is the function of the *consilium* in the thomist psychology of human acts), beside the organs of government charged with the *judicium ultimum* and the *imperium*, and free of any other preoccupation than that of the common good.[1]

[1]The political conception indicated in these few lines implies in my mind: (1) a *personalist democracy* (based on universal suffrage, and the

[168]

Is it necessary to add that these considerations, which concern the essence, the nature of a conceivable new christian order and which I hold are founded on reason and the logical necessities of this standpoint, at the same time exhibit the difficulties against which the effort to realise such a conception in fact will come, in the degree to which Christians will have to deal, not only with a civilisation in religious and philosophical division, but, on the one hand, with forces violently hostile to Christianity and, on the other, in the christian world itself, with univocal prejudices heavily enforced by history, and finally with the irrational currents of the masses, blinded by the contradictions of a civilisation no longer measured by the measure of man?

II

THE AUTONOMY OF THE TEMPORAL

The second characteristic feature of the temporal regime I am envisaging bears on what could be called a christian conception of the lay or secular State; this would be an affirma-

right to vote and eligibility of women as well as men) where the citizens would not only have an electoral right, but would be vitally engaged in an active way in the political life of the country; (2) the substitution for the worn-out parliamentary system, which belongs to the age of individualistic liberalism, of a *representative* regime in which the legislative and the executive (which correspond to the *judicium ultimum* and the *imperium*) would be united in the same governmental organs (emanating from the multitude by indirect suffrage, confirmed, for its supreme organic rector, by popular referendum); the representative assemblies would then have the task of preparing the legislative and executive work (the function of the *consilium*) in close collaboration with these organs, and of exercising a controlling and regulative function (e.g. by the vote on the budget, the right of demanding, in certain given conditions, the revision of a law or the accusation of a citizen, the right of final decision in certain cases concerning in a major degree the life of the country....).

[169]

tion of the autonomy of the temporal order as an *inter-mediary or infravalent end,* in conformity with the teaching of Leo XIII in his declaration that the authority of the State is supreme in its order. I recalled in the preceding chapter the distinction between the intermediary end and the means, and that between the secondary principal and the instrumental cause. And we have observed how, in the order of mediaeval Christendom, the temporal very often played the part of a simple means, a purely instrumental or ministerial function with regard to the spiritual.[1]

By virtue of a process of differentiation in itself normal (although vitiated by the most erroneous ideologies[2]) the secular order has in the course of the modern age built up for itself an autonomous relation with regard to the spiritual or consecrational order which in fact excludes the notion of instrumentality. In other words, it has come of age.

This is again a historical gain, which a new Christendom must know how to preserve. Certainly this does not mean that the primacy of the spiritual order will be disregarded! The temporal order will be subordinate to or underlie the spiritual no longer doubtless as an instrumental agent, as so often happened in the Middle Ages, but as a *principal agent on a lower plane*; no longer will the common good of the temporal order be treated primarily as a pure means with regard to eternal life, but as what from this standpoint it essentially is, i.e. as an *intermediary or infravalent end.* A real and effective subordination,—thus contrasting with modern gallican or liberal conceptions; but a subordination which is

[1] Cp. *supra*, chap. iv, p. 127, n. 1, and p. 142.

[2] These had already begun in the Middle Ages. Cp. Georges de Lagarde, *La naissance de l'esprit laïque au déclin du moyen âge* (I. Bilan du XIIIme siècle; II. Marsile de Padoue), ed. Béatrice, 1934.

in no instance purely ministerial,—and in this it is in contrast with the mediaeval conception.

We can thus disengage and make precise the notion of a *vitally christian lay commonweal* or a *christianly constituted lay State*, i.e. a State in which the secular and the temporal will play their full part and have their full dignity as an end and principal agent,—but not that of the final end or of the highest principal agent. This is the sole sense in which a Christian can understand the words 'lay State', which, otherwise, are a pure tautology,—the lay nature of the State then implying that it is not the Church,—or are erroneous, when the lay nature of the State signifies that it is either neutral or definitely antireligious, i.e. either at the service of purely material ends or of a counter-religion.

On several important points these indications will be found further enlarged and made more precise in the subsequent section.[1]

III

THE FREEDOM OF PERSONS

The third characteristic feature of a conceivable new Christendom will be, together with this insistence on the authority of the temporal order, a conjoined insistence on the extra-territoriality of the person with regard to temporal and political means.

Here we shall meet with the second central fact, this time of an ideological order, by which the modern epoch is in opposition to the Middle Ages. The idea of force in the service of God has been displaced by that of the conquest or realisation of freedom.

[1]See pp. 172-5.

But what freedom is it that is primarily in question for a christian civilisation? Not that simple freedom of individual choice (which is only the beginning or root of freedom) of the liberal conception; and not the imperial or dictatorial conception of the freedom and greatness and power of the State; but, before all, the autonomous freedom of the person, which is at one with his spiritual perfection.[1]

Thus at one and the same time the centre of unity in the temporal and political order is lowered and there rises above that order the dignity and the spiritual freedom of the person.

A whole change of perspective and *style* thereby ensues in the sphere of temporal organisation. The Christian knows that the State has duties towards God, and that it should collaborate with the Church. But the mode in which this collaboration is accomplished can vary in its type with historical conditions: once it was primarily by the use of temporal powers and legal constraints; in the future it will probably be, even in politico-religious connections, by way of moral influence. St. Albert the Great[2] and St. Thomas[3] explain by the diversity of states or ages of the Church the fact that in the time of the apostles and the martyrs it was not appropriate to make use of forcible means and that subsequently it became so. That in yet another age it will again be appropriate to make no use of them is explicable in the same way.

It is necessary that Christ should be made known: that is the work of the Church, not of the State. But, be its type

[1]On this expression, 'autonomous freedom', which I use in an at once aristotelian and pauline sense, but in no degree in the kantian. Cp. *Freedom in the Modern World*.

[2]Prologue to the Apocalypse; Commentary on St. Luke.

[3]Quodlibet XII (*c.* 1268), a. 19, ad. 2 (Utrum una sit Ecclesia quae fuit in principio Apostolorum et quae modo est).

sacred or secular, a temporal christian city knows that it is its duty to assist the Church in the free accomplishment of this mission.

In the case of a civilisation which is consecrational in form this assistance is of an instrumental order: the secular arm puts its sword at the disposition of the spirituality. It is then normal that the coercive force of the State should come into play to protect the faith and the community against disintegrating influences; and this is not in the least surprising when the consciousness of the community is vitally impregnated with the same unanimous certitude. It may even happen that the intervention of the State in such matters will moderate and curb the excesses of spontaneous popular reaction; what more natural impulse to the crowd than to lynch the heretic?

In the case of a civilisation of the secular type, it is in the pursuit of its own proper (infravalent) end and as the (subordinate) principal agent that the temporal city acquits this office with regard to the Church: then it is rather in integrating, according to the pluralist method which I have described, christian activities in its own temporal work (e.g. in giving christian instruction its just place in the scholastic curriculum, or in asking religious institutions of charity to take their rightful part in works of public assistance), and in so receiving itself, as an autonomous agent in free accord with an agent of a higher order, the aid of the Church, that the city will assist the latter in the fulfilment of its rightful mission; and 'the mode of activity which belongs most properly to the eternal city, that is, moral and spiritual activity', will thus be the dominant note in the collaboration of the two powers.[1]

[1]*Freedom in the Modern World*, p. 67.

An earthly city which, without recognising a right in heresy itself, assures the heretic his liberties as a citizen, and accords him the juridical status appropriate to his ideas and his habits,—not only in the desire to avoid civil discord, but also because it respects and protects human nature in him and the reserves of spiritual force which dwell in the universe of souls,—will do less to promote the spiritual life of the citizens than one that is less tolerant from the point of view of the *object* of that life, the level of wisdom and virtue beneath which the social body will not tolerate evil and error being thus lowered (but indubitably less so than in the *neutral* city of liberalism); on the other hand, it will be the more favourable from the point of view of the *subject*, whose privilege of extra-territoriality with regard to the socio-temporal order, —in his quality as a spirit able to be instructed from above by the Author of the universe,—is raised to a higher level.

In this connection the declaration made by Cardinal Manning to Gladstone sixty years ago should be remembered: 'If Catholics were in power to-morrow in England, not a penal law would be proposed, not the shadow of a constraint put upon the faith of any man. We would that all men fully believed the truth; but a forced faith is a hypocrisy hateful to God and man. . . . If the Catholics were to-morrow the "Imperial race" in these Kingdoms they would not use political power to molest the divided and hereditary religious state of the people. We would not shut one of their Churches, or Colleges, or Schools. They would have the same liberties we enjoy as a minority.'[1]

[1] *The Vatican Decrees*, London, 1875, pp. 93-94: cited by Fr. Michel Riquet in his pamphlet *Conquête chrétienne dans l'état laïque*, Paris, 1931.

Here again the historic ideal which I am striving to characterise is in contrast at once with the mediaeval and the liberal
ideal. If the conception of the liberty of the person rises above
the political structure of the city, it is by virtue of the very
nature of what I called a moment ago a vitally christian lay
State, and not in the least because of any neutrality, any idea
of the claim that the State should be neutral: by virtue of an
authentic sense of liberty, not of any liberal or anarchist
doctrine.

Freedom of expression

It is amusing to observe how Marx in his youth began by
fighting for the freedom of the press, which was then regarded by the young hegelians as a social panacea, and to
consider the degree of liberty enjoyed by the press to-day in
marxist Russia. Like the Russian State the other totalitarian
States have taken to other methods than those of the Prussian
kings and their censors, which primarily served to make the
government ridiculous and martyrs of their opponents; they
have understood that the law is only good when it is potent.
The lesson must not be lost, though it must needs be applied
in other fashion.

When the Papacy, in the time of Gregory XVI and Pius
IX, condemned the idea that the liberty of the press or of the
expression of opinion was an end in itself and an unrestricted
right, it was only recalling an elementary condition of
human government. These liberties are good and correspond
to an essential quality in human nature: but they need to be
regulated, like everything else which does not belong to a
truly divine order. The dictatorial or totalitarian method of
regulation—by annihilation—seems to me detestable; the
pluralist method—by justice and a progressive self-regula-

tion—strikes me as good, being no less strong than just. If, for example, the various groups of journalists and writers gathered in an autonomous body with an institutional status had a progressive power of control over the deontology of their profession, it could be seen whether, by virtue of that natural severity with which a potter criticises the works of a potter, they would not be able to exercise a most effective control: indeed it would rather be for the protection of the individual against his peers that the supreme judicature of the State would need to intervene. . . .

But the best adjusted solution is another. That a policeman judge works of art gives small satisfaction to our sense of the hierarchy of values: the judgement of another artist and a reliance on his decision is almost as little satisfying. All exterior regulation is vain if its aim is not to develop the sense of the person's own creative responsibility, and his sense of communion. To feel responsible for one's brothers does not diminish our freedom but weights it with a deeper responsibility.

The pluralist city and the law

This pluralist commonwealth, though less concentrated than the mediaeval, is much more concentrated than the liberal conception. It is an authoritarian State; the law, whose office is to constrain the *protervi*, the foolish, to a bearing and behaviour of which they are themselves incapable, and also to educate men in such a way that in the end they cease to be under the law (since voluntarily and freely they do what the law prescribes,—which only happens with the wise), the law will there recover its moral authority, its function as the *pedagogue of liberty*, which it has almost totally lost under liberalism. And, without doubt, those

[176]

supreme values by reference to which it regulates its scale of sanctions and prescriptions will not be those consecrational values which ruled over the mediaeval concept of the commonweal, yet they will in themselves hold something sacred: not the sacred material interests of a class, nor the sacred prestige of a nation, and still less the sanctified productivity of a State-controlled bee-hive,—but something which is truly and already by nature sacred, the vocation of the human person for spiritual accomplishment and the conquest of true freedom, and the reserves of moral integrity which this requires.

It is the thomist doctrine of analogy, in particular the analogical nature of the notion of the common good, which, again, here in connection with the thomist doctrine of the law, furnishes the justification for these remarks. Unlike the divine law, which is called immaculate, *lex Domini immaculata*, because it allows no fault and is directed to a common good which is the life of God itself, human law cannot, says St. Thomas, forbid and punish every kind of evil; and being ordered to a common temporal good it is natural that its manner of regulation and measurement, of interdiction and punishment, should be in proportion to the varying specifically different types in which this common temporal good, like the city itself and civilisation, is analogically realised. *Diversa enim diversis mensuris mensurantur* (i-ii, 96, 2); *distinguuntur leges humanae secundum diversa regimina civitatum* (ii-ii, 61, 2).

The ownership of earthly goods

Two other points which are related to the eminent part played by the person in the new Christendom which I have envisaged must here be summarily considered: the one concerned with the ownership of material goods, the other with the condition of women in marriage.

In the matter of property, St. Thomas teaches, as we know, that, on the one hand, primarily by reason of the needs of human personality considered as working in and elaborating matter in subjecting it to the forms of reason, the appropriation of such goods should be individual or private, since without it the working activity of the person would be hindered; but that, on the other hand, by the primal destination of material goods for the benefit of the human species, and the need which each has of such means in order to direct himself to his final end, the use of the goods which are individually possessed should serve the common good of all. *Quantum ad usum non debet homo habere res exteriores ut proprias, sed ut communes.*[1]

This second aspect was entirely concealed in the epoch of liberal individualism, and one may hold that the violent reaction towards State socialism which we see around us today will recall to men's minds the thing they have forgotten: the law of *common use*.

Nevertheless this reaction is in itself abnormal, and in its turn disastrous. To anyone who gives personality the rank and value that it merits, and understands to what degree it is precarious in the human species and constantly menaced by environment, the law of personal appropriation (either in a strictly individual or a social form) will appear no less imperious than that of common use. So that the remedy for the abuses of individualism in the matter of the use of ownership must be sought, not in its abolition but, on the contrary, in the diffusion, the popularisation of the defences which it

[1] *Sum. theol.*, ii-ii, 66, 2. On the interpretation of this formula, see *Freedom in the Modern World*, Appendix I.

builds up round the person. The point is to give to each human person the real and concrete possibility of achieving (in ways which can remain very diverse, and which do not exclude, where they are necessary, certain collectivisations) the advantages of the private ownership of material goods; the evil being the reservation of these advantages to a small number of privileged individuals.

This way of setting out the problem can also be found in Proudhon and even—by accident—in Marx; but the marxist solution is false in principle, because it finally makes the essence of man, which is alienated by private property and reintegrated thanks to communism, exist purely in the common good or communion which characterises political life. There are, in Marx's first communist writings,[1] such as the theses on Feuerbach, striking indications which reveal the metaphysical basis of his communism, in that social monism allied to atheism which was discussed in an earlier chapter,[2] and which ignores the highest values of human personality. Marx is profoundly absorbed by man and by the human: and one might say that the essence of human personality,—of the human person as individual, which in the degree to which it is individual constitutes a unity,—escapes his view. Hence the congenital weakness of his humanism. Hence his strangely monist and immanentist conception of work itself, as a sort of common and absolute substance in which the essence of man is actualised, and which has reference neither to specifying objects or goods, nor to the creative activity of the person as such with its own rightful exigencies.

[1]Cp. A. Cornu, *op. cit.*, p. 292. 'Historical materialism ... considers that the true nature of man is constituted by his social activity.' *Ibid.*, p. 391 (ninth thesis on Feuerbach).

[2]See *supra*, chap. ii.

One might here recall certain ideas of Proudhon, without pretending thereby to make any use of Proudhonism. In order to extend to each and all in a properly adapted way the advantages and guarantees with which private ownership endows personality, it is precisely *not* the form of any State ownership or communism, but a form (as I think) of *association* that ownership should take in the sphere of industrial economy, so that co-partnership is in as far as possible substituted for a salary list, and the servitude imposed by machinery on human personality compensated for by the participation of the workers' intelligence in the management and direction of the enterprise.

In this way a possible solution may be found for the problem, usually so feebly handled by socialist theory, of the inducement to work in a system of collectivised industrial production: for this incentive would then come neither from the application of the methods of parliamentary democracy to that form of technical commonwealth which is a great industrial enterprise, nor from any form whatsoever of forced labour. Nor would it proceed *only* from that generosity and joy in work which presuppose a mystical basis and which can be stimulated by christian faith as much as by communism, but of which stricken humanity is not easily capable, and which avoids, but does not suppress, that element of punishment which is equally included in work. It would proceed *also*, and this humble human foundation is indispensable, from interest, changed to new forms, and neither necessarily egoist nor grasping, but bound up with the sense of operative responsibility,—would also proceed from the interest of proprietorship, or rather co-proprietorship, which the workman would have in the wellbeing of the concern: which presupposes an organisation of this latter in accord with a somewhat biological series of superimposed and mutually inclusive circles, the individual molecule being directly interested in the life of the cell,—of the workshop, for example,—the cell in that of the tissue, this again in the life of the organ, and that in the life of the whole. The problem is not how to suppress private interest, but how to purify and ennoble it: to hold it in a social structure directed to the common good, and also (and this is the capital point) inwardly to transform it by the sense of communion and fraternal amity.

The title of the worker

When I spoke of an *associative* form of industrial proprietorship, what is in question is a *society of persons* (workmen, technicians, investors) entirely different from those capitalistic companies which, under the conditions of the present time, the notion of co-partnership raises in our minds: I have in mind a society of persons where the co-proprietorship of certain material goods (means of production) (1) would above all be the guarantee of a form of possession of more human significance, I mean the possession which has its title in work; and (2) would have as its fruit the formation and development of a common patrimony.

According to a very just comment of M. Paul Chanson, capitalist co-proprietorship, far from confirming the liberty and activity of the proprietor as a person, has rather instituted a kind of *plebs* in the world of property and of savings; the subscriber to a limited company is as such as little a 'person' as may well be, his creative activity is reduced to a detaching of coupons. A working co-proprietorship in the means of production, if it is understood in a purely material fashion and without any concrete reference to the persons concerned, runs the risk of ending in a similar illusion and of

[181]

only offering to the person of the worker a fictitious homage: the example of large-scale co-operative enterprises is from this standpoint of considerable significance, and Henry de Man was able to write that in general the direction of co-operative enterprises is perceptibly more hard-hearted than that of privately owned concerns.

For a form of collective ownership to represent an effective defence of personality it is necessary that its end should n't be a depersonalised possession. What does this mean? From the standpoint which I have taken up, the co-proprietorship of the *means of work* should serve as the material basis of a form of personal possession, the possession no longer of a thing in space, but of a form of activity in time, the possession of a 'trust' or *worker's title*, which assures a man that his employment is rightly his, is juridically linked with his person, and that his operative activity will there have room to progress: it should serve to give a title and a social guarantee to the bringing into action of what is functionally and inalienably the property of the worker: his personal powers, his intelligence, the skill of his hands. That was the profound human truth understood by the mediaeval guilds and which, in agreement with Paul Chanson, I hold should reappear under new forms and ways: it was the rediscovery of La Tour du Pin with his idea of 'property in one's craft'.[1] I have used the words right or title of work as the right or title of nobility was used in the times when this implied an effective function or trust. Such a form of possession rouses in us those primordial feelings which are at the base of the natural law: the desire to see work well done, the

[1] A justification of this extension of the idea of property could be found in the theory of 'functional' proprietorship expounded by Semprun y Gurrea, *El Sentido Funcional de la Propriedad*, Madrid, 1933.

[182]

sense of the dignity of work; it represents for those who enjoy it an effective economic defence for the activity and liberty of the person, which essentially demand that they should not be at the mercy of the moment; it is implied in that participation of the workers' intellect in the management of enterprises of which I spoke briefly a moment ago. But I hold that it necessarily in itself presupposes,—in order to be effectively and really guaranteed, and also, and more radically, in order to belong to an economic order freed from capitalism, in which it could alone bear its full fruit,—the 'associative' ownership of the means of production, the co-proprietorship of the undertaking: which is why I spoke in the first instance of this latter.

Again, the conceptions which I have sketched evidently imply a corporative organisation of production, without which the working person's accession to a progressive 'qualification' would be impossible. Such organisation would naturally bring with it, for the workers associated in the undertakings comprised in it, the possession of a common corporative patrimony which would be concretely translated by various kinds of personal allowances, and which would have for the workman and his family a personal significance and direct personal interest.

From the point of view here taken up, this corporative organisation needs to be conceived as established from below upwards, according to the principles of personal democracy, with the suffrage and active personal participation of all the interests at the bottom, and as emanating from them and their unions;—the higher organs of the total Body of Production co-ordinating with those of the total Body of Consumption for an 'endogenous' regulation of economic life, in harmony with more universal regulations concerned

[183]

with the common good of men (considered as citizens, and not only as producers or as consumers), and assured by the higher organs of the total Body of political life. While fully recognising the general principle of the subordination of the economic to the political sphere, the corporation which is in view here is thus totally different from the State-directed corporations (so in fact, if not in theory) of contemporary political totalitarianism: it is founded on the notion of a moral personality which is at once autonomous and subordinate, and of that of an endogenous development; it does not suppress the liberty of trade-unions, it emanates from them; and it presupposes the preliminary liquidation of modern capitalism and the regime whose first consideration is the profit of investment.

A regime consecutive to the liquidation of capitalism

To escape from any misunderstanding, I must insist on the point that these various considerations here put forward are concerned, in my mind, with a state *subsequent* to the liquidation of capitalism and only have a meaning with regard to such a state. They presuppose a radical change not only in the material[1] but also in the moral structure and in the spiritual principles of the economic sphere: for capitalism itself does not fully comprehend the spirit that informs it. Is it necessary to indicate, among so many others, two characteristic features by which, to my mind, this new state of culture will be opposed to our present one?

In our present civilisation everything is referred to standards which are not human but external to man: primarily to the laws of material production, to a technical domination

[1]Not by suppression, but by the passing over of private capital into the service of work. Cp. *Religion and Culture*, Note II.

of nature, to the utilisation of all the resources of the world for the fecundity of money. In a truly humanist condition of culture, man would represent the standard of the terms of reference of all the things of this world: and the vocation of man is great enough, his needs and desires capable of such growth, that no one need hold that such a standard would imply any renunciation or diminution of scale or fall from greatness.

Greatness demands at once abundance and poverty; nothing great is done without a certain abundance, nothing great without a certain poverty. Is there any understanding at all of human life if one does not begin with the knowledge that it is always poverty which superabounds in greatness? The tragic law, not of man's nature, but of his sin, makes the poverty of one create the abundance of another: the poverty of misery and servitude, the abundance of covetousness and pride: the law of sin, which we must not accept, but fight. What would be in conformity with nature and what we ought to ask in the social order of new forms of civilisation is that the poverty of each (assuredly neither want nor misery, but sufficiency and freedom, the renunciation of the spirit of riches, the gaiety of the lilies of the field), a certain individual poverty create a common abundance, superabundance, luxury, glory for all.

Meanwhile, and this is the second feature which I wish to stress for a moment, it is an axiom for the 'bourgeois' economic order and mercantile civilisation that one *gets nothing for nothing*: an axiom bound up with the individualistic conception of ownership. In a regime where the conception of property which I have tried to sketch was in force this axiom, I hold, would no longer be possible. Rather, on the contrary, the law of *usus communis* would lead to there being, at least and first of all in what is concerned with the primary spiritual

[185]

and material needs of human being, *as many things as possible for nothing*, in virtue of a distributive office exercised, not by the State, but by the various organic communities, beginning with the family community, integrated in the economic structure of society. That the primordial necessities of the human person should so *be served* is, after all, nothing but the first condition of any economic order not meriting the name of barbarous. The principles of such an economy would lead to a better grasp of the profound meaning and essentially human roots of the idea of inheritance, and would, at the same time, call for an immense transformation in the modes of hereditary transmission, so that, on the one hand, while all the while assuring to the children the fruits of their father's work, this would not be able to lead to the making or the remaking of a privileged monied class, and that, on the other, every man on coming into this world would effectively enjoy, in some degree, his condition as heir of the preceding generations.

Human personality and the economic community

Turning to the consideration of another great problem which the predominantly industrial character of social life brings to-day everywhere before us, that of the at once syndical, corporative and co-operative organisation of production and consumption, I would point out that, in the first place, the opposition between the corporative and syndicalist conceptions has its acuteness only under a system of individualist 'profit-making', when the profit on the capital invested in an undertaking is set over against that of those on the pay-roll[1]; in the second place, that the technical necessities of

[1] If it is true that class-antagonism is consubstantial with such a regime, we can understand why trade-unionists fear that under a capitalist system

social life only determine the main *generic* lines, the *specific character* of a social structure comes from its ethical dominant conceptions: and indeed, from the standpoint of a christian philosophy, the great task which will rest on us in the future in the face of the organic regime, which the economic process would seem to render inevitable in one form or another, will, it seems, be in the first place to guarantee that character of a moral person which, particularly in a pluralist society, belongs to the trade-union or corporation, against any form of State control; in the second place, while assuring the advantages of such a system for the general community, to defend the person *against* the corporative collectivity: i.e., on the one hand, to assure the goods of which human life has need, and above all the elementary necessities, to the individuals not incorporated in or not able to be incorporated in syndical and corporative categories[1]; on the other, to guarantee the rights and liberties of the person inside these very organisms.

More profoundly, the crucial problem here is that of knowing how to make technical means, the machine and industry itself, subordinate to man. Grand-nephews of Descartes, the final heirs of rationalism and anthropocentric humanism, the communists believe they have found an easy answer: by the admission, on the one hand, that the new civilisation should be, like the capitalist one and even, if poss-

corporative organisations would run the risk of being primarily utilised as a means for abolishing the liberty of the workers. I may add that in the opinion of the catholic social school, in particular that of La Tour du Pin, corporative organisation can only be founded on a basis of free trade-unionism.

[1] This is what Henri de Man calls 'a rising *fifth estate*' composed of 'workers lacking any "qualification" and chronically under the menace of unemployment' (*L'Idée Socialiste*, p. 476).

ible, more so, an industrial one; on the other, that science in the rationalist sense, science as apart from wisdom,[1] suffices, by means of a perfected planning, to make industry serve man, the inevitable result has been, despite themselves, to make man the slave of industrial and technical development. A non-human science, a science of the production of things, when it becomes the ruler of life can only impose inhuman rules. The prime work of the social body, if not ordinated to the higher good of the person, can only look to claim the entire man for itself and jealously dispute the claims of God and of man himself: 'for God is the supreme and overmastering interest of human personality.'[2]

The truth is that it is not the business of science to regulate our life; that is the office of wisdom: the prime work of civilisation does not belong to the order of transitive activity, but to that of immanent activity: really to make the machine, technical developments and industry serve man implies making them the servants of an ethic of personality, of love and of liberty. It would be a grave error to repudiate the machine and technically developed industry, things which are good in themselves and which should, on the contrary, be used to produce an economy of abundance. But it is the very illusion of rationalism to fail to understand that *we must choose* between the idea of an essentially industrial civilisation and an essentially human one, for which industrialism would indeed be only a means: and thus subject to laws other than those of industry.

The idea of planning thus changes its meaning; it is there from the moment the need is recognised for industrial organisation and rationalisation. But these should be the work

[1]Cp. *Science et Sagaesse*, chap. i.
[2]*Freedom in the Modern World*, p. 214.

[188]

of a political and economic wisdom which is above all a science of freedom, proceeding by the dynamism of means to ends, and in continuity with the nature of human beings, not a so-called mathematical universal provision[1]; and which would aim to regulate industry, not only in accord with its own laws, but with those higher ones to which they are subordinate; and primarily always to regulate the movement of supply by the real needs and capacities of consumption.

I do not forget that the technical aspect of social life, though the most subject to necessity, is also the one which changes most rapidly, and that the economic structure of a new Christendom may be very different from the scheme of which the dominant features of the industrial economy of to-day suggest the outlines in the not too distant future. But the aim of this digression has only been to suggest that the *subordination* of these technically dominant forces to those of a higher ethic is what alone gives, as I suggested a moment ago, its typical morphology and ultimate specification to an economic structure, and that when we adopt a christian philosophy of man, of work, and of the ownership of material goods, the whole aspect of these most important economic problems changes, so to speak, its meaning.

The condition of women in marriage

My second consideration is concerned with the condition of women in marriage, envisaged from the point of view of that christian personalism which is the third fundamental

[1]In his essay *La Sagesse du chef d'enterprise*, M. Georges Cazin has shown that already, even within the limits of a particular enterprise, it is wisdom which should take the lead rather than a mathematical technique. Cp. Lucien Laine, *Une communauté économique, le Tapis*, 1934.

feature of the new regime of culture whose image I am endeavouring to trace.

It is a platitude, which is nevertheless very exact, to say that Christianity has endowed woman, otherwise and particularly in the East regarded as an object of property, with a sense of dignity and personal liberty.

This gain, of an immense historical importance, has been realised in the spiritual order: it is there, in that universe superior to this world, that it has its prime value, and from thence that it has passed little by little into the temporal order and our juridical structures.

This progress took place with an inevitable lag, which the intensity of the life of faith rendered less hurtful in the christian centuries, and which has been felt much more cruelly since the Renaissance.

What I want here very briefly to point out is that the family of what we may call the *bourgeois* type, by which I mean one uniquely or principally founded on the material association of perishable economic interests, is like a caricature and a mockery, truly speaking the decaying corpse, of the *christian* family, which is essentially founded on the primarily spiritual and sacramental union of two persons who engender for an immortal destiny other living beings endowed with imperishable souls.

In the same way, in the present-day crisis affecting marriage and the family, a crisis principally due to economic causes, but also to a certain moral ideology, one may say that a pseudo-individualism, destructive of domestic society, whereby woman claims an equality with man which is in some sort material and quantitative in its terms, and which otherwise is only too comprehensible as a reaction against that non-christian but bourgeois conception of the

[190]

family, is like a caricature and a mockery of christian personalism.

It is notable that socialist theorists in general accept these dissolving and inhuman results of the capitalist system (in particular, for example, the factory work of women), as in general they accept the economic heritage of bourgeois economy and push it farther. Thus marxist theorists announce a radical transformation of the family and of marriage in the society of the future, where the equality of economic conditions between men and women will give their life of affection the dignity and the freedom of an earthly paradise. The new Christendom of which we are speaking can draw a like profit from the experiences of to-day, but in rectifying them in an entirely other sense.

For that progress on which certain thinkers of the school of Proudhon and Sorel insist,[1] and according to which woman, —having passed from the juridical condition of a *thing* (a condition imputed to the *ancien régime*) to that of an *individual*, due to her unhappy reactions and revolts in the bourgeois epoch,—should finally come to a full juridic status as a *person*,—it is only in a civilisation which is christian in mode that such a progress can achieve its aim, this full *juridical* status as a person then corresponding in the socio-temporal order to the *spiritual* condition of a person set up by the Gospel from the beginning in the moral and religious order.

In such a conception, which is one of a qualitative and *proportionate* equality, the married woman has not, except in exceptional cases, the same economic functions as a man; she cares for 'the humble kingdom of her house'[2] and it is in the

[1]Cp. Edouard Berth, *op. cit., infra.*

[2]'Over the humble kingdom of thy household with wisdom hast thou reigned....' Raïssa Maritain, *La Vie donnée.*

order of private life, and in the domain of all the humanity, the vigilance and firmness implied by these private personal relations, that she will exercise her primacy. But the experiences of individualism, however disastrous they may otherwise have been, will here also doubtless bring beneficial results. Woman will have taken cognisance in herself of that personality which the pagan and, above all, the bourgeois conception of marriage so bitterly disputed with her. And this consciousness is something which cannot be taken away. If in the order of the economic relations concerned with material goods it is normal that the married woman be *nourished* by her husband,[1] she will not thereby lose her liberty as a person, which, moreover, should have a full juridical recognition, implying a complete equality of rights in everything concerned with the institution of matrimony; and it is in order to realise, at the same time as her functions as a mother, that capacity on which the Bible insists, of assisting, as a person like to himself, the man to live, it is in order to *nourish* him in her turn in the order of a more secret and more profoundly human economy, that she and he are made as one.[2]

[1]Again, the work accomplished by woman *in the household*, in particular in her function of maternal education, has an incontestable *economic* value, which gives her, by this very fact, a right to her husband's earnings, earnings in themselves ordained for the benefit of the family.

[2]Cp. Raïssa Maritain, *Histoire d'Abraham* (Nova et Vetera, No. 3, Fribourg, Switzerland).

'In this story of human progress which we are endeavouring to read word by word in Genesis, be it noted, whatever be the possibility of other interpretations, that woman has jumped a stage. She was not made from the earth, from "the dust of the earth" like man. Dust by the intervention of man's flesh, as man is dust through his animal flesh, she was made of human stuff, created in the heart of paradise, while man only entered therein after his creation.

'Thus, according to the Bible, the physical origin of woman is nobler than that of man. The price of this privilege is that the claims of God and

Thus, in a new Christendom and thanks to the conditions of a new civilisation, the spiritual riches included in the state of christian marriage, which are to-day so regularly misunderstood, will at length come to their fullness and their flower.

IV

THE UNITY OF SOCIAL RACE

Authority and fundamental equality

After this parenthesis, let us come to the fourth characteristic feature of this new Christendom. It is the fact that a certain parity of essence (between the leaders and the led), an essential parity, I mean, in the common condition of men bound to labour, will then be at the base of all relations of authority and the hierarchy of temporal functions, whether it be a question of political or any other social forms of authority.

One might say that this conception of authority finds its type not in the benedictine system, but rather in that of the Dominicans, the Order of Preachers standing on the threshold of the modern world as the Benedictine Order did on

of man are by so much the higher with regard to her, and even, dare one say, in the eyes of God. It is Eve who took, by her fault indeed, but also in that hardihood of decision which is proper to an adult, took the initiative which, accepted by Adam, decided the fate of humanity. And it was again a woman who, without any human counsel, and by the plenitude of her faith, compensated in a way for the fault of Eve, and turned again towards God and towards the Saviour the humanity that had gone astray. For the same reason God has permitted the laws which man has made, either by himself or under His inspiration, always to demand a greater humanity, abnegation and purity from woman. The traces, the memory of his animal and earthly stage press more heavily on man. But Eve is full of resemblances to the better Adam.'

that of the Middle Ages: an order of brothers, where one of them is chosen as chief by his fellows.

In the political order (whatever be the form of the regime, that is a wholly different question), the organs of government will then be regarded by the Christian as having, like all legitimate power, their source of authority in God, without thereby taking on, even by participation, a sacred character; once designated, authority resides in them, but by virtue of a certain *consensus*, of a free and vital determination of the multitude whose personification and vicar they are: *vices gerens multitudinis*, in St. Thomas's words. This consensus itself may, moreover, be understood in varying ways, it can be formulated or unformulated,—in a system of hereditary monarchy it is given once for all for an indeterminate future, both in regard to the form of the regime and the eventual holders of its power,—in the democratic system it is given once for all for an indeterminate future in regard to the form of the regime, but it is periodically renewable with regard to the holders of power; still, in any case of the acceptance of a purely secular and 'homogeneous' conception of temporal authority, the head is simply one who has the right of command over others who are his equals or companions.

In the economic order, fellowship in work will not, in this new Christendom of which I am speaking, be resolvable into the domestic society, as in the Middle Ages, nor into that confrontation of two classes alien to each other of the age of bourgeois liberalism; but it will constitute—the liquidation of the capitalist regime being assumed as a preliminary—a specific institutional form, corresponding to a natural association or *collaboration* of those engaged in the same work.

There is a reverse to every medal. Granted that the necessary order of political life is more difficult to obtain in a common-

[194]

wealth where authority has to live in terms of one and the same 'social race' than in one where it comes from a higher 'social race', the weight of social responsibility will there be heavier, the tension of its discipline more severe.

A personalist democracy

Here again we find a conception at once in opposition to the false liberal one of modern times and to the consecrational ideal of the Middle Ages. If the word democratic is taken in Rousseau's sense, such a regime will be clearly anti-democratic, since it is not by an abstract liberty, an impersonal liberty, but by concrete and positive liberties, incarnated in institutions and in the social body, that the inner freedom of the human being asks to be translated on the exterior plane of social action. But, on the other hand, it is indeed one of the values included in that most equivocal word democracy that is here achieved: I am thinking of a sense of this word which is rather affective and moral, having reference to that personal dignity of which the crowd has taken cognisance in itself, not, doubtless, in the sense of truly meriting or possessing it, but at least as being called thereto; that popular civic consciousness which excludes as a natural consequence any separate (albeit good) domination of one social category over the mass of the people considered as minors, and implies on the plane of social life itself respect for human personality in each of the individuals of whom the crowd is made up.

I have just said that the crowd has become conscious of this personal dignity in modern times, not as something they truly merit or possess but as something to which they aspire; and yet most often it is in symbolic or figurative terms, terms which are often very deceptive, that in fact modern democracies profess a respect for the personality of each of the

[195]

individuals in the mass of the people. This is exactly the drama which the communist revolution claims to bring to a dénouement, and which Christianity alone—socially lived to the full—can indeed truly resolve, in making real what as yet has only been a symbol and an image. This is why it is only in a new Christendom, in the future, that this ethical and affective value of the word democracy, which corresponds to what may be called a popular civic consciousness, will be *really* achieved. If, moreover, the present *class*-divisions[1] will then have been overcome, this society without a bourgeoisie and without a proletariat will not be a society without any internal structure or any differentiations and organic inequalities. But the hierarchy of functions and advantages will no longer be bound up with hereditary categories fixed heretofore by blood (which is in principle a healthy solution), nor as to-day by money (which is an unhealthy solution). And it is by a veritable aristocracy of work (in all the amplitude and qualitative diversity of the word)[2] that a temporal system which is vitally christian will learn (without doubt even then none too easy a lesson) respect for human personality in the individual and in the crowd.

[1] I take this word *class* in the strict and very exact sense, as Briefs, for example, uses it in his studies of the industrial proletariat: a *class* implies a hereditary and permanent condition; the proletarian being unpossessed and constrained to alienate his forced labour for a wage which is not sufficiently high to allow of any accumulation, it is inevitable, save in exceptional cases, that his condition should be transmitted to his descendants from generation to generation. Cp. Goetz Briefs, *Le Prolétariat industriel* (Paris, Desclée de Brouwer, 1936).

[2] Cp. *Freedom in the Modern World*, pp. 57-60.

V

THE COMMON AIM: THE REALISATION OF A
FRATERNAL COMMUNITY

The temporal city and brotherly love

Finally, the fifth and last characteristic: in what is concerned with the city's common aim, let us say, in accord with the indication given in a previous chapter,[1] that for a christian civilisation which can no longer be naive the common aim is no longer that of realising a divine work here on earth by the hands of men, but rather the realisation on earth of a human task by the passage of something divine, that which we call love, through human operations and even through human work.

Thus the dynamic principle of the common life and task of such a civilisation will not be the mediaeval idea of building God's empire in this world, and still less the myth of a class or of a race, a nation or a State.

Let us say that it will be the idea—not according to the stoics or Kant, but according to the Gospel—of the dignity of human personality and its spiritual vocation, and of the fraternal love which is its due. The task of the commonwealth will be the realisation of a common life here on earth, of a temporal system truly in conformity with that dignity, that vocation and that love. We are far enough away from any such end to be sure that the need for work will not be lacking! This task is arduous, paradoxical, heroic: it claims no tepid humanism.

Such a conception would be utopian indeed if the fraternal love of which I have spoken were to be regarded as the sole

[1] See *supra*, chap. ii.

[197]

bond and basis of the temporal community. Indeed I am well aware that a certain material weight and, as it were, a biological community of interests and passions, a social animality so to speak, is indispensable in common life. And I have sufficiently stressed in the preceding sections the organic character which from this standpoint a new Christendom will necessarily hold. I know also that if it is not founded on a conception of human nature at once pessimistic and exigent, which makes the most important end appear the most difficult, and what is best in the political order appear to require the greatest care, an ideal of fraternal love can be the most pernicious of illusions. It is not easily realised in religious communities, where men and women are vowed to seek perfection: it is still less so, without doubt, in the order (a humbler one, it is true, but one nearer to the elementary realities of life, though much less careful of virtue) of secular and temporal life. But if it is absurd to ask the commonwealth to make all men, taken as individuals, good and fraternal one to another, we can and should demand, which is quite another thing,[1] that it should have in itself social structures, institutions and laws which are good and inspired by the spirit of fraternal love, and that it should orientate as potently as may be the energies of social life towards such an amity which, natural as at bottom it may be, is very hard for the sons of Adam. Thus, first of all, if one may have recourse to the word, it is as a 'myth' giving its primordial direction to the common life, as its typical end to be pursued, as a heroic aim to be realised, as the animating theme of a common enthusiasm, which brings into action the deep energies of the crowd, that fraternal love shows as an essential dynamic principle of this new Christendom of mine. It is because it

[1]Cp. p. 104, n. 1.

[198]

will be truly *orientated* in its entirety towards a socio-temporal realisation of the Gospel that it can rightly apply itself to a secular christian common task.

The solution of an antinomy

At the beginning of the previous chapter[1] I underlined a characteristic paradox of the political life of human beings: on the one hand human persons as parts of the political community are subordinate to it and to its general common aim; on the other, the human person, at the core of his personal life, is superior to this common aim and gives it its end. We can now see the solution of this antinomy.

It is not sufficient to say that justice demands a certain re-distribution to individual citizens of the common good (which is common to the whole and to the parts); it is necessary to say that the common temporal good being the common good of *human persons*, by that very fact each, in subordinating himself to the common task, is subordinate to the accomplishment of the personal life of *others*, of other *persons*. But this solution only holds a practical and existential value in a commonwealth where the true nature of the common task is recognised, and, at the same time, as Aristotle divined, the value and the *political* importance of fraternal love. It would be a great misfortune if the failure of the vain optimistic 'fraternity' inscribed on the banners of the bourgeois revolution made us forget such a truth. There is no more fundamentally anti-political frame of mind than the profound distaste for the idea of fraternal amity entertained by the enemies of the Gospel,—whether by great indignant souls like Proudhon and Nietzsche, or the cynics who adore what they are pleased to call order.

[1]See *supra*, chap. iv, p. 130.

[199]

But a problem rises here which must be swiftly scanned: that of the collaboration and participation of unbelievers in the life of a christianly constituted temporal commonwealth, of a vitally christian lay State, which comprehends, as I pointed out before, at once believers and unbelievers.

To seek to establish a *common doctrinal minimum* between them which will serve as a basis for common action is, as I have equally pointed out, a pure fiction. Each gives, and should give, his whole self, and give his maximum.

It is not to the search for a *theoretic common minimum*; it is to the effectuation of a *practical common task* that all are called, believers and unbelievers. Here we see the dawn of a solution.

This practical common task, as I have just said, is not consecrationally but *secularly christian*. Comprehended in the fullness and perfection of the truths which it implies, it takes in all Christianity; yes, the whole of christian ethics and dogmatics: it is only through the mystery of the redeeming Incarnation that a Christian sees the proper dignity of human personality, and what it costs. The idea which he has of it stretches out indefinitely, and only attains the absolute fullness of its significance in Christ.

But by the very fact that it is secular and not sacred, this common task does not in the least demand in its beginning a profession of faith in the whole of Christianity from each man. On the contrary, it includes in its characteristic features a pluralism which makes possible the *convivium* of Christians and non-Christians in one temporal city.

Hence, if by the very fact that it is a christian work it pre-

[200]

supposes by hypothesis that those who take the initiative will be Christians, with a full and total comprehension of the aim to be attained, yet it calls to work all men of goodwill, all those to whom a grasp more or less partial and defective,—very defective it may be,—of the truths which the Gospel makes known in their plenitude, disposes to give their practical help (which may not be the least devoted or the least generous) in the achievement of this common task. It is here that the text has its fullest force and application: *he that is not against you is with you* (Mark ix, 39).

VI

The Spiritual Attitude of St. Thomas and the Philosophy of Culture

Such then is the concrete historical ideal which we ought to have in our minds of a new Christendom: such is the way, I believe, in which Christianity can save in order to transmit to the future, while purifying them of the mortal errors in which they are involved, the truths towards which the modern age is striving in the cultural order. It is obvious, at least in the degree to which I have made myself understood, that in my eyes this purification is wholly different from any simple empiric arrangement or patchwork. Modern civilisation is a worn-out vesture: it is not a question of sewing on patches here and there, but of a total and substantial reformation, a trans-valuation of its cultural principles; since what is needed is a change to the primacy of quality over quantity, of work over money, of the human over technical means, of wisdom over science, of the common service of human beings instead of the covetousness of unlimited individual enrichment or a desire in the name of the State for unlimited power.

[201]

In this quest I have sought inspiration in the general principles of St. Thomas Aquinas, and tried to feel, if I may put it so, what would be his personal reaction to the conflicts of human history. Did not he constantly fight against two eternal and opposite inclinations to error: on the one hand, against the *accumulative inertia* of a backward scholasticism which clung to the accidental and passing elements of the christian tradition; and on the other, against an instinct of *spendthrift disassociation*, represented in his time by the Averroist movement and which came to its full flower in a later era in the anthropocentric humanism of modern times?

St. Thomas, and it is the particular note of his genius, was always able to discern at the core of the firmest order, and of the most oecumenical and catholic tradition, vital energies, the most potent impulses of revolution and renewal. Hence his attachment to his central intuition of analogy as the truly living and universal instrument of research and of the truth. And this is also why he was able to take up and to save in the catholicity of a perfectly free and pure doctrine all the truths, without depreciating one of them, pursued by pagan thought through the dimness of its shadows and by the systems of the philosophers with their discordant clamour.

To-day, in that order of the philosophy of culture or of civilisation we are dealing, on the one hand, with conceptions due to a univocal inertia which clings precisely to what is dead and done with in the temporal ideal of mediaeval Christendom; and on the other, with a whole ideology of revolutionary destruction, which rises in opposition to the very idea of Christendom. Here also, to my mind, the truth must be sought in an apex between these two opposing errors. It is towards the inauguration of a veritable and authentic Christendom, faithful to the immutable principles of every vitally christian temporal order, and free from all the errors springing from anti-christian ideologies and that instinct, as I called it a moment ago, of spendthrift dispersion, that our minds should be directed: but towards a *new* Christendom, realising in a specifically different type from that of the Middle Ages the unchanging exigencies of a temporal christian life, exigencies which I say are analogical, not univocal. Taken in its essence, the mediaeval ideal of a consecrated christian society is certainly not evil, since it *has been* good. But existentially it corresponds to something come to an end. If I may be allowed to use in paradoxical fashion the language of metaphysics in the context of the philosophy of history, I should say that this ideal or prospective image has been truly an *essence*, i.e. an intelligible complex capable of existence and inviting realisation, but that now and in relation to the concrete and *dated* existence of the historic age we are entering it is no more than a logical entity conceived *ad instar entis* and incapable of existence.

If St. Thomas had lived in the time of Galileo and of Descartes he would have taught christian philosophy to free itself, in order to be the more faithful to the metaphysical thought of Aristotle, from the worn-out fantasies of the mechanics and astronomy of Aristotle. May he in our day teach christian philosophy, in the social and cultural order,—in order to save among the broken forms of history the imperishable substance of the past, and above all of the christian past of Europe, in the elaboration of a christian historic ideal capable of existence and inviting realisation under a new historic sky,—to free itself of the images and fantasies of the *sacrum imperium*, which, once effective and necessary in its hour to the growth of history, has to-day become an *ens rationis*, only able once more to make truth serve falsehood, and to drape and conceal with a christian appearance the form of temporal systems long grown strangers to the christian spirit! The fecundity of the analogy in this domain is obviously not exhausted by the historic ideal whose main outlines I have here tried to sketch. Others doubtless will arise, in other historic circumstances of whose conditions we have no idea. And there is indeed nothing to prevent those devoted to a consecrated christian conception from admitting the hypothesis of an eventual cycle of culture in which it will once again prevail, under conditions and with characteristics which we cannot foresee.

CHAPTER VI

THE HISTORIC POSSIBILITIES OF THE
REALISATION OF A NEW CHRISTENDOM

The ideal which occupied us in the preceding chapter belongs to what I have called the 'intelligible constellations dominating human history'. If I have succeeded in expressing it as it should it belongs to the order of essences or of intelligible structures *possible in themselves*, i.e. not implying any feature which is incompatible with existence,—with the dated existence of the age on which we are entering. And it suffices that such an ideal be *possible* for it to serve as an effective orientation for human energies in a useful labour in the field of history. But this study would not be complete if we did not consider, as rapidly as may be, and precisely because in good doctrine the very nature of the essence is defined by its relation to existence,—*potentia dicitur ad actum* —the conditions of realisation of this ideal.

I have already pointed out that this ideal, by the very fact that it belongs to the wide horizons of the philosophy of culture, is concerned with a relatively indeterminate future. But its roots are in the soil of our own day: hence from to-day it should exercise its dynamic value and should orientate our action, even though its realisation must belong to a distant future and come in a more or less defective form, or give place, under a new historic sky to-day unforeseeable, to another concrete ideal.

I

INTERNAL DIMENSIONS: THE IMPULSE OF THE SPIRIT IN SOCIAL LIFE.

A refraction of the truths of the Gospel in the temporal order

Let us therefore come to an examination of the conditions of realisation of the concrete historical ideal whose major typical features I have sketched.

This question has great practical importance in relation to the aim and to the prudent ordering of our action. Speculatively it may seem vain enough, for the issue depends not only on the material conditions and determinations of history, but also on human freedom, which can enter in in so many diverse ways. Here at any rate we may adopt the famous formula of Marx: 'Man makes history, but under conditions which are determined.'[1] Scientific German Marxism forgot the first half of this formula. The fact remains that these 'determined conditions' referred to in the second half allow of certain previsions of possibilities, at least allowing for a sufficiently wide margin of indetermination. What is in any case certain is that the passage to a new Christendom implies much deeper changes than are implied in the ordinary use of the word revolution. We thus come to the supremely important question of the *internal dimensions* of such changes. In a word, they consist of the penetration into the temporal and cultural order of a real *refraction* of the Gospels.

[1]'Men make their own history, but they do not do so at will in conditions of their own choosing but under given conditions, left to them by tradition. The tradition of the dead generations weighs on the brains of the living like a nightmare. . . .' *The 18 Brumaire.*

We have to do with changes in the regime of human life which are at once external and internal, to be accomplished at once in the hearts of men and in their cities and institutions, which affect together, although in different ways, the domain of social and visible things and the spiritual, moral and invisible one; and first of all, the spiritual domain. Such changes have often been under consideration in the previous chapters, as well as the transmutation of the scale of values which they imply: the end of the disintegration which prevailed in the modern world, and the historic necessity we have found for a new impulsion of the spirit and of faith to raise the socio-temporal order. Now I wish to turn to one particular aspect, in stressing the need for a transcendence not only of *economics*, but of *politics*.

Economism transcended

The idea of such a christian renovation is opposed to the *economist* conception of social development and even of economics, according to which great social transformations of history consist essentially in a transformation of economic technique.

This conception is false, even in regard to a materialist economy like that of capitalism. As Amintore Fanfani has recently pointed out: capitalism itself is above all things of the mind or spirit.[1]

Politics transcended

The idea of a christian renovation is as opposed to *politicism*, which is indeed the corruption of politics. I understand by this word 'politicism' a conception which consists not only in regarding the winning of power by a party, or the

[1] A. Fanfani, *Catholicism, Protestantism and Capitalism* (Eng. trans. 1936).

conquest of political power by a class, as essential for a 'substantial transformation' of the order of civilisation, but more profoundly one which invokes a purely technical idea of political activity,—political and social activity being then regarded as intrinsically amoral and social facts as special instances of purely physical facts, which it is sufficient to deal with according to purely technical rules, while private conduct remains subject to the rules of personal morality. In this conception political knowledge is essentially identified with a pure and simple *art*, with a technique; an art which is perhaps subordinated by such a one to some external moral system, but whose ends and particular texture are strangers to morality: ends, for example, such as the purely material existence, the power and material prosperity of the State.

If we wish to give a name to this conception, one can, if one wishes, attach it to that of the great political writer who is also the great political heresiarch of modern times,—Machiavelli. Every error has its truth; the truth of machiavellianism is a reaction against a false conception of ethics, against what may be called *supermoralism* (meaning by this the melancholic claims of a pharisaic morality, one which is purely formal and geometric, which denies at once nature and life). It is also and above all an attitude of mind or of the soul, a certain force and metaphysical freedom in the concrete judgement of events and of men, of which, indeed, the style of the Old Testament furnishes a divine example. A man of this character understands that God brings forth good from evil, and takes into consideration the weaknesses and violence of men, and the metaphysical dictates of nature and history, in the course of events and the designs of providence.

But this character, this attitude of mind differs absolutely from a doctrine or philosophy of immoralism, as a senti-

[208]

mental and purist attitude is something absolutely different from a doctrine or philosophy which recognises the just claim of ethics over the whole domain of human life. And it is the misfortune of human nature that this character, which is in itself good, finds expression too often in an amoral and evil philosophy, just as the other attitude which is evil too often decks itself out with the truths of ethics, which are good. In any case, we can recognise that the Conquistadors served in a way the growth of history, and at the same time share Las Casas' condemnation of their faults. We may comprehend the surrenders to which a political genius, fascinated by the greatness of the work to be accomplished, makes to temptation, but that need not mean that we approve or excuse these surrenders. We can realise how immense a part is played in politics and incorporated in its ends by art and technique, without thereby confounding political activity with a pure technique and perverting it in itself.

For the political and social sphere is not only technical, but primarily and essentially human, i.e. ethical or moral. The achievements of men in that sphere are intrinsically human and moral. 'Political and social virtues have an essentially moral character. . . . Social life should by nature be built upon the same rules of integrity, of justice, of love for one's neighbour, as rule the moral building up of our own personalities. These laws have assuredly differing modes of application in the social and personal spheres: but their substance and their rigour remain the same.'[1]

The political good is a BONUM HONESTUM (*worthy in itself of being an end of human action*)

There are some who will take what I have just said amiss, since they misunderstand the sense of the word *moral* in the

[1]The manifesto *Pour le Bien commun*, Paris, Desclée de Brouwer, 1934.

use made of it when one says that the political sphere is as such a moral one.

They assume that *morality* means uniquely, exclusively *individual* morality, the rules of private conduct between single personalities. And they imagine that we seek to reduce politics to morality *so understood*, which would obviously be to empty it of its proper content. No, I do not say, and no one, I believe, has ever had the naïveté to say, that politics is reducible to individual morality or a simple application of the latter: but I do say, and Aristotle said it long ago, that political science represents a special branch of ethical science,—not that which concerns individuals, nor that which concerns domestic society,—but precisely that which is specifically concerned with the good of men gathered in a commonwealth, the good of the social whole: this good is essentially human, and thus is measured above all by reference to the ends of the human being, and is occupied with the manners of men as free beings who should make use of their freedom for right ends. The ancients defined it as the right life of the assembled multitude. It is not a simple bundle of *utilities*, advantages and prosperities. As in all things that are truly human, the useful is there taken in relation to ends good in themselves and for themselves, that good and worthy social life, of which I have spoken, and a good and worthy common task for men to accomplish. This is why an act of treachery, the murder of the innocent, no matter what iniquity which seems favourable to the *utility* of the State, goes in reality against the common good and tends in itself to destroy it; because the common good is not only what is useful to the State, but a righteousness which is higher than utility, good in itself and for itself, in the life of the human multitude.

Thus it does not suffice for a man to be pious, just and holy for him to be a good politician. He must also possess the knowledge of techniques that are useful for the common good; but he must also and above all possess a knowledge of the human and moral values involved in this common good, the knowledge of the field of social and political realisation, or so to say, the *political aspect* of justice, of fraternal love, or the respect due to human persons and the other exigencies of moral life.

It is not sufficient to be just to be a good politician, but justice is a necessary *condition* of every political good as such: to such a point that, according to St. Thomas,[1] it is necessary that the prince, in order to be able to govern, should be purely and simply *bonus vir*, a virtuous man in every sense of the word.

The specific character of political ethics

Here again there is another misunderstanding belonging to the same order of ideas, or another sophistical manoeuvre, which must be indicated.

There are some who imagine that morality measures our acts, not in accord with the just human ends to which these should be proportionate in the given circumstances, but by a forest of abstract formulae which should be copied to the letter. This is that supermoralism or moral pharisaism that I referred to just now. And the partisans of machiavellianism are the first to ascribe this impracticable purism to morality, turning it into a ritual, as it were, of human sacrifice demanded by a fidelity to principles which are all the purer in being isolated from any connection with life and action, and enthroned like idols or like theorems. In truth minds of this class make it a point of honour to declare that the

[1] *Sum. theol.*, i-ii, 92, 2.

first condition of existence for politics is a rejection of morality.

The principles of morality in reality are neither theorems nor idols, but the supreme laws of a concrete activity which aims at something to be done in such and such circumstances, and uses more proximate rules and also the prescriptions, which are never *set out in advance*, of the virtue of prudence, applying the principles of ethics to the particular instance under the influence of a will disposed to right. They do not seek to devour human life, but to build it up.

The particular object of politics is the common good of the social body: that is its measure. This common good, as I pointed out a moment ago, is in principle moral and thus is incompatible with no matter what intrinsically evil means. But it also demands, by the mere fact that it is the right common life of a multitude of sinful and weakly beings, that in order to procure it one should know how to apply the principle of the lesser evil, and how to tolerate evils whose interdiction would bring greater evils in their train. Finally, politics is not an affair of abstract entities; the good and evil with which it has to deal are incarnate in historical energies whose intensity, duration and concrete scale are fixed. Faced with the forces in action in the field of history it must not only appreciate the truth and falsehood of the values which they present *as such and in the abstract, in their timeless significance*: it must also estimate the energy of *historical realisation* and the coefficients of *future* good and evil contained in them. And this estimate may lead to conclusions which are in practice very different from those to which a purely abstract consideration would in itself have led. The tendency in the French mind to see things through the eyes of a logician or in logistic terms makes it necessary to recall these proper conditions of political thought, i.e. of the most authentically pure political wisdom and ethics, as a St. Louis, for example, would have understood them.

Hence we see that the subordination of politics to morality, to true morality,—exactly because it is morality,—is something human, practical and practicable, and not in the least inhuman or antihuman, impracticable and geometric.

Essence and existence in politics

Indeed, going a step further, it is to the old debate between essence and existence that the preceding reflections belong. They signify that political and social life belongs to the world of existence and contingence, not to that of pure essences: and goodness knows the risks that essences, those essences the philosopher considers apart, must run in the actual life of things. In a final reckoning, if history were nothing more than an unfolding of logical necessities, the automatism of essences would suffice, and the governance of God, the free head of free agents, would become superfluous. None knows that better than the great makers of ecclesiastical policy. An ideological policy, be it jacobin or clerical, knows only pure essences (duly simplified), and we can have a firm confidence that its platonism will always lead, with an infallible rectitude, to non-existence. In history, as I recalled a moment ago, it is not theses that confront one another, neatly set out on the pages of a book, or as in some academic discussion, where all ends to the intimate and meritorious satisfaction of the man who is in the right and makes himself clear: it is concrete forces charged with humanity, heavy with their weight of fatalities and contingencies, which are born in events and die in events, whose existential significance it is the office of politics to measure.

But if it is an error to forget that essences come to act only in existence, i.e. in ceasing to be pure essences, if it is a fault to deal politically with Great Britain as one would deal theologically with Puritanism, with Germany as if it were Racism, with Soviet Russia as if it were Marxism,—it is no less grave an error to forget that existence is where essences are realised, and that in the measure in which they there are realised they develop their internal energies and their logic, while all the while combining with other forms and with the whole historical inheritance of the matter which receives them.

The utilisation of morality

These comments could be developed and deepened. Good things are difficult to manipulate: nothing is more difficult to handle than morality, above all since it became kantian in so many minds who are unaware even that this is so, and when it is separated from nature (which, indeed, it has to rule by reason, and which is yet, in the degree to which it springs from the eternal Law, the measure of reason). The sorest disasters can result when, instead of acting from within as consubstantial with the vital movement of our pursuit of the ends of human life, morality strives to act on this movement from without, i.e. in a word, when moral laws *external to life* are imposed on the *amoral* movements of life. The sorest disasters can result in the life of a people when, instead of acting as consubstantial with politics, it essays to act on them from without, i.e. in the imposition of *apolitical* moral laws on an *amoral* conception of politics.

Morality demands that before a man does evil we should do everything to prevent it; and afterwards everything to undo it without inducing a greater evil; but, if this is impossible, that we should recognise facts: the existence of the evil a man has committed, and the fact that it is there, that it has taken its place in the course of the events of this world, together with the good on which it is a parasite. And if it is there we are perhaps in some unknown way responsible. And what is then demanded of us is that we do everything to heal and to repair it, and to turn to good the consequences of this *fait accompli*. In its own order the ethic of politics works in the same way. On the same principle the rules of prescription legitimate in numerous cases the ownership of worldly goods (which have often been acquired by very dubious means). The evil is not effaced: God will punish, either in this world or the next. But a state of fact consequent to this evil dealing is legalised, when once the connection between this actual condition and the evil which led to it has become so woven into a nexus of relations with human wellbeing that restitution would not be possible without evoking greater injustice, and when the good (e.g. ownership) which was in the first instance unlawfully acquired has made sufficient new connections with lawful activities for it in the end to be healed, as it were, and scarred into the stuff of existence.

Pursuing such reflections, we can see that there is another solution to the debate between history and morality than hypocrisy or cynicism, or an endless oscillation between the two. It is morality itself, it is laws and principles equally and essentially moral, which require that we should seek with all our force to promote what is good and just in history and also that we should not claim to impose these by force when they would be the cause of greater evils or the result be a treason to higher duties. It is at the heart of the same intrinsically ethical development that we are given the double commandment, first to devote all our energies to the raising of the level of goodness and justice in the current stuff of his-

[215]

tory, i.e. make it render an active witness to God; and secondly, not to act as if it was our office, in the endeavour to separate the wheat and the tares, *to close the account* and so the very movement of historical existence in which we live: in other words, not to constitute ourselves at each instant the auditors of God's judgement on history.

In fact men often make very ill use of the principle of the lesser evil, because they see in it a pretext for doing nothing for the ends of justice. Nevertheless it is essentially an ethical principle, like the demand for justice. And of that also man can make very evil use, in turning it against the stuff of existence and so augmenting, despite themselves, the weight of the evil they would resolve.

Finally, if men often make an ill use of morality, they also neglect to take into consideration another moral truth, which is a primary one: morality demands that we apply its laws to our own conduct, not that we revenge it on the person of another when that other has been in default: that is the business of the eternal Judge, and, in a very imperfect measure, of human judges and human educators: it is no business of each one of us in relation to each other.

Man, thou art not thy brother's judge; thou art a sinner as he is, and he is thy brother: there, in a general way, be it a question of private or of political ethics, is the fundamental basis of our bearing towards others. *Omnes quidem peccaverunt, et egent gloria Dei.* We can judge the moral value of another's acts, but not his soul. We should not be silent, we should cry out against injustice and that loudly: but we have not been charged with dispensing the retributions of God. Christ, who hated sin, was the friend of sinners. When another is culpably at fault we may change our conduct with regard to him, because we no longer have confidence in him, because he brings into danger a wellbeing over which we have to watch. But, unless we *have by some right or another a jurisdiction over him*, we have no call to exhibit in our conduct towards him our reprobation of his fault. As though we should be accomplices in his fault if we did not treat the man who has committed it like a criminal and so manifest the purity of our social consciences! This naïve form of pharisaism belongs to the 'herd morality' of a social group; it is the more developed in the degree to which the society in question is a primitive one, and is only morally justified in itself by reflex considerations of social pedagogy, and in relation to a certain vital good, which is, the creation of public opinion. But it in no way constitutes an absolute and unconditional moral rule: for the Gospel has taught us once and for all: 'Let him that is without sin cast the first stone.'

Politics and the providence of God

There remains yet another problem, which gives rise to considerable difficulties, and whose solution, indeed, inevitably depends on our religious position.

Everything that is human in us declares that politics, however large a part is played in it by skill and technical ability, is, as I have just been recalling, something intrinsically moral: a perfidy, an iniquity committed in the so-called interests of the State, is a *political blunder*. The first political condition of a good policy is that it be just.

But it is easy to see that justice and virtue do not as a rule lead to success in this world; and, on the other hand, the commonwealth has not an eternal life, where it can receive the price, like the poor man Lazarus, of the injustices, the unmerited disasters, the death inflicted by evil men in this world: the only good it knows is in the temporal order.

Is it necessary then to recognise an inevitable conflict between the prosperity of the commonwealth which, as an integral part of the common good, is the aim of political wisdom, and that wisdom itself in the degree to which its first condition is justice?

We cannot, I hold, find a valid solution to this question if we do not admit a supreme political government of the universe, which is, truly speaking and in this very order of things, divine (for God is the first cause of this particular order which is that of ethics), and which makes for peoples, cities, nations, good and evil bear their fruits *here on earth*. Hence we can affirm that the political exercise of justice and the other moral virtues, though it may lead to temporary suffering and disaster, must finally serve the common good of the city, which normally implies a certain measure of prosperity.

But this consideration is *super-empiric* and the solution remains mysterious, for the good in which the city's justice comes to fruit has nothing to do with the immediate and visible results, *duration* must be taken into account; and, precisely because it is the government of the first cause which is here in question, the temporal good in which the city's justice fructifies, the temporal evil in which its iniquity bears its fruit, may be quite different from the immediate results which the human mind might have expected. It were as easy to tell at a river's mouth among its waters which come from which glaciers and which tributaries.

Pseudo-realism

There is thus an inevitable division between the christian conception of politics and one which is non-christian. I regret that I must add that many Christians reject the very idea of a vitally christian politic. They call themselves realists.

Just as, generally speaking, the 'practical man' is the dupe of every form of utopianism, so the man who calls himself a 'realist' with a certain tone of assurance and gloomy satisfaction gives himself that name because he is most often at odds with reality. Only believing in force, but also only believing in what can be immediately seen, he will trust himself to anything of sufficient scale so long as it has neither roots nor foundations underground. Many who believe themselves 'realists' are, in fact, empiricists and nominalists who think in dialectical platitudes.

Their whole political standpoint is based on a series of momentary cross-sections taken in time, a series of momentary, of disconnected instants,—of abstractions: however perfect be their estimate of chances, they lack what is essential, the element which belongs to the continuity of real time, the sense of what may be called the 'physiology of development' of history. They would be in the right if politics were nothing but a game of cards, or the art of drawing the best possible hand for a discontinuous series of distributions taken at hazard, had neither a real past nor an internal principle of evolution. When they succeed their successes are deceptive and without any roots in reason and burden the cause they defend with a heavy historical debt, and prepare for it a more disastrous failure.

Very different from these banal and pointless pseudo-realists there are others of a different kind, at once more consistent and more profound. Their successes are more durable and wellnigh scandalise the righteous, who cry against them to God: what the latter are up against is the fairplay of God, who gives those who have freely chosen injustice the time to exhaust the benefits of such a choice and the fulness of their energy. When disaster comes on these victors the eyes of the righteous have long gone to dust and men know not the distant source of the disaster.

This pseudo-realism is that of machiavellianism. Since it is a pure empiricism in a science, i.e. politics, which is concerned with the direction of human life, machiavellianism implies a form of atheism in our temporal existence. It denies in practice that man comes from the hands of God, and that, in spite of everything, he still keeps the greatness and the dignity of that origin. Its pessimism, which is founded on incontestable empiric truths, turns these truths into ontological lies, because for it the fact that man comes from God does not count. Hence they despair of man for the benefit of the State. It is the State which will create man in God's place. It is the State which by its constraints will compel man to issue from the anarchy of his passions and lead a righteous and even heroic life. In his *Preludio al Principe* M. Mussolini, who seems to find a form of sombre intoxication in 'Machiavelli's bitter pessimism with regard to human nature', cites several passages exhibiting Machiavelli's 'negative judgement' of man, his 'desolating and just appraisal', and he adds: 'Machiavelli had no illusions and he does not endow his prince with any. To Machiavelli's mind any antithesis between the prince and the people, the State and the individual, is fatal. What has been called his utilitarianism, his pragmatism, his cynicism proceeds logically from this initial position.' And he also writes: 'I assert that Machiavelli's teaching is more living to-day than it has been for four centuries.'

There is, finally, a third form of pseudo-realism, as profound and vigorous, as murderous as this last: that of the idealists who have turned cynical, of a reversed idealism, of a utopianism become 'scientific' and 'dialectical'. Its metaphysical origins are not pessimistic but optimistic; they spring

[220]

from Rousseau, not from Machiavelli and Mandeville. These also in practice deny that man is God's creation, but this is because they refuse to accept his origin in nothingness: if man does not enjoy the state of a god it is because there is an abomination in the world which binds him: and against this abomination, by whatsoever name it may be called, all means are good; doubtless those who serve this abomination are irresponsible instruments, they are doubtless not more wicked than others; but from the moment they have taken part with the powers of darkness and have renounced human nature, i.e. the duty to live as gods, they became alien to the values implied by the name of man. Hatred for hatred: if for the rich the poor are not human, for the *class-conscious proletariat* neither is the bourgeois a man, nor the *koulak*, nor the heretic to the revolutionary cause. And they will be treated so as a consequence,—as lacking the claims of men. A pitiless hardness towards human personality, a radical contempt for its destiny, are thus bred in the name of universal brotherhood against those who belong to the category of the disqualified or the disgraced: and at the same time a pragmatism, a cynicism, a utilitarianism, exactly equal to those derived from the 'initial position' of Machiavelli.

In short, taking certain typical attitudes in their purest meaning, there is a positivism of the Right which acts as though it were false that man comes from God and belongs to God; it obliterates God by the degree of its contempt for men. And there is an idealism of the Left which acts as if it were false that man comes from nothingness and belongs to nothingness: it removes the Creator in order to divinise man.[1] These opposite tendencies, whose direction is seen by a study

[1] If one pursued this analysis, we should doubtless see that National-Socialism shares at once in both these practical atheisms. It despises

of their ideal limits, explain many of the contradictions of modern history: Fascism springs from the one, Communism from the other. Both, for all that, call themselves realist and indeed their power of political realisation is grandiose. But it is tragic and in itself without issue. A realism which does not take into account, even maybe despite itself, what is deepest in man can indeed be nothing but a pseudo-realism. To hold firmly to this truth however, despite the false evidence of marvels, and to conceive of another realism, one that will be this time authentic, man has need that faith teach him wisdom, and to reckon time not by hours and days, but by weeks of years.

II
INTERNAL DIMENSIONS: THE REINTEGRATION OF THE MASSES
The symbiosis of the true and the false

To what do the foregoing considerations lead if not to the conclusion that the future of a new Christendom primarily depends on a full and inward realisation of a certain lay christian vocation in a certain number of hearts?

This future also depends, in fact, on knowing whether a great christian renaissance will take place, not only among the intellectual élite, but also in the wide range of the popular masses.

This leads to a second, complementary consideration. If the idea of a temporal christian renovation making us quit the age of anthropocentric humanism, and in particular human personality, refusing to treat it as God's creation, but man must serve the apotheosis of the earthly element primitive and divine (daemonic) which develops in and through him, i.e. in and by the predestined *blood* of the race.

[222]

the epoch of capitalistic bourgeoisie, in order to enter a new world, implies a revolution whose internal dimensions (so to say) are of incomparably greater height and breadth and depth than any others, it is necessarily bound up with a vast historic process *of integration and reintegration*.

It is a fact that in the course of the nineteenth century the working classes have in large degree turned away from Christianity. I have already briefly referred to the causes of this fact and the responsibility for it of the christian world.[1] Let me now try to draw out the main lines of this problem as in my view it appears to the eyes of a Christian.

One of the most instructive chapters of a christian philosophy of history would deal with what I might call the intermingling of masks and offices. Not only is the part of iniquity often played under the mask or figure of justice, but masks of iniquity can fill (and mar) the rôles of justice. Not only is evil historical work and useless work done by those who carry the banners of truth, but good work is done (and spoiled) by the adversaries of truth. It is so because the full truth is too heavy for human weakness: the latter, everywhere except among the saints, has need of abatements for error. Historic processes normal and providential in themselves, which tended as such to move along christian lines, are thus found in the course of the modern age, at once by the fault of Christians and of their adversaries, cornered, masked, perverted by anti-christian forces.

In the same way as in the intellectual order, since the sixteenth century, rationalism and the most erroneous philosophies have at once energised and deformed, by a sort of parasitism or symbiosis, something as normal and good in itself as the admirable development of the experimental natural

[1] See chap. iii, *supra;* also *Freedom in the Modern World.*

sciences, so in the social order the growth of socialism in the course of the last century,—automatically called forth by the excesses of capitalism, but in itself expressing a new and typical reaction to evils which had been in motion for centuries in the underworld of history, and proclaiming with a potent voice the immense anonymous cry of the poor,—the growth of socialism has energised, masked and distorted certain historic acquisitions which were good and normal in themselves.

In both cases the historic phenomenon in question was bound up with that tendency towards a rehabilitation of the creature which I have pointed out as typical of the modern world.

The growing consciousness of the dignity and solidarity of labour

What in the case of socialism is the primary acquisition and historic gain that is in question?

It is not primarily a question of the claim for or conquest of better material conditions, an amelioration, as it is called, of working-class conditions.

No, however right and just this claim or this conquest may be, they are only concerned as such with particular economic points, and are so little typical of socialism that they are to be found in reforming or paternalist conceptions, and supposing them entirely possible of fulfilment under the conditions of the actual system, might even lead to a bourgeoising of the proletariat.

On the contrary, it is rather because of the misery and *social not-being* in which they have been held during what may be called the golden age of liberal individualism and capitalism that the proletariat has been able, under the colour of illusory systems, all the more illusory in their very

[224]

claim to be scientific, to realise the gain I have in mind. While primarily affecting the order of temporal and earthly civilisation, this gain is of a spiritual order and that is what gives it its importance. It is a certain *growth in self-consciousness*, a recognition of an offended and humiliated human dignity, of a historic mission. Marxism was created to activate and to distort this awareness. And I would assert that it is impossible to attach too great importance to this, for all the great forms of progress of the modern age, be it a question of art, of science, of philosophy, of poetry, of the spiritual life itself, seem largely to exhibit this growth of self-consciousness, this awareness.

The consciousness in question has been given a name in the vocabulary of socialism: the proletariat's achievement of *class-consciousness*.

Two errors may be pointed out in the socialist or communist notion of *class-consciousness*: one an error which is liberal or *bourgeois* in origin (and thereby Proudhon remains *petit-bourgeois*; yes, and Marx also!), which makes the liberation of the workers a final episode in the struggle for liberty against Christianity and the Church, regarded as forces of servitude and obscurantism; the other an error which is revolutionary-eschatological in origin, the marxist conception of the class-war and the messianic rôle which thereby devolves on the proletariat.[1]

[1] As I wrote recently, 'the existence in modern society of two formations with conflicting interests is a historic fact which, like all the facts of history, presupposes beforehand, together with given conditions independent of the human will, long sequences of contingent events and free acts which have come thereby to their fruit: the social and economic structure to which it belongs once posited in existence, such a condition can only disappear in the replacing of that structure by one which is totally different.

'Following this trend of dispositions so created, another wave of con-

[225]

But detached from these errors and considered in itself, this growth in self-consciousness appears as a considerable

tingent events and free acts was sure to give to the existence of this class-conflict, which is bound up with the structure of the capitalist economy, a particular theoretic and practical interpretation, i.e. that of socialism. In this interpretation, not only is it a normal progress that the proletariat reach their "class-consciousness", but that this should at the same time be an accepted consciousness of moral division, and include the will to pursue its proper ends, which refuse to subordinate themselves, as the very nature of social life demands, to the general good of the commonweal. And since we are here dealing with human affairs, where symbols in their turn affect the nature of the realities they signify, this interpretation was not only one of the fact of class antagonism, but contributed to giving a certain real configuration and certain typical characteristics to this latter.

'According to the very just comment which M. Edouard Berth has often stressed, the division of society into "classes" is a totally different thing than its division into "orders", and it is necessary for the *orders* to have been abolished for these *classes* to appear. Each order of the old regime represented a defined social function, destined to pursue, in its given place in the hierarchy, a common good which was that of society as a whole; the modern proletariat, on the contrary, tends to become an independent totality, which refuses to recognise any common ground of public good between it and its opposing class.

'And indeed so that it should not be so, i.e. that the proletariat while being fully self-conscious should *in spirit*, in the present, surmount this conflict by which it suffers, and strive to transform radically the modern economic system otherwise than by an exasperation of the conflict, a sufficient tension of free energies on its part is needed to dominate the inclinations and dispositions born in the stuff of history,—a tension in a sense heroic, of which man is certainly capable, but which we have no right to expect unless in connection with a living faith in eternal realities which raises our nature above itself' (Preface to the French translation of Goetz Briefs' *The Industrial Proletariat*).

The *secessionist* conception of class-antagonism, to which Proudhon had also come, but with regret and much less decisively, was, from the point of view of revolutionary effectiveness, Marx' stroke of genius. Nevertheless in itself it is deeply erroneous: not only because it fundamentally misinterprets the natural human links and indestructible aspirations, in the natural and moral order, which continue to unite the proletariat with the whole political community, despite the cleavages due to

[226]

historic progress; it signifies the ascension towards liberty and personality, taken in their inner reality and their social

this economic antagonism and despite the condition of the proletariat so created, whom a *freedom without possessions* reduces to a peculiarly inhuman form of servitude; but it insists as a way of escape from this evil on a solution of despair, on a moral scission fully and decisively accepted by the proletariat with regard to the common good of the political commonweal. *Acheronta movebo.* Henceforth the '*damnés de la terre*' shut themselves up in the bounds of that reprobate condition to which they have been driven, and will know no other common good than that of their own disinherited class: and it is from the very excess of this evil that, thanks to their 'final war' and titanic struggle, the liberation of the human race is to arise.

This apocalyptic conception which, instead of merely seeking to rouse the workers of all countries to a class-solidarity, which is right in itself but keeps a due subordination, converts them into a mystical body in internal warfare with the existing political order, remains latent under all the scientific paraphernalia of Marx's terminology. It may be said that it was the blindness of the opposite class in the nineteenth century which projected thither the great mass of the proletariat: the latter had only too many excuses for so doing, believing that no other resource remained open to them. But they will have to suffer for the errors and functional illusion of all policies of distress; they have committed the world to a disastrous schism, and socialism itself to a strife without an end; for either, as we saw in the last war, national structures and their sense of solidarity must needs prevail over the 'general good of the proletariat'—whence, in great measure, the disasters suffered by socialism in Europe; or, as has happened in Russia, its very triumph in the State entails in itself—at least in the State in question—a choice between the (so-called) 'common good' of the universal proletariat and the 'common good' of *that* political city (socialism in the terms of one country), a choice for one and so against the other.

Finally, it may be pointed out that if the *nationalistic* tendencies manifested in actuality by the communists are, from the point of view of the historic processes analysed in this note, a paradox, they also represent a change which may be of extreme importance in the internal evolution of socialism, and prepare on the side where one least expected it certain preliminary conditions, however remote these may be, of a solution of the conflict between the general good of the proletariat and that of the political commonwealth. It seems, however, highly improbable that the internal logic of communism will not rouse some form of *secessionist* reaction, of which the Fourth International is perhaps a prelude.

[227]

expression, of a community of persons, of the community which is at once nearest to the material bases of human life and the most sacrificed, the community of manual work, of human persons set apart for this form of labour.

Naturally I am speaking of a fact typical for this community as such, and not necessarily for each one of the individuals who make it up. We may hold with Aristotle that there will always be men who find themselves constitutionally incapable of working otherwise than in the service of another man or group of men, and as in some way *organs* of the latter. The fact remains that this collective consciousness claims for the working community (whose most typical expression under actual circumstances is the proletariat) a form of social coming of age and the concrete conditions of freedom.

In a word, the historic gain of which I speak is this recognition of the dignity of work and of the worker, of the dignity of the human person of the worker as such. This is the point to which the enlightened elite among the workers hold above all. To maintain the sense of this dignity and the rights which are bound up with it they are ready to face all forms of evil, and also to sacrifice themselves to the most murderous ideologies.

It is the tragedy of our time that a primarily spiritual gain such as this should appear as though essentially part of an atheistic system such as Marxism.

The historic rôle of the proletariat

Meanwhile let us look at one of the consequences of this awareness. If the proletariat claims to be treated as an adult person, by this very fact it is not in a position to be succoured, *ameliorated* or saved by another social class. On the contrary, the principal part in the next phase of historic evolution belongs to it and its own upward movement.

We know with what energy Marxism insists on this consequence—on the one hand in incorporating it in its erroneous social metaphysic, and not only proclaiming that the emancipation of the proletariat will be the work of the proletariat, but that it will be the work of the proletariat *alone,* so rejecting every other form of community than the single form of class-consciousness; while, on the other hand, it has in fact made the proletariat a passive means in the hands of a party and of the 'revolutionary thinker', who plays a no less extravagant part among the marxists than his *legislator* did for Jean-Jacques Rousseau.

Truly, without falling a prey to this marxist messianism, a Christian can recognise that there is profound insight in this idea that the proletariat, by the very fact that its part in the capitalist regime has been one of suffering and endurance, and not of profit in the exploitation of men's capacities as a form of merchandise, is the bearer of unused moral reserves which endow it with a mission in regard to the new order of the world: a mission which will be (or would be) truly one of liberation if the consciousness of it is not (or were not) falsified by an erroneous philosophy.

The Christian accuses the marxist of a false conception, at once material and mystical, of work; with not seeing in work anything but an effort of production, the transformation of matter and the creation of economic values, and, on the other hand, endowing it not only, which is entirely true, with great dignity, but with the greatest of all dignity for human being, i.e. in treating it as man's essence. And he also charges the marxist with a false conception of the class-war. That classes exist without any organic unity between

[229]

them and therefore are in conflict (it is a fact due to the structure of the capitalist regime), and that this conflict must be overcome,—on all these points the Christian and the marxist are in accord. But *how* is this conflict to be surmounted: that is the question. For the marxist, by a physical warfare which turns the proletariat into a military organisation, a Jerusalem of the revolution voluntarily cut off from communion with the rest of mankind, crushing, annihilating the other class.

For the Christian, by a spiritual warfare, and by a social and temporal strife which ought to be waged by all those who share the same human ideal, in the very waging of which the conflict in question is indeed already overcome.

For the Christian what makes the bond and the unity between those who should labour for a temporal renovation of the world is, first of all,—to whatever class, race or nation they may belong,—a community of thought, of love and of will, a passion for the accomplishment of a common aim, the achievement of a community which is not biologically-material as that of the race, not sociologically-material as that of the class, but justly and truly human. There the idea of classes, of the proletariat, is transcended.

Yet, precisely because man is at once carnal and spiritual, because every great historic and temporal undertaking has biologico-sociological material foundations, where the very animality of man and a whole irrational capital is at once borne along and exalted, it is natural that, in the transformation of a regime such as the capitalist system, the working classes should furnish this sociological basis: and in a sense one may speak of their historic mission, may hold that the destiny of humanity depends largely, in actual fact, on their attitude and action.

But to what end in fact? That is another question, and depends, in the first case, on the philosophy, the spiritual attitude which inspires the masses.

Here it is interesting for us to look to the witness of certain independent socialist writers, doubtless regarded as unorthodox by the Marxist Party, but whose thought remains, nevertheless, very representative, for they have carried further than others their consideration of the principles underlying revolutionary movements. I am referring to the small group of the disciples of Georges Sorel who range themselves among the 'revolutionary syndicalists'.

A highly significant book by Edouard Berth has recently appeared under the title *From 'Das Capital' to the 'Réflexions sur la Violence'*.[1] It contains various passages highly relevant to our theme. While remaining attached to the errors I have noted above (a confusion of social progress with the war against religion, and the marxist conception of the class-war), the school of Sorel has clearly disengaged that element of truth of which I have spoken. For them, as they say, it is a question of passing 'from the pole of capitalist fatality to that of working freedom'. They regard socialism as 'a metaphysic of working-class freedom and even of freedom as such, of human freedom'. 'In the last analysis', writes Edouard Berth, 'what is important is the human factor, man, his energy, his firmness of character, his capacity for sacrifice and for sublimity, in a word, his freedom.' This is why this school thought that the revolutionary transformation of the world would come from the creative energy of proletarian thought and action operating through the trade-unions.

[1] Paris, Rivière, 1934.

[231]

Now the hour of disillusion has come for these Sorelian socialists: they have loyally recognised it,—if also naively, for they do not ask if their own premises are not in some sense to blame for the conclusions they deplore.

Not only has the proletarianisation of the middle classes on the one hand and, on the other, the diminution of social effectiveness to which the progress of mechanisation has subjected the working class, had the result that the latter can no longer feel that they are called to tread the winepress alone, but still more socialism itself and that very recognition of working-class self-consciousness of which I have spoken have come to a moment of internal crisis. It is the very idea of freedom and autonomy itself which seems in danger. Instead of a proletariat marching forward to its hour of social manhood and personality, Edouard Berth depicts for us 'a proletariat in part plutocratised and ready to accept the more or less gilded place allowed to it by an americanised bourgeoisie, and in part a proletarianised swarm ranging itself under the banners of a demagogic, fanatical and sectarian communism', driven by the bureaucratic big stick; and Georges Sorel's hopes in the creative personality of the revolutionary proletariat (Sorel regarded the proletariat as 'the hero of a drama whose happy end depends entirely on his energy, his devotion and his capacity for sacrifice and sublimity' and wished that its acts of violence should be *acts of war*, of a noble and pure war, almost a holy war), these hopes seem at the moment in grave danger indeed.

It is immediately obvious how moving such a tragedy can be to the eyes of a Christian. A conscious realisation of the dignity of the human personality of the worker, the conquest of a freedom and social personality externally translating a true interior freedom and personality, the liberating

[232]

mission of the poor and the disinherited come to a sort of historic majority,—are there not here echoes of Christianity, and a significance originally christian?

'Is the working class', asks M. Berth, 'in fact capable of becoming a *person*?' Yes, without doubt, but on one preliminary condition: neither a man, nor a nation, nor a class can be saved by man alone; and if the pelagianism and practical atheism of the bourgeoisie are adopted and exalted by the proletariat, this will entail the latter's historical bankruptcy. Its apparent triumphs will but augment its servitude. Man can achieve his freedom and personality, but only by opening his heart to that Life whence he draws the springs of his being. It is possible that, despite the pessimism of Berth, trade-unionism is at the moment the most considerable and the most promising force of social renovation.[1] But it will only keep these promises if it rejects the atheism of certain of its initiators.

To my eyes the dilemma is inevitable: either the popular masses will become more and more attached to the materialism and the metaphysical errors which have been for nearly

[1] The philosopher, in any case, should not neglect the studies of the theorists of syndicalism whose origins are socialist and proudhonian, of Georges Gurvitch for example, nor the works of the militant syndicalists (I would refer to an article by Raymond Bouyer, 'Les Féodaux du tantième,' in *L'Homme réel*, August-September 1935). On its side the Catholic social school has long ago established a doctrine of trades-unionism. No less than socialist-minded trades-unionism, christian trades-unionism and the christian movement among the workers may play in certain countries an important historical rôle. In matters of professional claims and technical arrangements, there is a high degree of convergence between these two forms of trades-unionism. There is a notable instance of this in the similarities between the 'plan' of the C.G.T. (Confédération Générale du Travail, i.e. the French form of the Trades Union Congress) and that of the C.C.T.U. (the Confederation of Christian Trades Unions).

a century the parasites on their movement of historical progress, and then that movement will develop along lines that will lead to deception in the long run.

Or it is by the principles whose deposit Christianity maintains among us that they will shape their philosophy of the world and of life, and by the formation of a theocentric humanism, whose universal value will be able to reconcile, even in the temporal and cultural sphere, men of all sorts and conditions, that their will for social renovation will come to its fruition and they will achieve the freedom of a full-grown personality, the freedom and personality, not of a class absorbing man into its limits for the destruction of another class, but of man communicating to his class his proper dignity as a man, for the common inauguration of a society from which, I do not say all forms of differentiation or any hierarchical order, but the present-day severance into classes, will have disappeared.

A historic reordination

It is useless to insist on the scale of the historic reordination which such a hypothesis implies. On the one hand, potent centres of spiritual and religious renewal must be formed among the masses. On the other, Christians will have to free themselves from all more or less unconscious sociological prejudices, christian thought will have to integrate, in purifying them from the antichristian errors among which they have been born, the truths seen or adumbrated by the effect of social emancipation which has been going on throughout the whole modern age; the social and political action inspired by this thought will need to develop on a tremendous scale.

It is much more than a realignment of alliances; it is a

general redistribution of historic forces of which, in such perspectives, we are led to think.

It may be that thus that enigma, which is so irritating to the mind, of the temporary opposition which has occupied so large a place in the modern centuries and particularly in the nineteenth, between a christian world more and more separated from the sources of its true life and an effort to transform the temporal regime orientated towards justice and nourished by the most false metaphysics—it may be that this crying scandal of the nineteenth century, of which Pius XI has spoken, will then become intelligible in once more becoming part of an infinitely deeper and greater mystery. Does not St. Paul tell us, in reference to the temporary rejection and final reintegration of the Jews, that God has included all under sin that He may have mercy upon all?[1] If we think that a new temporal christian order can only arise in full and durable fashion after the 'disobedience' and the 'sin' in which the christian world of the anthropocentric epoch is 'included' will have called forth a new effusion of 'mercy', we can then form some idea of the scale of the historic transmutation with which the inauguration of a new Christendom is bound up.

III

THE DIMENSIONS IN TIME

Of the philosophy of history

The question of the scale of the internal dimensions of the changes presented by the idea of a christian renewal in the

[1]'Conclusit enim Deus omnia (in the Greek: *tous pantas*) in incredulitate: ut omnia misereatur' (Rom. xi, 32); 'Sed conclusit Scriptura omnia sub peccato . . .' (Gal. iii, 22).

temporal order brings with it another, that of the scale of the *chronological dimensions* implied by the same idea.

Here we must pause for a moment for a consideration of the question of the possibility of a philosophy of history. In the hands of a pure philosopher, who only recognises the light of the natural reason, the philosophy of history, to my mind, must either shrink to a very insignificant object or run the risk of inevitable mystification: for it necessarily presupposes prophetic gifts and where shall the pure philosopher lay hold on these?

To my mind this question is only susceptible of a positive solution if we admit the idea of a philosophy of man where the philosopher looks for light on his philosophy and his understanding of a natural order from a higher science, given by faith and theology.[1]

The ages of christian history

On these very questions with which we are at the moment occupied it seems that a christian philosophy of history cannot fail to give us certain valuable indications.

The first is, as I suggested a moment ago, that a historical transmutation of world proportions would seem to be the inevitable result of that interior drama which has been developing in the Western world since the meeting of the Graeco-Roman world and the Gospel, whose tragic quality first became apparent in the sixteenth century. The exposition given in the first chapter of this book of the tragedy of humanism sufficiently illustrates this assertion.

In particular, the accumulated fatalities of the capitalist economic order, the dislocation of human life consequent on the industrial conquest of the universe, and, on the other hand,

[1]Cp. *Science et Sagesse*, pp. 255-305.

the age-long development of anti-christian forces, like the social bankruptcy of the christian world which I have earlier pointed out,—all these things make it necessary, to my mind, to regard the inauguration of new Christendom, which I regard in itself as *possible*, as highly *improbable*, at least with any degree of general and stable success, before that historical transformation of which we are speaking. For the acts and conflicts of historical forces must bear their fruit in time. And it is impossible to see how the religious servitude of man to material things, whether its form be scientific or in terms of the State, can come to an end without a supreme effort—an inevitably catastrophic one—of human initiative to save by and for itself alone a world without God.

The second indication which can be furnished by a christian philosophy of history is that the end of *a* world, even if its proportions are truly universal, is not the end of *the* world and the end of history. On the contrary, one who connects human history with the government of a wise Providence, ought to regard the denouement of which I have spoken as the opening of a new age of history.

On the one side (and this is of value only for a Christian) the state of culture of christian peoples surely lags very far behind the social possibilities of Christianity, and any full awareness of the claims of the Gospel with regard to the temporal structures of the commonwealth? In terms of an effective realisation or refraction of the Gospel in the socio-temporal sphere, we are still truly in a prehistoric age!

Again (and this affects the philosopher as such) are we not driven to a similar declaration in all that is concerned with the natural possibilities of the cultural and intellectual development of humanity? In relation, in particular, to all the matters of man, and all thereby that is most interesting to us,

[237]

it would not be hard to show that our speculative and practical knowledge and our general way of behaviour,—I am not speaking of an illusory materialist knowledge but of one which is truly spiritual and of the behaviour which would correspond to it,—are still extraordinarily primitive.

Is humanity on the verge of its final decline, near the end of history? If so the end is premature and the book stops in the middle.

The age on whose threshold we stand can be called 'a new Middle Age': but the phrase is likely to create illusions. Rather it should be called *a third age*, regarding the world of christian antiquity as the first, which endured for eight centuries, and characterising the Middle Ages as the time of formation and education, as the historic coming to maturity (in good and in evil) of christian Europe; the modern age will then show as primarily the crashing dissolution, in a formidable outburst of energy, of the long preceding epoch; and the third age of our era of civilisation one can hardly say is yet begun, rather we are taking part in the prelude, the far-off anticipations which announce it. It is such a division into three ages that in the second commentary on the *Canticle of Canticles* St. Thomas (or the author who wrote in his name, if in contradistinction to Mandonnet's opinion we hold the treatise apocryphal) admits with regard to the history of the Church: the Church of the thirteenth century is in his eyes 'the modern Church', and he sees in the reintegration of Israel the characteristic sign of the third age of the Church and of Christendom.

From this standpoint one may hold that this third age will primarily see the general liquidation of post-mediaeval humanism, and none knows for how many centuries this will yet endure. I am in no wise imagining it will be any golden

[238]

age, as do some millenarian dreamers. Man will remain what in himself he is, but under a temporal regime, a new historic heaven, destined also to come to an end, for all the things of time wear out in time: and it is only under that regime that there will begin the flowering-time of integral humanism, of that humanism of the Incarnation which has been in consideration in the preceding chapters, and which carries the sign of no theocracy other than the gentle dominion of God's love.

A first chronological moment

What consequences can be drawn from the preceding comments with regard to the theme of our present researches, i.e. in regard to the conditions of realisation of a christian renewal of the temporal order, or the historic chances of a new Christendom?

It is necessary, I think, to distinguish in this instance two different moments of time.

Before the liquidation of the present epoch, it seems to me we can only reasonably hope for momentary realisations or the partially sketched outlines in the midst of non-christian forms of civilisation of any such new christian order. Without speaking of the other conditions which render the general and durable inauguration of a new christian life in this world actually difficult and relatively highly improbable, and which belong, above all, to the potent development of collective energies of a quite other inspiration, the first condition, on the side of the christian world itself (naturally, I am not speaking here of the Church, which has never been bound up with or into any temporal regime whatsoever, but of the *christian world*, which is something temporal), would be that the christian world of to-day as a whole should have broken with the regime of civilisation spiritually founded on bourgeois humanism and economically on the fecundity of money, while at the same time keeping itself immune from the totalitarian and communist errors to which that regime leads as its logical catastrophe. In fact, by the very degree to which the christian world is something of this world, subject to-day to the law of class-interests which has become the predominant note of modern civilisation, any general fulfilment of such or similar conditions seems something exceedingly remote. For, if it is true that nothing is more injurious to the progress of Christianity and nothing more contrary to its spirit than the prejudices and blindnesses due to class or race among Christians, it is equally true that there is nothing more prevalent throughout the christian world. Instead of the spirit of the Gospels vivifying the socio-terrestrial order, the things of the socio-terrestrial order stifle the spirit of the Gospels.

Another condition would be that a sufficient number of Christians should understand that the temporal inauguration of a new christian order demands *means* which are proportionate to that end.

The question of means

I have several times already dealt with this question of means,[1] and I only return to it to remove certain misunderstandings. Indeed it includes three distinct questions, to which I shall briefly endeavour to give an answer: the question of the morality of the means as such, that of the morality of the context, and that of the hierarchy of means. It was of this last that I was above all thinking when I spoke of the

[1] Cp. *Religion and Culture*; *Freedom in the Modern World*.

purification of the means. Some people have thought that I condemned as impure in themselves, i.e. as intrinsically evil, means not evil in themselves, but of an inferior degree, whose exclusive or predominant employment in view of a higher end introduces an impurity into our action. These are two very different things.

In the matter of the *morality of the means*, it is clear that force and, generally speaking, what I have called the physical means of war[1] are not intrinsically bad, because they can be just. Theologians and moralists explain to us on what conditions these are just, and thereby they perform a work of mercy, enabling us to live on this earth. They do not take the lead, it is not their business to open new doors to violence; but once these doors are open, they justify what can be done, and give us light whereby to advance down the shadowy paths of history. Force and the use of force implies also violence and terror and the use of all the means of destruction. These things also can be just in certain defined conditions.[2] With the progress of science and technical development on the one hand, on the other the growing importance of the part played by the masses in political conflicts, the physical means of war invented by men have become, I will not say more and more cruel, the ancient world was well instructed in cruelty, but more and more grandiose, almost astronomical in scale. The most obvious example of this are the means of modern warfare in the

[1]Cp. *Freedom in the Modern World*, pp. 153-63.

[2]It is then necessary to understand by the word 'violence', 'not, as is often done, the unjust use of force, but every use of force which lacks the character of an instrument of a positive law; a just war, a just strike, a just insurrection, are in this sense acts of violence'. Yves Simon, *La Campagne d'Ethiopie et la Pensée Politique Française*, Lille, 1936.

[241]

narrow sense of the term, of military war;[1] there are others.[2] The most terrible anguish for a Christian is precisely this of knowing that there can be justice in the use of horrible means.

[1]On this question of war I would like to quote a page from a catholic manual of an official character which seems, to my mind, to perfectly sum up what is to be said on this subject. '*Can war be legitimate?* War in itself is a great Evil. It is in effect organised violence and its inevitable effect is the destruction of human lives and the accumulation of the worst catastrophes on men's heads.

'More, it is in fact inapt to show the right or to avenge it. It does not in effect necessarily result in the triumph of innocence and the defeat of injustice. In itself victory rather goes to the most skilful, to the strongest and sometimes to those favoured by fortune.

'Like duelling it is a "stupid and unreasonable" act, because it does not achieve what is asked of it, i.e. a declaration or avenging of a right.

'It has become a much greater evil since scientific inventions and the quality of modern warfare have added almost infinitely to its powers of destruction.

'All the more so therefore we must say that war can only be legitimate in one single case: *the case of legitimate defence.*

'And for this case of legitimate defence it is necessary:

(a) that a country should have been unjustly attacked;

(b) that the object of this unjust attack should be a proportionate good, i.e. a good whose loss would be equal to a veritable physical and moral disaster to a nation;

(c) and that there should be no other means of defence.

'A country, in effect, like an individual has a right to live, to what integrates and constitutes its existence. And when this right is unjustly attacked, or violated, or denied its realisation, a people can, should indeed, defend itself.

'But the evils of all wars are so terrifying and to-day moreover the struggle can so easily be extended, that other peoples have the duty in charity and prudence of as far as possible preventing war and, *if they can*, of imposing, but by honest means, a pacific solution on the conflict' (*Petit manuel des questions contemporaines*, Paris, 1935).

In the matter of resistance to unjust laws and of sedition, the same manual says in another place: 'Sedition is a collective violent struggle against a government. Such a struggle paralyses or tends to paralyse the whole activity of the government. If theoretically it can be legitimate

What I have called the *morality of the context* is not concerned with the means themselves, but with the accidental connections they contract in human history. History is impure and dark; it is the history of evil mixed with good more often than of good, the history of an unhappy humanity on the march towards a most mysterious deliverance, and of progresses towards good made in the midst of evil and by evil means.

The Christian is *part of* history, he is *in* history; since he is to witness there to a supra-historic world *to which he belongs*, he wishes only to use good means: thus we have good means employed in a context where evil means predominate, and running the risk of being themselves mixed up in such a context. For when a man performs an action in this world he knows well what he wished to do, he does not know what he has done nor what end it will serve.

This man, if he fears God, should only employ means that are good in themselves; and he should in any case envisage the context also, so that this may have the possibility of being evil in the least possible degree. After that, let him be at peace. The rest belongs to God.

The fear of soiling ourselves in entering into the context of history is a pharisaical one. We cannot touch human flesh and blood without staining our fingers. To stain our fingers is not to stain our hearts. The catholic Church has never

against a government whose tyranny is such that each citizen can consider himself as being in grave danger, we must say that in practice, in a general way, all sedition rightly so called is illegitimate, because the anarchy and the trouble engendered by it are ordinarily worse than the evils for which a remedy is sought.'

[2]I have in mind here, in particular, the measures which a regime, either legitimate or not, which is the result of a revolution may employ to defend itself against its adversaries.

[243]

feared to lose its purity in touching our impurity. If, instead of dwelling in the heart, purity mounts to our heads, the result is sectaries and heresies. Some seem to think that to put our hands to the real, to this concrete universe of human things and human relations where sin exists and circulates, is in itself to contract sin, as if sin were contracted from without, not from within.[1] Hence they claim to interdict the use of all means not evil in themselves to which men have given an impure context (the writer must not publish, for modern publicity is impure; citizens must not vote, for Parliament is impure); they insist that men should not co-operate in a common aim when impure means are mingled in it by accident (as always happens)[2]: the crusaders should not set out for the Holy Land for rapine and cruelty have had their part in the crusades. This is pharisaical purism: it is not the doctrine of the purification of the means.

This doctrine relates back to the question of the *hierarchy of means*. It rests on the axiom that *the order of the means corresponds to that of ends*. It asks that an end worthy of man should be pursued with means worthy of man. It does not so much insist on the rejection of the use of certain means as on the positive will to raise up means not only good in general, but truly proportionate to their end, truly bearing

[1]'Non quod intrat in os, coinquinat hominem; sed quod procedit ex ore, hoc coinquinat hominem. . . . Quae autem procedunt ex ore, de corde exeunt, et ea coinquinant hominem: de corde enim exeunt cogitationes malae, homicidia, adulteria, fornicationes, furta, falsa testimonia, blasphemiae. Haec sunt, quae coinquinant hominem. . . .' Matt. xv, 11, 18-20.

[2]This rejection would become necessary if, for the common aim in question (as is the case in an association of bandits) evil means were required as such, or in fact principally employed. The discernment of the difference is indeed sometimes difficult, supposing it is a question not of an association of bandits, but, for example, of financiers or politicians.

on them the stamp and imprint of their end: means in which that sanctity and sanctification of the secular which was in question in an earlier chapter are incarnate. That such means can and should be used for temporal ends, and by men fighting on the plane of the temporal itself,—'those only will be astonished at this apparent paradox who fail to appreciate the intrinsic and essential dependence of politics and sociology on ethics, and of temporal on spiritual things; and who do not see that the evils from which mankind is suffering in our time are incurable if divine principles and remedies are not applied to the deep sources of human life and of the profane and secular order'.[1]

Are such principles applicable to the great mass of mankind, who are far from any preoccupation with sanctity? They concern the small number of those who may undertake the social and political guidance of this mass: a political fraternity of the future, who will have with regard to the inauguration of a new Christendom that *vocation of leadership* of which I spoke in a previous chapter. How will such a fraternity purify its means?

Earlier in this book[2] we had to do with the use of human means, and we pointed out how in one epoch of our civilisation the primacy was given to them for the defence even of divine things, and that it was good that this experience should have been. It failed. Another time has come. To claim to renounce human means and the use of human energies would be an absurdity. In my belief what is needed is not to cut ourselves off from them, not to turn away from them, nor the superimposition on them in a static way of means of a higher order: it is to lay them open

[1] *Freedom in the Modern World*, p. 151.
[2] Cp. chap. iv.

to that great movement of the descent of the Uncreated Love among men which is the very consequence of the Incarnation.

When I distinguished between the means of patience and the courage to suffer and those of aggression and the courage of attack, and preferred the former to the latter, it is not, as I have already expressly pointed out, that I claim to condemn, like Gandhi, any recourse to force (physical or coercive force). The question for us is to establish an order among the various means, not to exclude one category. 'Force is the midwife of society': this statement roused no problem for Karl Marx, other than that maybe of acquiring force. It sets a problem to the Christian, a problem all the more grave in that force, even when it is just, is of all human means the one which entails a historical context most charged with suffering and sin, and that it always implies, even when it is just, the eventuality of those horrible necessities and horrible means of which I spoke above and of which even the justice is obscure.

For myself I hold that the Christian should not refuse such a use of *just* force, when it is absolutely necessary. But such means, if they are connatural to our carnal and wounded nature, are against nature in regard to the *pneuma* which introduced us into the ways of God: the Christian will tremble at the necessity of having recourse to them. If they are Christians, and if their aim is a really humanist transformation of the world and the inauguration of a new Christendom, the men on whom the initiative of a recourse to force will depend are not only bound to impose the bridle of justice with an unshakable will on these means which come from the world of wild beasts, and to reject in a way that is absolute any use of force as a means of persuasion or of complaisance. They must also do violence to force itself to compensate

[246]

for the violence to which it subjects the spirit; in other words, subordinate force in such a way to love that it really becomes the instrument of love in act, so that, in the action which they direct, the just use of the physical means of war will really never occur except as a last resort and in a case of veritable necessity.

And it must also be, and here a truly christian reversal of values enters in, that before force, and those means of aggression and coercion which are the sole ones known to men of blood, there should have been a recourse and a setting into action of a whole world of other means, among them those I have called the means of edification and the means of spiritual war: the means of patience and voluntary suffering which are, *par excellence,* the means of love and truth. Only so can that inferiority, which coheres for the Christian in the carnal means of warfare from the fact that he is obliged to rule over them by justice and that they offend in him the instincts of the spirit, be compensated for and *turned back* into victory. As I have tried to show before, the state of a world where every form of violence is let loose will at once reduce to impotence and self-abdication those Christians who, wishing to act upon the temporal plane, do not on that very plane set the folly of love at the head of all their means of action.

All of which presupposes indeed a sort of 'Copernican revolution' in our conception of political activity: not to be content with acting in the way of the world, to win from the world machinery that is christian in external appearance, but to begin with *oneself,* by thinking, living, acting politically in a christian way; bringing to the world a truly christian life. Such a reversal is perhaps in preparation; even if limited to the narrow formations capable of exercising an animating action, time will be necessary for its effective accomplishment.

A second chronological moment

Hence it seems probable that the new Christendom we hope for must needs be slowly shaped and prepared. Meanwhile, if, in that first moment of which I spoke, it will in effect be only realised in a partial, inchoate and virtual fashion, and in the heart of civilisations whose form and inspiration is non-christian, these inchoate expressions and virtualities will none the less be of great value and will testify that the men who work towards the inauguration of a new Christendom are at the same time, by a generous co-operation, ready to devote themselves to the work of rendering more human and more just the world in which they are involved.

And, moreover, there remains a possibility that they will realise something more and, in perhaps taking a decisive part in the near future, will enable that historic liquidation of which I spoke a moment ago to be fulfilled in a crisis of growth exempt from catastrophe, and so lead to a new world without subjecting men to too cruel experiences.

In a second moment of time in any case, *after* this historic liquidation, it is a full realisation (I do not say a perfect one) that we are, to my mind, justified in hoping for the historical ideal of a new Christendom. But in ways which it is not easy to foresee or imagine, and by means of a 'revolution' which must imply, as I stressed already, singularly *more* than is usually included in that word.

An endeavour for a christian socio-temporal renovation can thus find, and this is not without importance, a scale and points of reference by which it may become defined. And whether it is a question of a more or less precarious realisation in the relatively near future, or of a full realisation in the distant future, it is in time and in earthly history that it has its aim and application, as different from the spiritual and religious effort, in the strict sense of the words, which looks directly towards eternal life; hence it is *now* that the historic ideal to which it belongs should exercise its dynamic value and orientate our action.

A second aspect of the notion of a new Christendom

I have spoken of two different periods with regard to the inauguration of a new christian order.

Up till now I have used the expression 'a new Christendom' in a wide, cultural sense. But this expression can be understood in another and narrower meaning. If we recall the distinction which was made in an earlier chapter between the *intermediate end* which, while being a means is also an end on its own proper count, and the pure means or *pure instrument*, we see in fact that we should distinguish in the ideal of a new Christendom two different aspects or instances, according as this ideal concerns profane and temporal formations having the rank of *ends* in their own order (i.e. what I called a vitally christian lay State, and a secular christian civilisation, a new Christendom in the sense which up till now I have given to the words) or, on the contrary, temporal formations which are only *instruments* of the spiritual order.

If we consider this second instance or aspect, the idea of a new Christendom, while being concerned altogether with the temporal and cultural sphere, in a way spiritualises itself. What is then described is a sort of christian *diaspora*, a Christendom not grouped and united in the body of a homogeneous civilisation, but spread over the whole surface of the globe like a network of centres of christian life disseminated

[249]

among the nations. The temporal means of this Christendom are primarily poor and humble, they can be pared down as much as you please, it will allow them to pass through all obstacles. Though secular christian endeavour may fail, at least before the liquidation of the modern epoch, to inaugurate, even in a partial and momentary fashion, a new christian life in the world, to renew the visible structures of this world, in any case it will not have failed with regard to this diaspora of christian civilisation.

It is possible that before those supreme reintegrations of which I have spoken, the world will in fact know only an epoch of terror and offended love. It is possible that all the efforts of Christians in the temporal order may be limited to rendering less evil regimes of civilisation which rather resemble Behemoth and Leviathan than the face of human personality. It may be that the christian community, after having been in the condition to be persecuted by the pagans, then of persecuting heretics, will again and anew know the state of being persecuted. It will remain to them to testify, in the midst of the vicissitudes of history, that all that is not love will perish.

And, on the other hand, if, as I believe, a full and temporal christian flowering (under the conditions of deficiency and imperfection proper to this our life) is promised for the period of history which will succeed the liquidation of anthropocentric humanism, it will indeed be the fruit of all the hidden travail which will have taken place in this sense, and which the Christians of to-day are called to undergo with a holy energy and a profound patience. Is it not a self-evident proposition, or at least one that becomes so when we consider it, that in the end it is those who have the greatest patience who will conquer?

[250]

CHAPTER VII

THE MORE IMMEDIATE FUTURE

I

ON POLITICAL ACTION

On political action having an immediate objective

Whatever may be the distant perspectives, certain questions arise concerned with the attitude that men conscious of the temporal tasks of Christianity and anxious to act in the secular sphere,—let us say, if you will, to become something resembling the *cives praeclari* of the old philosophers, an enlightened political element,—need to take up in our own day.

Let us first of all distinguish, it is essential to the matter in hand, between what may be called political action *with an immediate* objective and one whose *objective is distant*. By the former I mean a political action which, even if it seeks to work for a long distant future, is determined with regard to its action and the power of its impetus by an immediate realisation which gives it its aim.

Now if it is true that, by the fact of its interior vices and denials, our actual regime of civilisation is enclosed in contradictions and irremediable evils, it seems that political action with an immediate objective, depending on the immediate future and setting its course by reference to near events, has a choice between three forms of treatment: one of parley, which will be content, for the maintenance of civil peace, with the lesser evil and will have recourse to palliatives; a draconian one which will claim to save a sick world by immediate revolution inaugurating the communist dictatorship of the proletariat; and another, also draconian, which will set its hopes on an immediate revolution or defensive reflex action leading to a totalitarian recasting of the national State.

It is possible that at certain moments and in certain countries, the first method may accommodate itself to modifications by the second or the third (which for the rest strongly resemble one another, save that for the one the proletarian community is to be given precedence over the existing political commonwealth, and in the other this is reversed). But it does not seem as though men of the sort I have in mind would easily link up with any of the three. Does not the first method suffer from all the faults of empiricism and opportunism, and like all policies made from day to day does it not presuppose an acceptance of the existing system of civilisation? Is not the second bound up with a philosophy and a mystical feeling which are expressly atheistic, and does it not expose the person, the family and the national community to their dangers? Does not the third (without speaking of the obstacles in fact which, like the second, it sets in the way of an active christian expansion in politics) claim for the mending of certain evils of the actual regime the aggravation of other evils, and is it not totalitarian like the second and does it not risk the destruction of one of the first conditions for the inauguration of a vitally christian temporal order, I mean that return to Christianity of the mass of the working classes in their advance towards that social coming of age which was in question in the preceding chapter?

Faced with these major difficulties it may come about that our *cives praeclari* will be tempted to fall back upon what is still a temporal activity, but one which is superior to political parties (because it is solely concerned with the events of the temporal and spiritual spheres, and only indirectly touches on political life in the exact sense of the term), I mean to the strictly limited ground of the temporal defence of religious interests and religious liberties, leaving the others to look to themselves. Such activity is certainly indispensable, it is necessary; it is not sufficient. It is imperiously required of a Christian, he should not withdraw to it. He should not absent himself from any field of human action; he is needed everywhere. He must work at once—inasmuch as he is a Christian—on the plane of religious action (which is indirectly political), and—in that he is a member of the spiritual community—on that plane of action which is properly and directly temporal and political.

On political action having a remote objective

But how is this to be done? In my opinion our *cives praeclari* will be led to political action *having a remote objective* or at *long range*. This would be neither a method of parley nor a draconian treatment; it is a case rather of a heroic treatment.

But when we speak of the *realisation* of a christian-temporal historic ideal the meaning of the words must be well understood. A concrete historical ideal will never be realised as a *term*, as a thing which is fulfilled (of which we can say: 'There, that is done, now we can take our rest'),—but as movement, as a thing in the making and ever requiring to be made (as a living being, once born, continues to make itself). When will the 'realisation' of this ideal, its 'inauguration' take place? When it crosses the dividing line of historic existence, when it is born into historical existence, when it begins to be recognised by the common conscience and to play a motive part in the work of social life. Previously it was in preparation, afterwards it will continue in the making. I have already drawn attention to the difference between a *utopia* and a *concrete historical ideal*. A utopia is a model to be realised as an end and a resting-place—and it cannot be realised. A concrete historical ideal is a dynamic image to be realised as a movement and a line of force, and it is exactly as this that it is realisable. Hence, we see, its realisation may be far off and yet serve in the present as an aim, and govern during what may be a long continued period of preparation action at each moment proportionate at once to a future end and to present circumstances. This is what I have called political action with a remote objective.

This alone enables us to escape the contradictions pointed out a moment ago. Political cities, existing national communities, are other than the regime of civilisation in which they are set at such and such an epoch: it is an essential distinction. And our enlightened political elements will neither need to sacrifice these to the abolition of the present system of civilisation nor sacrifice to them the inauguration of a system less unworthy of the human being. The problem set before them, which is insoluble for any political activity with an immediate objective, is to lead—by means of the profound changes, the reshaping of structures which that requires, and also by those limitations of sovereignty which are necessary for the establishment of a veritable international community —the existing political cities, through the vicissitudes and

[254]

dissolution of the present regime, to a new regime of civilisation, fundamentally different from the present one since it produces in the socio-terrestrial order an effective refraction of the exigencies of the Gospel.

Let us then suppose that these men form—and this would strike me as much to be desired—not a political party with a religious label as was the German *Centrum*,[1] but one or more political groups truly and specifically political in fact and in name (which implies a certain concretely determined point of view with regard to the general common good as such) and authentically christian in spirit;—I say, various groups, for on this plane men united by the same religious faith can have marked differences and oppositions between one another.

If the considerations here set out are at all exact, those among these groups who base themselves on a good political philosophy and a good philosophy of modern history would work for a scheme of political action *at long range* which, instead of being hypnotised by the present moment, would reckon on *duration*, and take into account the necessary time that is required for the maturing of any integrally humanist renewal of the temporal order.

This action would have an effect here and now. It would not be without care for the present necessities of the social body,—we are under an obligation to provide for the present necessities of men, those who are here before our eyes and will not wait. But this obligation does not mean that we should sacrifice everything to present necessities; for example, a general in the thick of a battle thinks more of the final victory than of the immediate sufferings of his soldiers. How then can we provide for present necessities without compensating one evil for another, without too heavily burdening

[1] Cp. *Freedom in the Modern World*, chap. iii.

the future? By measures which, while serving the common good, also arrange for and prepare deeper changes, and which, if they require patience, if they can only, before the liquidation of the present regime, seem to be palliatives, are in reality more than palliatives and transcend both empiricism and opportunism, because they positively prepare a new regime of civilisation. This is how the form of political action of which I am speaking would in this regard proceed, advancing by stages, proposing, and in the measure to which it would succeed in directing events, executing its 'plans' of approach and its own programmes, specified by the end to which they are ordinated.[1]

But this end will be a remote one. Master foresters work for a future state of their forests which is calculated precisely but which neither their eyes nor those of their children will ever see. In the same way it is in relation to a distant end that the form of political action in question measures its impetus; it will determine its end by reference to precise realisations in the far future, and it is with regard to this end that it will order all the rest.

Christians and political activity

To avoid any misunderstanding, it must be clearly understood that a sharp distinction needs to be drawn between the notion of political activity as *exercised* (and legitimately exercised) by *Christians* and a form of political activity (of no matter what political school) which is *inspired* by christian principles. It is not the former idea which is the theme of these reflections.

If we consider the political activity *effectively exercised* on the political plane by men who in the order of religion are

[1]Cp. Henri de Man's reflections in the last chapter of *L'Idée Socialiste*.

Christians, we are faced by a question of fact, and all is then reduced to two observations: first, with regard to the established political regime, whether it be new or old and whatever be its characteristic tendencies, and even if it entirely fails to correspond to the christian temporal ideal or more or less gravely goes against it, the pauline *principle* of the respect and loyal service due to the authority which has charge of the common good will, in fact (however propitious or unpropitious may be the diverse circumstances proposed by way of minor proposition to the practical reason) lead a more or less large number of Christians to accept public offices and so give, in view of the country's good, a personal, active and devoted collaboration to the regime. And this (and also the opposition to it) is a normal thing. The question of the legitimate nature of the regime must evidently, in certain cases, come up; but most often, particularly in an epoch like the modern one, the empiric consideration of the lesser evil will settle the question; and even if the regime is disputed, even if it be tyrannical, it is probable that there will always be found a greater or lesser number who will decide the issue in its favour, for reasons which are valid for their consciences.

The second observation has regard to the parties and diverse political formations which are active in this world; given, on the one hand, the very complex synthesis of truths and duties which the christian conscience is obliged to make; on the other, the extreme variety of aspects presented by political problems, and above all the fierce divisions made by the parties, each of which more or less misunderstands the high values affirmed by the other: the prevalence of one or another aspect according to intellectual grouping, professional position, social category, will have as a consequence that, in fact, we shall find Christians taking part in the

[257]

most diverse political formations, often the most contradictory ones, supposing always that their conscience has not decided that to adhere to such and such formations would be to co-operate with what is evil.

Further, if it is a question of giving rules and precepts for the formation of the christian conscience, in other words, if we are considering the question of the political activity *morally permitted* for a Christian, it is the office of Christ's Church to give such rules and precepts and to particularise them according to the situation, i.e. the teaching Church; without any one else, clerk or layman, having any right to set himself up as an authority and to add to these at his will.

But all this lies outside the field of the problems which are here under discussion. These problems do not concern the political activity effectively exercised by Christians and morally permitted to Christians, in other words, one which essentially affects *religion* in its relations with politics. They are concerned with a much narrower question, and one which essentially belongs to the field of politics itself and of political philosophy: what they are concerned with is the question of a *political activity* which, in the very degree to which it is political, is of christian inspiration and ordinated to a christian temporal ideal; i.e. the question of what ought to be, in the conditions of the modern age, a just political activity in the eyes of a christian philosophy of culture and society; and the answer which is here proffered does not claim to be the only one possible, for there can be on this point as great diversity as there is among philosophical schools: it has reference to a certain cultural conception which appears to me to be just, and which corresponds to what I have called an integral humanism.

This form of political activity, as I have often explained,

does not need all Christians, nor only Christians: but only those Christians who have a certain philosophy of the world, of society and of modern history; and such non-Christians as recognise more or less completely the cogency of this philosophy.

It is normal that on the plane of action these men should constitute autonomous political formations; this evidently does not mean that they would refuse on principle, except in certain exceptional cases, to co-operate with the established regime, or join in agreement with other political formations or collaborate with them. But it does imply that at the same time they will guard the germ of a vitally christian policy from anything that tends to injure it. 'The more fragile and hidden and contested this germ is the more intransigence and firmness must be devoted to keeping it pure.'[1] Hence they should always maintain their liberty and freedom of action: since their very collaborations, alliances and accords are all part of that *long range* policy which I have striven to characterise, as are their whole political activity and the deepest of their temporal engagements.

The proper demands of a policy centred on the future

Every authentic revolution presupposes that one day men have begun to turn away from the present and, in a sense, to despair of it. This transfer of the specifying ends of activity to a state incompatible with the principles of present conditions, to give one's heart to this future which can only be born of an essential rupture, to care for it above all, and to be interested in the present primarily in regard to this future, to prepare for it by every conceivable means, the elaboration of doctrine, work in other minds, social and cultural work,

[1] *Lettre sur l'Indépendance*, p. 51.

[259]

political action, these are the first rudiments of a revolutionary attitude in the widest and most legitimate sense of the
words.

In regard to those who would add to this list of civic
duties a sort of duty of civil war, and would constrain each
one of us to choose between contrary illusions (however comparable on many points) of immediate temporal salvation,
the men who take this attitude will perhaps seem to make
a schism; and it is not they who will have sought this appearance, and indeed it is only apparent. For there is indeed, without doubt, a certain separation, but only in the degree to
which the present condition of the world fails to furnish
their aim and their determining objective: but there is no
schism, there is no severance or secession, there is only (and
nothing is more truly human) a refusal to sacrifice the future
to the present, there is a *conversion* towards an end and a *con-
centration* on a centre which does not belong to the present
order,—but is a new Christendom which demands a long
preparation and period of ripening.

Indeed there is nothing which rouses more scandal and, in
a sense, is more revolutionary (for this is revolutionary even
with regard to the revolution) than the belief in a form of
political action which is intrinsically christian in its principles, in its spirit, in its methods, and the claim to advance
in the world to a form of political action which is vitally
christian. But the man conscious of these things knows that
the first way of serving the common good is to remain faithful to the values of truth, of justice and of love which are its
principal element. He knows that after the season of the con-
centration of vegetative energies comes the time of germina-
tion and the glorious expansion of life. And with as much
ardour as the disciples of Marx or of Proudhon guard and

[260]

brood over in their hearts, at the price of the necessary refusals, the future of their revolution, he guards, he tends in his soul and in his action, the seed and the ideal of that new civilisation which we are all called, each according to his measure, to prepare in time and for time, for the earthly history of this poor world of ours.

II
PROBLEMS OF TO-DAY
'What should A do?'[1]

Certain critics[2] have reproached me with not formulating a rule of conduct for A, for not telling 'the individual Catholic as such' what he should do *hic et nunc*. My reply is that the conduct of Catholics as such is a question for the Church, and that, moreover, the giving of such instructions is hardly the business of a philosopher. Also, if A asks what he should do, B will ask the same thing, and who will assure us that A and B should have the same form of activity? Each has his particular gifts, his own situation and significance in the context of existence. And the law of the division of

[1] In English in the original (trans.).

[2] In particular Mr. Charles Smyth in *Christendom*: this criticism had interesting echoes in *Colosseum* and in *Blackfriars*. 'What should A do?' Mr. Smyth asks; and he reproaches me with preaching in my book *Du Régime Temporel* (Eng. trans. *Freedom in the Modern World*) 'a sanctified detachment'. I had thought that I had made myself sufficiently clear on this theme, but it must be taken that for some readers 'the famous French clarity',—at least where it is concerned with philosophical questions,—is indeed, in effect, 'a smoke-screen' concealing impenetrable obscurities. A distinguished and sanctified detachment is, in my eyes, the very contrary of a christian attitude; it is to the exigencies of a freedom caught up in the conflict of history that the christian is held, but it is not sufficient to say: *mucking in*, we must also make the declaration that the world expects from us.

[261]

labour operates in the field of socio-temporal activity as in all others.

Thus these reflections rather bear on the epoch in which we are or the one we are entering than on the present moment and on 'what should be done' at the present moment.[1] More-

[1] I have elsewhere indicated that, in the order of political action, it is the creation of a 'third party' which seems, to my eyes, principally required at the present moment.

In the matter of this 'third party', 'which must not be regarded as a party disputing the field with other parties, but as a great gathering together of men of good will', overcoming their conventional prejudices and ideologies and turned towards a positive work of social and international justice, acting in concert with professional groups and ready, whatever may be their political preferences, to collaborate in things useful for the common good and for the success of the enterprises undertaken by the country, 'looking to and sustaining reforming measures realisable at the moment, and tending at all times, whatever be the fluctuations and movements of political life, towards what truly serves the ends of peace and justice' (*Lettre sur l'Indépendance*, p. 38), it is clear that, originally roused by the menace of civil war and to counteract this, such a gathering together would belong to that 'method of compromise' which was in question in the previous section, in the sense that its primary aim would be the avoidance of the most pressing perils by immediate remedies and the maintenance of civil peace.

The very work of transformation or profound revolution which is needed to lead our system of culture to good in itself demands also for its success a certain pause in which the world can take breath and give space for new formations and for youth to try its hand. The birth of a new world marks the death of the old one, and hence it is necessary that the latter should not die too soon, nor of a fever which will leave its inheritors nothing but physical defects.

In speaking of this 'third party' I speak of what, in my eyes, it *should have been*, because the more time goes on without the initiation of such a gathering together the more the chance of it is lost. Truth to tell it is the absence of political education in certain strata of the population which would seem principally responsible: many of those who would have made the force of such a 'third party' having, on the contrary, thrown themselves into one or other of the camps which now divide the crowd, or into formations without political consistence or compre-

over, between the moment when an author hands his book over to the printer and the moment when it appears the present moment may, particularly in this epoch in which we live, have changed unrecognisably. In fact it is the pressure of the necessities of the hour which most often dictate to men what they should do: and often it dictates very ill and, in any case, in ways which are unforeseen.

My aim, in the second part of this chapter, is, taking into consideration the actual historical period in its main outlines, to make more precise what has hitherto been said with rehension of the real conditions of unity in the country, which only resemble in an illusory way a coming together of the type described above.

For the rest, if it is still possible for France to escape, otherwise menaced as she is by so many external perils, the eventuality of a crisis of civil war, or a communist one, or a crisis of dictatorship, the eye of an impartial observer can, in any case, see no other way to attempt this than the political action which *would have been* that of this 'third party', and which as such impresses itself on all reasonable minds: a policy in accord with the instincts of freedom, of initiative, of good sense in a population in which, despite the incitements of the press and of political partisans, the instinct for the mean remains intensely characteristic,—until the moment when it loses its self-control and passes under the domination of a violence drunk with logic. To what degree,—so long at least as party passions will not have provoked convulsions in which elementary reactions will alone have place,—will the spontaneous movements of good sense and national feeling, the devotion and personal activity of men who have a true understanding of the public good, be able to take the place, with regard to such a policy, of the work of this 'third party'? Facts alone will give the answer to that question.

This 'third party' is, or was, an improvisation to my mind necessary and one for whose lack we are likely to pay dearly. The political groupings in name and in specification truly and really political and in inspiration intrinsically Christian, which were in question in my *Lettre sur l'Indépendance* and which we are dreaming of here, correspond to other and more profound and organic necessities and suppose another personnel and other leaders. But with them it is neither the present moment nor the immediate past, but a more or less distant future which is in consideration.

[263]

gard to those activities on the temporal and political plane whose initiative will be christian: in other words, to determine more approximately the physiognomy of the new political formations whose eventuality has been envisaged in the preceding section.

Catholic action and political action

Let it be recalled at the outset that we are dealing with the strictly temporal plane; and that if I naturally address those who are Christians, being a Christian myself, I am not only addressing those who are Christians, nor Christians *inasmuch* as they are Christians; but those Christians and non-Christians who, in the order of the philosophy of culture and of society, hold as founded on reason those conceptions which I have here gathered together under the name of integral humanism. The considerations I am proffering belong to a wholly different plane from what, since its initiation by Pope Pius XI, Catholics of various countries know under the appellation of *catholic action*, which belongs essentially to the religious and apostolic order.[1]

If it has been said that Catholic Action should lead to political action and prepare the solution of social problems, it is in the degree to which it belongs to it to shape, in the heart of their respective temporal communities, Catholics truly and fully instructed in the common doctrines of the Church, notably in social matters, and able to transfuse our life with an authentically christian inspiration. But it would be to confuse the spiritual and temporal spheres to imagine that the common doctrine of the Church suffices in itself to resolve the conflicts of temporal history and to bring those temporal and concretely determined solutions which men have need

[1]See Appendix, *infra*.

of *hic et nunc*. Beneath this doctrinal sky a social and political philosophy, and its practical elaborations, are necessary. It is the same in the sphere of action.

It is important here to guard against taking up old errors in new forms. If the mediaeval Church directly formed and shaped political Europe, it was because it had first had need to raise the temporal order from chaos: a task, moreover, which it could not refuse, but of which from the beginning it had justified apprehensions and never desired. To-day a highly differentiated temporal organisation exists. It is not for the Church but for Christians as temporal members of this temporal organism to strive directly and immediately to transform and act upon it in the spirit of Christianity. In other words, it is not for the clergy to hold the driving-wheel of truly political and temporal action. The proper task of Catholic Action, as its authorised organs have never ceased to proclaim, is to create an essentially christian state of mind, and it is only when 'politics touches the altar' that it is (by a sort of modern adaption of the old *potestas indirecta*)[1] to intervene on the political plane. In the order of strictly temporal, social and political activities, it is the normal course of things that the initiative should come from below, that is from laymen acting at their own risk and peril.

The necessity for new political formations

It seems normal, and inevitable, that the appropriate organs of action should correspond to new social and political conceptions. The awakening of the christian conscience to

[1] Cp. Mgr. Paul Richard, *Notions sommaires sur l'action catholique*, Paris, Spec, 1936, p. 47; and the collection of papal utterances published and commented on by the Abbé Georges Guerry in *L'Action Catholique* (Paris, Desclée de Brouwer, 1936).

those strictly temporal social and political problems implied by the inauguration of a new Christendom will entail, I hold, the birth of new temporally and politically specified political formations, whose inspiration will be intrinsically christian.

These new political formations should, to my mind, be conceived as temporal fellowships of an entirely new type,—which will be purely secular and so differ from the religious orders or the military or hospitaler orders heretofore, and which will be founded on the principle of respect for human personality and the spiritual force of evangelical love, so differing from a secular and atheistic order like, for example, the Communist Party of to-day. They will be devoted to a long-distance work of transformation, which requires, together with much of the spirit of sacrifice, that difficult renovation of means which has on various occasions been referred to in this book. They will evidently be at the beginning in the form of a minority, which will act like a leaven and depend on the initiatives of a few. In one sense one desires their immediate coming into being, for external circumstances might in the future make this singularly more difficult; yet when we consider the interior preparations required, this can only be hoped for at the moment when the spiritual and doctrinal conditions will be adequately secured, and when new generations will give rise to personalities with a real call for such work. An outline idea can be already formed; this is already visible to those who follow attentively the indications of new growths: 'since even now, under the most unpromising conditions, and with the awkwardness of first attempts, the first steps have been taken.'[1] The work itself will take time to appear.

[1] *Lettre sur l'Indépendance*, p. 52.

These new political formations indeed presuppose a profound spiritual revolution, they can only come into existence as one expression of the resurrection of religious forces in men's hearts. They also presuppose a vast and multiform work of preparation, in the order of thought as in that of action, of propaganda and of organisation. They presuppose the penetration of these new conceptions into the working-class and peasant worlds, for it is from a collaboration between the proletarian élite and the 'intellectuals' that they must take their rise. If A asks what he must do, he will find in all these things matter to employ his talents.

The historic situation of these new formations

Let us imagine that these new formations have come into existence.

In the order of movement and action they can evidently, like all political entities, make all the alliances, pacts, or momentary accords which seem to them required by the circumstances: the French monarchy formerly made alliances with the Turks and with heretical princes; the Holy See has never been afraid to sign concordats with States far from practising the christian maxims. That is a question of the opportunities of the moment; these are subject to an ethical rule, but that does not mean that we should only treat with men of whose ideas and conduct we approve, but that the object of our treaty should be an intrinsically good concrete effect and should not compromise a greater good, i.e. in the concrete historical future, and a taking into consideration of the concrete connexions of the forces at play.

But another question, at once more general and more fundamental, must be asked apropos of these new formations here envisaged: it is that of their effective *situation* face to face with fascist or racial totalitarianism and face to face with communism, presupposing those doctrinal positions which the analyses contained in this book have defined.

Their concrete situation (and hence their practical attitude) with regard to the forces of communism and with regard to those forces which, for lack of an appropriate generic name, we will call 'fascist' (Italian fascism representing the first form of the manifestation in history of certain fundamentally common energies, which are yet of very diverse specification), will, to my mind, be primarily determined by the following conditions of fact: on the one hand the various forms of fascism are all, by their original tendency and their State-centredness, opposed to the historic ideal in which our political formations will see their specifying end, and opposed both to their existential basis in itself and the primordial necessity itself which they will recognise,—by this 'existential basis' I mean the movement of history which leads to a substantial transmutation where the 'fourth estate' will come (by good or evil means, that still greatly depends on the human will) to ownership, to real freedom and a real participation in political and economic enterprise; and by this 'primordial necessity' I understand the historic necessity for the 'reintegration of the masses' in a civilisation whose spirit is christian. On the other hand, communism certainly recognises this existential basis, but falsifies it by its erroneous philosophy of man and of society, and hence falsifies the direction to be given to its evolution: where our new political formations will proclaim the primordial necessity of reintegrating the masses in a civilisation whose spirit is christian, it affirms the necessity of their integration in an atheist one; where they will recognise the necessity for a large degree of economic collectivisation to allow the per-

son to live a supra-collective life, it undertakes a total collectivisation and one of such a kind that the whole life of a
human being will find itself collectivised.

Thus it is the very aim and *raison d'être* of the whole movement which are falsified in one case, the historic basis
(and the aim) which are rejected in the other. The basic opposition of such new political formations to the two contrary forms of politico-social totalitarianism will thus spring
in part from the same theoretic reasons (above all concerned with the dignity and the liberty of human persons
and the values which belong to them); but in part also from
conflicting though equally pressing reasons of actual concrete circumstance. It follows that any accord with one or
the other of these forces can only be envisaged in relation to
objectives which are not only limited but neutral, or which
have only a 'material' significance. Since what is in question is 'formal', i.e. the specifying and animating impulse
of their action, it is their independence and fundamental
irreducibility that these new political formations will, above
all, have to affirm. If, in particular, in face of a communist
dynamism already powerfully developed, they do not always
maintain their independence and liberty of movement, they
will run the risk (after having given a moment's romantic
stimulus and the freshness of a mystical humanism to their
allies of a day) of being absorbed or devoured by them, as
has happened in Russia to those non-marxist elements which
at first took sides with Lenin in the name of the spiritual
revolution. For, in good revolutionary practice, the friend of
yesterday quickly becomes the enemy of to-day, and the
most hated.

But, between the millstones of fascism and communism what will then be the destiny of these new political

[269]

formations? Minority formations, will they not inevitably be crushed by the triumph of the one or of the other?

Things are not quite so simple as that. There will be chances—and what way can we look for more than chances? —for these minority formations, if they exist, of becoming in some countries sufficiently strong, I do not say to cease to be a minority (any more than the other parties themselves with which we are comparing them), but to take an initiative[1] in action (and of perhaps acting on communism itself and inclining it, not only to extend a godless hand towards Christians, but to deliver itself from the atheism which is the root of its other errors). Here it is necessary to take into account the aspirations of a despairing world for something that is really new and both better and more human than the existing forces, and where the deep and vital claims, and the great irrational energies with which the sorrows of many

[1]The activity of these formations would be, moreover, it seems, the best means of escaping that singular subtilty of the followers of Lenin, who put Christians in the dilemma *either* of collaborating with Communism for certain temporal ends which are at once immediate and, more particularly, good in themselves, but in doing so allowing themselves to be led or directed by it, *or* of refusing such collaboration and so letting slip occasions which are perhaps highly favourable for acting for men's good, thus furnishing evidence of bad will.

It goes without saying that, in the sphere of public assistance, limited collaborations, such as those the ecclesiastical authorities have permitted between certain parish priests and communist municipalities to help the unemployed, lack the point of difficulty indicated above. But, in general, the question for Christians is not, truly speaking, so much one of accepting or refusing the collaboration proposed by the communists, but of themselves fulfilling in the social order, as their bishops recommend, their proper obligations of justice and fraternal amity, and of so working on their side for the birth of a new order. And that is of itself of a nature to dissolve many prejudices, and perhaps change notably certain psychological situations.

generations have filled the men of to-day, will find at last one form of truth. Evil and error are by nature versatile, having no roots in being. And the moment is perhaps at hand when men, having put all the hope of their heart in the glamour of matter and being dreadfully deceived, will cry out for the truth.

In what concerns more particularly my own country, the historical vocation of a nation such as France must also be taken into account. No one has ever been able to act there otherwise than in the name of liberty. More even than the illusory liberties invoked by bourgeois liberalism, by the parties of personal and collective dictatorship, true freedom can move the great instincts of the heart of France,—and by this true freedom I mean at once the supra-political freedom to which human personality tends, and the social and political liberties which it needs as the basis of collective organisation.

But, in the end, the fact remains that the coming of a totalitarian regime, be it dictatorial or communist, will result in the legal annihilation of all independent political formations. The risk is uncontestable. It does not signify that the formations I am speaking of will thereby be suppressed out of any effective existence, or that they will have no chance of getting through the meshes of a tyrannical regime of whatsoever kind it be.

Fascist totalitarianism and communist totalitarianism

And now, supposing that *nothing is done*, and a policy whose inspiration is christian does not come into existence, or shows itself feeble and impotent, or deviates by the way, it seems more than dubious whether the peoples who are still ignorant of the benefits of the totalitarian regimes can avoid a domination of this kind, either a fascist or a communist one, in a form which is more or less violent, attenuated or mingled with other elements.

By an automatic reflex action, which is not human but mechanical, communism rouses and nourishes defensive reactions of a fascist or racist type, and these in their turn rouse and nourish communist defensive reactions, so that these two multitudinary forces grow in simultaneous opposition: the one and the other make a virtue of hatred,[1] the one and the other are vowed to war, a war of nations or a war of classes, the one and the other claiming for their temporal community that messianic love with which the Kingdom of God should be loved;[2] the one and the other bowing men down before some inhuman humanism, the atheist humanism of the dictatorship of the proletariat or the idolatrous humanism of Caesar, or the zoological humanism of blood and race.[3]

But communism would seem to be an erroneous system

[1]'This victory will be preceded ... by a universal class hatred with regard to capital. That is why christian love, which applies to all, even to one's enemies, is the worst adversary of communism'—Bukharin, Pravda, 30th March, 1934. 'There is a virtue which should be your stimulus, should be the flame of your youth, and the name of this virtue is hatred'—Prof. Bodrero (to the students of Padua). 'Yes, gentlemen, to hate our enemies and intensely love our friends. Not to hate, or still worse, to love our enemies, is a form of cowardice that no cause which leads to a lasting and serious victory can accept'—Scorza, the chief of the Fascist Youth, Gioventù Fascista, April 1931 (in response to an article in the Osservatore Romano, where it was said that 'hatred, a fascist virtue, is not a christian virtue').

[2]Cp. Charles Journet, L'Eglise et les Communautés totalitaires, Nova et Vetera, October–December 1935.

[3]On this notion of the race, which corresponds in anthropology, for the humanity of to-day, to no anatomo-physiological reality whatsoever, to no unity of 'blood', but only to a 'psychological unity', a 'mentality' typical of certain historical and social conditions, see the recent work by P. Lester and J. Millot, Les Races humaines, Paris, Armand Colin, 1936.

which at once stimulates and deforms a process given positively in existence: that process of historical 'generation and corruption' by which a new civilisation (the moral physiognomy of which depends, in great part, on human liberty) will be raised *outside* the—broken—shapes of bourgeois civilisation. It is, on the contrary, as a defensive reaction at once against this existential process and against communism that the various forms of 'fascism' have primarily been built up; hence they tend, by virtue of their original impulse, to keep the development of history *inside* the forms of capitalist civilisation, while carrying to a point of revolutionary intensity certain defensive reactions aroused by its disturbance, and having recourse to a large measure of State socialism; and they can only nourish their moral and emotional dynamism on a historical retrospect towards certain ideal forms in the past (the Roman empire of the Caesars for Italian fascism, the mythical world of primitive Germanism for German national-socialism, the Holy Empire for fascists of a catholic type).[1]

I have already pointed out that their specifications are very

[1] I have only mentioned these last forms of fascism in passing, since they keep in the background of history: in effect, historical conditions have limited their possibility to exceptional cases like that of Portugal; again, and above all, the spirit and the dynamism proper to fascist totalitarianism are then in a more or less degree attenuated, which gives them a higher moral value but deprives them of some of their expansive energy. M. Salazar's dictatorship, which is undoubtedly the most intelligent dictatorship of the fascist form now existing, keeps itself most carefully on guard against the totalitarian spirit of a Mussolini or a Hitler, but it is also the one in which the character of a *rational construction* (i.e. of something arranged by the reason, unpossessed of vital being) is most marked: up till now the army and the military leaders have been the sole effective support of this dictatorship. (Trans. It should be remembered that this was written in April 1936.)

diverse and it would be wrong not to recognise these differences, which often involve formal oppositions, not only between interests, but in spirit: while both imply the suppression of political and civil liberty, for the profit of an 'authoritarian democracy' and the dictatorship of a leader, Italian fascism springs from a much more political mode of civilisation than national-socialism, whose appeal to earth, on the other hand, stirs up much richer instincts of elemental life and sensibility; Italian totalitarianism even has perforce been subject to certain mitigations.[1] Nevertheless, despite their specific diversities, the various forms of fascism have in common those fundamental generic characteristics I have pointed out.

While fascist or racist totalitarianism thus rouses and employs powerful irrational forces, which assure for it a high degree of historical energy (and which tap for its benefit many authentic human values, such as the instinct of national community and love of one's country), the social and political truths it invokes,—and they are many, I have in mind the criticism of liberal individualism and the fictitious democracy of the nineteenth century, or the importance given to creative tension, or to the direct and 'popular' sense of authority, or to the almost vitalist notion of the community of the people,—these truths are realised in successes which doubtless may be grandiose, but which concern particular ends,—the reform of the State, the recovery of independence and sovereignty, imperial ambitions, the rousing of national energies or the psychic deliverance of a people's aspirations: with regard to more universal and deeper historic phenomena, those which concern a transformation of human civilisation, these are only realised in so far as they are involved, despite the efforts of corporatism, in the material

[1] See *infra*, p. 279.

process of decomposition and alteration of the capitalist system, without being able, for lack of an internal creative principle directed to a higher substantial form, to dominate this process. If they appear to nourish truly human forms of civilisation, it is much less in the forms which they invoke to-day, which are otherwise dehumanised, than in those retrospects which I spoke of a moment ago. For decadent capitalist civilisation to be succeeded by a new world superior to communism nothing less is needed than the principle of personalism and integral humanism in its widest significance, nothing less is needed than those energies of spiritual and social resurrection of which man becomes capable, not thanks to the State, but by a love which vivifies his freedom as a person and which fixes the centre of his life infinitely above the State.

It follows from those considerations that the fascist or racist totalitarian regimes cannot grasp what is most fundamental in the movement of history, to impress on it,—which is impossible, if one denies the principle of personality and of freedom[1]—a truly human and liberating direction. Hence they will, it seems, be led, on the one hand, to orientate their internal evolution in a way which is more and more close to the communist morphology (of which it seems certain tendencies of the extreme Left of Italian fascism are witness); on the

[1] I am speaking of freedom in the pure and simple sense, i.e. the freedom, which is in itself supra-social, of the human person. I am well aware that fascism and communism alike, and even national-socialism, lay claim to freedom; and there is, in fact, in these diverse regimes *a certain* freedom, more real perhaps than that of bourgeois liberalism, but it is a freedom *secundum quid*, a freedom, immanent in social life, of initiative aroused within the bounds of the groups making up the temporal community. It is not from this freedom *secundum quid* that those energies of resurrection of which I speak arise.

[275]

other hand, and finally, to carry their defensive tension to a maximum of violence and efficiency, in developing an ethnic or national imperialism and a policy of prestige which will shake to the roots what remains of a common European civilisation, or in disorganising more and more profoundly (as is only too tragically apparent in Germany) those internal structures of civilisation which are at once the most sensitive and most strong and which present precisely the most fundamental preventive of the growth of communism, since they affect the world of the soul and of freedom and are bound up with moral values inherited from Christianity.[1]

By virtue of this double process the fascist or racist regimes seem destined to lead, inside the forms of capitalist civilisation, not by dissolution and collapse like the liberal-individualist democracies, but by an excess of tension and stiffening, the nations belonging to the old Western culture to the requisite point for some communist or imitation-communist experience, as the product of fascist or racist totalitarianism or in reaction from it,[2]—at least if they do not lead quite simply to mutual destruction which will leave Europe as a

[1]'Italian and German politicians and publicists point to democracy as the first step to Bolshevism, and it must be admitted that a democracy, like the European, which has been misunderstood and misused, may well deserve this accusation, but present-day European nationalism is no "bulwark against Bolshevism".... The idea of applying Soviet principles to Europe is absurd, but the increasing distress of the European peoples caused by the application of false national principles will increase the danger of a communistic revolution to such an extent that the absurdity will become a fact. Events will prove this within a few years in some countries, within decades in others'—Ludvig Freund, *The Threat to European Civilisation* (Sheed and Ward, 1935).

[2]Inversely, it seems that communist totalitarianism may be led, in the degree to which it takes on the features of a national State, to borrow certain traits of fascism, while, on the other hand, it takes pains to stress to the maximum everything that is culturally opposed to national-socialism.

field for the conquering enterprises of other continents. They claim, as communism does on the other side, to bring the world new forms of civilisation: it would be rash to deny that this may be possible; neither do I wish to prejudge the unforeseeable evolutions which may take place under the pressure of the necessities of existence and the natural energies of human being. But the question for us is to know if these new civilisations, where as in all earthly things good is mixed with evil, merit in either case the name of *human* civilisations, i.e. if they reach man's heart not only to make use of him and burn up his reserves of heroism and exaltation, but to rouse there stable forms of virtue and to create in his conscience and in society structures which are vital and progressive, and not merely decorative: and of their very nature lead to something other than pride and war. For the historical philosopher, on condition that he takes sufficient account of duration, fascist or racist totalitarianism in its diverse forms shows as an inevitable historical process in reality evoking communism or historic misfortunes of like dimensions; because, while reacting *in toto* against communism with an immediate success which is striking to the imagination, it is incapable of rising above its level and of discovering that veritably human *form* called for by the movement of history: a discovery which can only be made by that free spiritual endeavour which overcomes the determinism of the material forces of evolution.

The spiritual bases |of the totalitarian principle

The like considerations are valid in the spiritual order. It should here be pointed out, first of all, that declared atheism is not the only form of resistance to the divine ordinances, of 'impiety' in the classic sense of the word; nor the only form of the practical negation of God. There is an atheism which declares that *God does not exist* and that makes a god of an idol; and there is an atheism which declares that God exists but which *makes an idol of God himself,* because by its acts, if not by its word, it denies the nature and the attributes of God and His glory; it calls on God, but as the protecting genius attached to the glory of a people or a State *against* all others, or as the daimon of the race.

We must guard here against falling into an error whose gravity I have already pointed out, against confounding an abstract principle and the historical realities in which it is embodied. We know that not only all sorts of political accommodations, but also a real good faith and human good will, a sincere belief in the true God and an unenlightened devotion to religion, can in the concrete compromise with the 'totalitarian' principle. We know that this can be realised in diverse ways, which more or less attenuate or aggravate its malice. Nevertheless the principle carries its own consequences which it is the duty of a philosopher to consider. Without doubt since the days of Constantine the civil power has always been seeking more or less to utilise, and divert to its own ends, the christian religion itself. But let us not be deceived: there is an abysmal difference between these disorders and deviations, grave as they may have been, and the devouring absolutism of to-day which claims the whole man in the name of the temporal community and of the State.

It is highly remarkable that in the very country where the totalitarian State first had that name, in Italy, the totalitarian principle has been in the sequel half broken by the resistance of the catholic Church, with which historical circumstances obliged it to come to terms. Its claim on the entire man in the name of the State is hence found perforce reduced to human activities in the temporal order,—as if man could cut himself in two so as to have the State for the soul of his soul in the order of temporal life, and have, in the order of spiritual life, another soul of his soul![1] Thus reduced perforce (if I may use a word as contradictory as the thing it describes) to a semi-totalitarianism or remaining a pure and simple totalitarianism,[2] political totalitarianism in any case wishes the State to become the absolutely sovereign reality and the absolutely sovereign regulator of the temporal life of men, and hence of the acts of conscience this implies—'all in the State, nothing against the State, nothing outside the State,'[3] and it wishes

[1] We find here a modern form of the Averroist notion which was in question in the first chapter of this book.

[2] This is the case with German national-socialism; in that case it is less a totalitarianism of the State than of the community of the people (a unity which is rather biological than political) which is in question.

[3] B. Mussolini. 'We are (members) of a State which controls all the forces which stir within the nation. We control the political forces, we control the moral forces, we control the economic forces, we are in the full meaning of the words a corporative fascist State' (*Scritti e Discorsi*, 1926). 'I affirm anew and with no less energy my formula of my speech in the Scala at Milan: all in the State, nothing outside the State, nothing against the State' (*Ibid.*, 1927). See also the quotation cited on p. 129 (note); and again: 'The fascist State, the highest and most potent form of personality, is a force, but a spiritual one. It assumes all the forms of man's moral and intellectual life. Hence it cannot be limited to the simple function of keeping order, as is the wish of liberalism; it is no simple mechanism which limits the sphere of so-called individual liberties. It is the form and interior norm and the discipline of the whole person: it penetrates the will as well as the intelligence. Its principle, the directive inspiration of human personality socially united, descends into the depths of our being and dwells in the heart of the man of action as of the thinker, of the artist as of the scientist: a soul within the soul' (*Dottrina*). Liberalism makes the State serve the individual; Fascism reaffirms the State as the veritable reality of the individual' (*Ibid.*). 'The State, considered as a universal ethical will, is the creator of right' (*Ibid.*). Turned back as it has in fact been by the papal counter-attack, the dynamism of these idea-

[279]

alone to inform, 'a soul within the soul', the energies of the soul in the conduct of earthly life, the only one which matters to it. Hence, by virtue of inescapable logical exigencies, it will demand that the spiritual order,—there at least where it meets the temporal and has an interest in the conduct of 'civil life', the order of civilisation,—should be integrated in conscience with the State[1] or the spirit of the people and serve them. Considering the totalitarian principle in itself, as a historical energy having its own proper laws, it is thus apparent that this principle includes a fundamental aversion to christian ordinances,[2] an aversion which is only rendered ineffective in the degree to which totalitarianism is effectively contradicted by the opposition of religion. Where it does not, as in its communist form, seek to exterminate the latter, it will seek practically to annex it by usurping men's consciences: it will render impossible the expression of a free christian judgement of the things of the temporal order, or the undertaking in this order of free christian action; it removes their means of defending moral values in public life: it even tends, in so far as this is in its power, to change their internal opinion of what is good and what is evil, just or unjust, measuring by the measure of the State, not by that of God.

Totalitarianism—and hence the anti-Christianity which I have here pointed out,—has, in fact, in Italy, as I recalled

forces remains as an essential part of fascist doctrine. It would be easy to find in national-socialist quotations evidence of similar totalitarian claims, often more vehemently expressed.

[1]M. Gentile has given this a most clear exposition in the terms of his own philosophical system; the fact that he is now held in disgrace as a source of official inspiration does not prevent the principles here indicated, which are independent of gentilian *actualism*, remaining central in the fascist conception of the State.

[2]Cp. Charles Journet, *art. cit.*

above, been subject to a grave check by reason of the papal intervention of 1931, before the energy of which it had to cede. As things remain what they are in nature, it follows that, concretely considered, the form of the State actually existing in Italy appears to the historical philosopher a totalitarianism stemmed by catholicism; we are in the presence of one of those mutual interlockings of adverse forms, with all their advantages and dangers, which are so instructive for the historian and the philosopher, and which the catholic Church accepts because she knows that God and time are on her side. While at the present moment in Germany the place allowed in social life to the works and institutions of the Church and the apostolate of the faith is more and more narrowed and invaded on all sides by persecution, in Italy, on the contrary, it remains very large, while the ethic of the State with its pagan virtues brings a contrary pressure to bear on it, and only allows to religion those concessions to which it is strictly obliged.[1]

It follows from these analyses that where religious forces, and above all the catholic Church, do not succeed in holding in check the forms of totalitarianism which claim to *protect* God, the real 'impiety' of this totalitarianism will grow like a dissolving force which, despite itself, prepares the way for the counter-offensive of open anti-Christianity and of atheism.

The solution of martyrdom

If, through the failure of temporal christian initiatives, things come to the pass indicated in the preceding reflections, the problem *What should A do?* may perhaps have a singularly simplified solution. Whether it be under a system of

[1]The Ballilas have been constrained to concede Sunday to religion and the family.

[281]

fascist or communist totalitarianism, A will in vain consent to taking part in the game, to collaborating, in order to foment good, in forms of civilisation which are more evil than good: if he claims to be a Christian in his life, and above all in his temporal life, he will quickly learn rather how to suffer than to act. ·

It is clear that so long as those christian temporal initiatives and new formations of which the world has such need fail to appear, each man can and should individually work at *preparing* them, and even by his private action in a measure to *supply their place*.[1] That, it goes without saying, is the task to be accomplished in any case.

But while in the properly political (not the private) order a temporal christian action is lacking in the world, something will be lacking in the organism of christian activities taken as a whole. The world will willingly supply the *dispensation* so rendered necessary. For men engaged in the matters of this

[1]'We believe that with regard to the common temporal good men are too apt to neglect the efficacy of those energies which spring from personal life and the duties corresponding to them. It needs great vigilance and critical attention to resist on all sides the solicitations of hatred or injustice, to keep one's spirit free in a time when conventional lies bring pressure to bear on every side, when the press which defends the established order rivals in its tone the frenetic excitations of the revolutionary press, when lying has been made the prime political weapon, as if in that domain calumny became a venial sin: it needs great vigilance to make one's soul a refuge for the truths despised by men, and to practise in our judgements of men and of events and the actors in the drama of time that *truthfulness* demanded of us by the Gospel.

'And this interior vigilance is externally translated in words and in deeds. And so each vigilant soul creates around it an active radiation of truth and peace. We hold it for certain that if there were a number of such centres of radiation throughout the world, many things would be changed in political life, many evils would be rendered impossible, many complications which seem inextricable would find an unforeseen solution' (*Manifeste pour le Bien Commun*, Paris, March 1934).

world, who find themselves cut off, by a failure for which they are not responsible, from the 'political' strife which is the activity most connatural to the world, the martyrdom (visible or invisible) dispensed by the world exempts from this combat: over those who are dead to time, time has no rights.

Who knows if, from a long habit of being victims, Christians do not count unconsciously on this solution? Martyrdom is a solution, but it is an extreme one (and for all those who by their omissions and their torpor prepare the martyrdom *of others* a solution by sloth). St. Thomas More would have held it pure presumption to claim the glory of being decapitated for God before all other ways of bringing his trial to an end had been exhausted. Martyrdom does not destroy, it calls for and enriches solutions proportionate to nature. It is abundantly necessary that one day these should be found.

In envisaging the hypothesis that 'nothing will be done' I have designedly taken things at their worst. I am confident, in reality, that something is being and will be done, and that by christian initiatives. The temporal christian forces called for by the world are in the phase of preparation, of long-distance preparation: it is impossible that one day they will not issue visibly in the world.

Is the Christian's position invincibly tragic?

If the world purifies the Christians by shedding their blood, the blood of Christians will at the same time purify also the world.[1] It is perhaps from this double purification that the new Christendom that is to come will be born.

[1] 'Even if the lay christian effort failed to renew the visible structure of the world, another task in the temporal order, closely related to the spiritual order, and which indeed takes precedence of the other since it is

Meantime, while the various and opposing forms of totalitarianism grow in the world, how can a Christian avoid the sense of a tragic destiny?

Not to speak here of those other forms of totalitarianism which are, as we have seen, primarily forms of reaction, and which, moreover, also include a fundamental error, the Christian sees in Communism, carried to an extreme degree of violence, errors which cruelly wound at once his intellect and his heart: the will to build a world without God, and to bring to life an equally godless individual, family and social ethic, the radical negation of contemplative values and the affirmation of the fruitfulness of hate, the eviction of wisdom sacrificed to the idol of science, the claim to socialise the entire man, a feigned forgetfulness of the soul and its destiny, the refusal to recognise any sacred reservations in human life and to conceive that there can co-exist with the temporal community the educative authority over human beings of a supra-temporal social body like the Church. He sees the hatred for religion, anti-religious propaganda obstinately pursued, or only modified in method, despite the proffers of collaboration extended to believers. He sees a multitude of men made in the image of God ready to offer themselves a molten lead to receive the imprint of materialist orthodoxy and atheistic conformity, and quick to obey other men with a total submissiveness only permissible in regard to God. But he knows also that in the man who professes them

more closely related to the proper realm of the spiritual, would always remain for Christendom: the task of infusing into the world almost secretly and from within a certain sap or spirit. Naturally it can be supposed that this christian sap will not be unmixed with blood' (*Freedom in the Modern World*, p. 115). Is it necessary to point out the calumnious use to which some have put these words, who have imagined that the blood referred to was that of the *adversaries* of Christianity?

these extreme errors witness rather to generosity than tepid-
ity, and that many do so by virtue of an inveterate ignorance
and a terrible misunderstanding of the identity of what they
hate: he sees in many young communists a hunger and thirst
after justice which knows not its own right name; and he
loves these ardent souls. He recognises in the destructive
horrors which menace the world the face of generations of
omission on the part of Christians,—of his own omissions: he
knows that communism is a parasite on a historic movement
of emancipation of the wage-slaves of labour which is at
once normal and inevitable in itself, and of those exigencies
of justice which are like 'the indignant soul of nature',
truths of christian origin which are worn by long waiting;
and, even when it makes it cry out against God, that it
is the voice of the poor and the have-nots it brings to our
ears; he knows that the poor have never won justice,—I am
not speaking of the saints, but of the mass of mankind
socially speaking, christian and non-christian,—except when
they have sought it by force. Nothing in all this diminishes
by one iota the gravity of the errors and of the dangers of
Communism. All these things prove that it is stamped with
the supernatural sign of the great strokes of the sword of God
in history, and that to get the better of it first of all the
Christian must conquer himself.

The Christian is not shut up in a tragedy from which there
is no issue. The solution, in the spiritual order, the saints
have taught him is a love stronger than the powers of hell.
In the temporal order also, I hold, there is a solution; it can
only be found by going ahead, by accepting the risks of
our creative freedom, by consenting to a form of trans-
valuation of values which in every sphere will give the
primacy to the real over the verbal, to the interior and sub-

[285]

stantial over the external and apparent; in the initiation, in the fullest possible sense of the words, of a policy which is intrinsically and existentially christian, in working here and now for the future, however far off it may be; preparing the ways of a new Christendom, a new christian order of which, to my mind, the notion of integral humanism expresses the distinctive character.

The course of the world

Or do the Christians of to-day think that Christianity can only be lived on paper, and that its energies are so enfeebled that they can do nothing for this earth, and that all that remains for us is to endeavour to please those devils which seem to us a little less evil than the others, to win from them the favour of their protection, and that there is nothing to be hoped from a resurrection of the forces of the soul? Have they decided not to understand the epoch they have entered, to refuse their pity to the more than human sufferings which rend the human being abandoned to itself? Hail, then, pestilence and famine! You are purer than we.

Truly there is no reason for us to be surprised if, faced by a state of history whose internal and social conflicts, if they are to be resolved, must be comprehended and penetrated *in spirit*, a nominally christian world should react rather ill than well: there is no need to be astonished that its behaviour should exhibit a very small element of the spiritual, I mean of intuition and of freedom, and a very large element of the social, i.e. of the reflections and mimicries of classes or groups to which good conscience gives a tone of spirituality. This is but the play of the statistical laws of human nature. But neither should we be astonished that christian civilisations perish as do other ones: and by the same abandonment to the fatalities of matter.[1] New births will come to be. It is also a statistical law that those difficult discoveries of which history has most need to grow are seldom made without the help and the energy of error and disaster.

The purifications which would have saved everything come after all has gone to ruin, and begun to bloom again. 'So runs the world away.' The same men who have assisted the saints to sanctify themselves by a slow torment draw a profit from their merits and feed on the glory of these crucified souls—once they have been canonised—the platitudes of their eloquence and the prosperity of their enterprises: and they do not fail to prepare new agonies and new canonisations for new saints. Worlds which have risen in heroism lie down in fatigue, for new heroisms and new suffering to come in their turn and bring the dawn of another day. Such is the growth of human history, which is not a process of repetition but of expansion and progress: it grows like an expanding circle, so stretching out to its double consummation,—in that absolute from below where man is a god without God, and the absolute on high where he is God in God.

[1] In his *Outline of History* Mr. Arnold Toynbee counts, leaving out primitive societies, twenty-six distinct civilisations in historic times, of which five have survived till to-day.

APPENDIX

THE PLANES OF ACTION

I

In a recent number of *Sept*, Etienne Gilson has perfectly shown how christian activity is exhibited on three distinct planes. I wish to further stress this point, by reason of its great practical importance.

The spiritual and temporal planes

On the first plane of activity, which is the spiritual in the most typical sense of the word, we act as members of the Mystical Body of Christ. Whether it be in the order of liturgical and sacramental life, of the work of the virtues or of contemplation, of the apostolate or of works of mercy, our activity has its determining object in eternal life, in God and the things of God, the service of the redemptive work of Christ in ourselves and in others. This is the plane of the Church itself.

On a second plane of activity, which is the temporal one, we act as citizens of an earthly city, engaging in the affairs of humanity's earthly life. Whether it be in the intellectual or moral order, scientific and artistic or social and political, our activity, while all the while, in so far as it is right, being turned towards God as its final end, has as its determining end a good which is not eternal life, but one which is generally concerned with the things of time, the work of civilisation or of culture. This is the plane of the world.

They are clearly distinct

These two planes are clearly distinct, as the things which are Caesar's and the things which are God's. It is obvious that the order of the redemption or of the spiritual of the things that are God's, should vivify to its most intimate depths the order of earthly civilisation or of the temporal, the things that are Caesar's: but these two orders remain distinct.

They are not separate

They are distinct, they are not separate. To make Christianity an abstraction, to put God and Christ on one side while I work in the things of this world, is to cut myself in two halves: one christian half for the things of eternal life— and for the things of time, a pagan or semi-christian, or ashamedly christian, or neutral half, i.e. something infinitely feeble or idolatrous of the nation, or the race, or the State, or of bourgeois prosperity, or of the anti-bourgeois revolution, or of science or of art made into final ends. Such a division of self is only too frequent in practice; it may even serve to characterise an epoch of civilisation of which the political philosophy of Machiavelli, the Protestant Reformation (considered in its cultural effects) and cartesian separatism illustrates the beginnings. When we take note of what it represents in reality, when we apply the light of the intelligence to the formula, we see that it represents a death-dealing absurdity.

What you do, says St. Paul, do it in the name and in the power of Christ. If we are regenerated by grace, if it makes a 'new man' out of each one of us, is it in order that we should make a bargain with the 'old man', who will serve Mammon with a secure conscience, fortified or exasperated by the consolations or deceptions dispensed by a civil society in itself detached from any connection with the law of the Gospels, while otherwise in the fulfilment of our religious duties we serve God in peace, consoled by the promises of the Gospel and the comforts of religion? In reality, the justice of the Gospel and the life of Christ within us want the whole of us, to take complete possession of us, to impregnate all we are and all we do, in the secular as well as in the spiritual order. Action is an epiphany of being. If grace takes hold of us and remakes us in the depth of our being, it is so that all our actions should feel its effects and be illuminated by it.

The temporal is subordinate to the spiritual plane

What does this mean? I am occupied on two different planes, by two different objects, by two different common goods, the one spiritual, the other temporal. They are different, but the one is subordinate to the other; the temporal as such needs to be vivified by the spiritual; the common good of civilisation requires of itself to be referred to the common good of life eternal, which is God himself. On the one plane as on the other my work will only be well done if I have in regard to the object in view the necessary competence and the needed instruments: but even where I act as a citizen of another city than the Church of Christ, the christian life and truth should permeate my activity from within, should be the living soul and direction of all the material whether of knowledge or means of realisation that I bring into play; whatever be the object of my work, be it, as in planting a vine or building a house, one which belongs in itself to a technique independent of the christian faith, be it, as are the things of the social and political sphere, one where, however large the part played by technical elements, the ethical order predominates, and hence one that intrinsically depends on the higher principles assigned by christian faith and the christian wisdom that comes from above.

A necessary distinction . . .

If I turn towards men to speak and act among them, it can then be said that, on the first or spiritual plane of activity, I come among them *as a Christian,* and in so far I engage Christ's Church; and that, on the second or temporal plane of activity, I do not act *as a Christian as such,* but I should act *as* a good Christian, engaging only myself, not the Church, but engaging my whole self, not amputated or inanimate,—engaging myself who am a Christian, who am in the world and work in the world without being of the world, who by my faith, my baptism. and my confirmation, tiny as I may be, have the vocation of infusing into the world, whereso-ever I be, a sap and savour of Christianity

. . . which allows us to judge more exactly the bearing of our actions

Let us have the patience to pause here a moment and turn our attention to the bearing of these two phrases: to act *as a Christian* and to act *as a Christian as such.* We shall obtain some enlightenment.

We shall understand the error of certain political apologists (of a *separated* pseudo-politics) who, trembling for nature, reason and patriotism, and even also for Holy Church, imagine that Christians who should want to act *as* Christians in the world will at one stroke precipitate the world into the blackest dangers of a catastrophic *supernaturalism,* and at the

[291]

same time encroach on the proper mission of the Church. These writers cannot distinguish between 'acting *as a* Christian' and 'acting *as a* Christian *as such*' and so committing the Church. And what does their logic come to if not to claiming that the Christian, when he acts on the temporal plane, should not act as a Christian? But what will he do if he does not act as a Christian? He will be a beast, a piece of human material utilised by the world's forces and interests.

And we shall also understand the wholly opposite error of certain unenlightened apologists of religion who are prepared to think that piety and the defence of religious interests cover the whole ground and that, to acquit all our duties towards the earthly city and the temporal order, it suffices for us to fulfil what is required in the spiritual order, falsely considered as *separate*. That is not true. Even religious who have quitted the world are called to open their hearts to all the misery and anguish of the world and to gather them into themselves to apply to them there the blood of Christ: so, in a way which is wholly spiritual, they still care for the things of time and act upon them. And for us, we who are still in the world, we must not only act *as* Christians and *as* Christians *as such*, as living members of Christ, on the spiritual plane; we must also act as Christians, as living members of Christ's Body, on the temporal one. Otherwise the weakness and abstention of christian energies in the things of time will result in the abandonment of the world into the hands of other energies who do not labour for its good.

The third plane of activity

But this analysis is not complete. There is, for a Christian, a third plane of activity which is, as it were, intermediate between the other two. Truly speaking this belongs to the same order as the spiritual one and implies a particular aspect or function of it: hence it is only distinguished from it by an 'accidental' distinction, which is concerned not with the essence of the activity expended, but with its application. This intermediate plane is that of the spiritual as inflected to the temporal one, the plane of the spiritual where it joins the temporal.

By the very fact that the spiritual order is at once in effect superior to the temporal order and in living relation with it, there is on the temporal plane:

(1) With regard to the temporal order itself, a zone of truths connected with the revealed truths of which the Church is the deposit, and which directs from above christian thought and temporal activity; thus the encyclicals of Leo XIII and of Pius XI have elaborated the principles of a christian political, social and economic *wisdom*, which does not descend to particular determinations of the concrete, but which is like a theological firmament for the doctrines and more particular activities engaged in the contingencies of the temporal sphere.

(2) With regard to the spiritual order, a zone of questions which in themselves (e.g. 'mixed questions', touching marriage, education, etc.) or in the circumstances of the case include a reference to that order: while affecting the earthly city, they also directly concern the good of souls and that of the Mystical Body; the Christian, as a member of that Body, has to consider them primarily and above all, not in reference to the temporal order and the good of the earthly city (which, moreover, suffers detriment if higher values are violated), but as they affect the supra-temporal good of the human person and the common good of the Church of Christ.

Here, then, is a plane of activity where the Christian's object is still eternal life and the order of divine things, either in seeking to safeguard the proper values of the spiritual in the temporal order, or as formulating from above the supreme rules on which the good of the temporal order itself depends. This is the plane of the *spiritual as adjoining the temporal*.

On this third plane the Christian acts as such and to this extent commits the Church

On this third plane as on the first the Christian acts and appears before men *as a* Christian *as such* and to this extent commits the Church. This is why the latter so insists on the independence which our action should keep with regard to the temporal activities belonging to the second plane, and in which we should ourselves participate (not *as* Christians *as such*, but *as* Christians).

It is on this third plane as on the first that the laity is called by *catholic action* to collaborate in the apostolate of the teaching Church. It is on this third plane that they exercise a catholic *civic* action (in the strict sense of the word), when they intervene in political affairs in the defence of religious interests and in the strict degree demanded by that defence, which is not at all the same thing as working towards a political aim directed to the achievement of a certain conception of the temporal common good. To rightly 'take part in politics' we must know how to discern political realities, and have a concrete idea of the means required for assuring the common good of the earthly city. To defend religious interests in the temporal order, it is sufficient to know how to discern these interests.

The place of catholic action

The whole work of catholic action is done on the first and on the third plane. If, by the teaching it dispenses and the spiritual formation it achieves, it *prepares* the laity for acting *as* Christians, for a participation in secular strife and a participation *as* Christians, for the assumption of those forms of social and political work to which they feel called and called *as* Christians, it guards itself with all the more care against in itself laying the shadow of a finger on the second plane. And it is not only because the Church will not, at any price, be enfeoffed to any one particular secular form. It is also because, in regard to the proper work of that second plane, with regard to work which must penetrate to the ultimate contingent realisations called for by the service of the secular common good, the competence of an activity whose order is wholly spiritual quickly finds its limits.

These precisions are doubtless dry enough. They are elementary and cannot be misunderstood without hurt. For this reason they had to be stressed at the outset. In what follows I shall try to show some important consequences to be drawn from them, notably with regard to the problem of a catholic press.

II

The three planes of activity of the Christian

As I have tried to show in the previous section, the activity of the Catholic is deployed on three several planes: the spiritual plane, the temporal plane, and the intermediate plane which joins the spiritual and the temporal. On the temporal plane, the Christian acts as a member of the terrestrial community, and he ought so to act as a good Catholic. On the spiritual plane (be it the purely spiritual plane or the plane on which the spiritual joins the temporal) he acts as a member of the Church of Christ and in the measure in which he appears before his fellows in his quality as Catholic, in that measure he commits the Church.

Two consequences follow immediately from these principles.

These three sorts of activity are all necessary

First consequence: These three forms of activity so placed and defined cannot be substituted one for another. They are all three necessary, each on its own plane.

I am well aware that they only apply to *each individual person* according to his circumstances. On the temporal plane in particular, on that of social and political activities, such properly political activity may for some reduce itself to voting on election day in conformity with their idea of the common secular good: for many a purely social or civic or educative activity will satisfy what they feel is required of them in the temporal order.

The fact remains that with regard to the catholic population of a country *collectively considered*, a complete temporal activity, one which is political as well as social and civic, of Catholics acting *as* Catholics, is normally requisite: from this point of view the lack of properly political formations, whose inspiration is authentically christian but specified by a certain conception of the common temporal good, makes itself to my mind everywhere to-day most cruelly felt.

Union on the plane of catholic action

Second consequence: On the third plane, on that of the junction of the spiritual and temporal ones, of catholic action and of civic action for the defence of the values of the city of God in the temporal sphere, *union* should evidently be the watchword. It is clear that this union can alone give Catholics sufficient force to establish among themselves a network of cultural works which would be the first beginnings of a virtual Christendom, and cause the civil legislature to respect religious interests,—it being well understood that this is a question purely of the incidence of the spiritual in the temporal sphere, and of authentic religious interests as these are determined *hic et nunc* by the Holy See and the Episcopate, and *not* by the particular judgement of no matter what person or no matter what party usurping the mission of speaking in the name of the Church, and sometimes thinking that they understand her interests better than she herself. It is impossible to conceal from oneself the fact that so long as the education of the catholic masses is not more advanced in this domain, so long as they have not learnt to distinguish better between what belongs to religion and what to the socio-temporal order, from the interests, prejudices and passions of the sociological order, the union of Catholics on the plane of the junction of the spiritual and the temporal spheres, however necessary it may be in itself, will raise the most difficult and delicate problems.

Diversity on the temporal plane

But on the second plane, on the temporal one, the rule is not union, but *diversity*. When the objective is the earthly life of men, when it concerns earthly interests and our temporal welfare, or such and such an ideal of the common temporal good and the ways and means of realising it, it is normal that a unanimity whose centre is of a supra-temporal order should be broken, and that Christians who communicate at the same altar should find themselves divided in the commonwealth. It would be contrary to the nature of things, and hence highly dangerous, to seek on this plane a union among Catholics which could *there* be only artificial, and obtained either by a political materialisation of religious energies (such as is too often seen in 'catholic parties' such as the German *Centrum*), or by a weakening of the Christian's social and political energies, and a sort of flight from general principles.

The problem of the catholic press

It is the business of a philosopher to insist in and out of season on those distinctions of species which practical life continually likes to confuse. But he is then being of service in the very order of practical life and of action. For not with impunity are such distinctions forgotten or misunderstood. Those I have just pointed out have become all the more necessary and exigent, need all the more to be rigorously respected, as the conditions of existence for Christians in the commonwealth have become more complex and differentiated. A particularly notable example is furnished by the problem of the catholic press.

It is a fact, and one not confined to France, that the existing catholic press excites many complaints, and that the very degree to which its existence seems indispensable is the measure of the scale of the difficulties confronting the fulfilment of its task. By a strange paradox we are witness to the insistence with which the highest authorities in the Church point out the importance of the work of the press, and on the other hand—at least in the order of culture and secular activities—the small degree of efficiency that, with the best will in the world and all the required professional capacities, it seems possible to realise in this domain.

Why is it so? Primarily, because the elementary laws which govern the truth of our action have been neglected, the type of action proper to the second plane (the purely temporal) and the type of action proper to the third plane (that of the junction of the spiritual and temporal planes) having been in practice almost constantly confused.

By the very fact that it gives itself out as *specifically catholic* and is addressed to Catholics as such, a professedly catholic periodical abides on the spiritual plane. By the very fact that it is a periodical, and that contact with actuality is indispensable to it, it necessarily runs the risk—if certain measures, at present only too much neglected, are not taken—of being drawn on to the temporal plane, and of giving voice to judgements on *temporal events as such*.

From this there spring two major difficulties, which often come together and between which we have a choice: (1) either Catholicism and the Church are implicated in political and social quarrels, so confounding religion with such and such a sociological projection of the latter, tying it up with the particular interests of a party or a class, claiming, for example, to rivet French Catholicism for the moment to one side in the Dreyfus case; (2) or, to avert in some degree this first defect, one will be led to abstain in some measure from engaging in the temporal sphere (in the strict meaning of the words), and strive to remain on purely spiritual ground, without explicitly renouncing the right of pronouncing on the temporal as such. And then, since temporal things, in order to be effectively brought to their end, require treating on their own proper ground, with the particular options and competence and means which this implies, one will inevitably be found to be in a weak position with regard to them; and since at the same time the reader is led to believe that he is being supplied with all the necessary means of judging and of directing his own conduct with regard to these things, he is likely, above all in times of crisis, to be led into serious and inevitable error and disappointment.

To speak as a Catholic having a certain temporal position and to speak in the name of Catholicism are two very different things

Hence let the equivocation contained in a formula like the following, not infrequently encountered, one be denounced: 'We wish to judge from a catholic standpoint all temporal, political or economic, national or international, artistic or scientific questions.' Such a formula, so as not to be illusory, must necessarily be taken in two differing ways: for there is a judgement *of Catholicism* on these questions, but this judgement only bears on certain principles seen from a very lofty angle, on which these questions depend, or, on certain spiritual values which they imply and will not tell me what attitude I should take up with regard to M. Flandin's wheat policy or the policy in foreign affairs of M. Laval. And there is a judgement of the *particular Catholic who is myself* on these questions which requires, if I am taking part in political action, that I make up my mind on the policies of M. Flandin and M. Laval. And this I should do *as* a Catholic, scrutinising my knowledge and my human passions which are engaged in these mundane affairs by the light and illumination of my catholic conscience; but it would be intolerable if in the so doing I claimed to speak in the name of Catholicism and implied that all Catholics as such should follow my road.

Let it be well understood that the need for such a distinction does not only lie in the fact that the Church will not be committed or bound up with temporal things. It is also because differentiations which belong to the nature of things are here in question, differentiations which precisely elucidate this standpoint of the Church. And finally it is because both the honesty and integrity of our action—spiritual action on its spiritual plane, temporal action on its temporal plane—suffer by a misreading of these differentiations.

Two essentially different types of periodical

What then? Must we needs fling out the baby with the bath-water and give up the very idea of a catholic press, or think that the only authentically admissible forms of it are the religious weeklies and the diocesan bulletins—and more, these in their official portions?

I do not think so, but I think it is urgent to take cognisance of the problem, and to resolve it by the distinction between two essentially different types of periodical, the one specifically catholic and religious, and as a result catholic *by denomination*; the other specifically political or 'cultural', which we must indubitably wish to be catholic, but catholic *in inspiration* only, not by denomination.

Specifically catholic periodicals

Periodicals of the first type belong to the field of catholic action. How should these be conceived? To my mind these should contain two clearly and explicitly distinct sections: one called *catholic action*, in which would be set forth, and would only be set forth, the common doctrine of the Church, not only in its speculative values, but also, and doubtless principally, its practical values, concerning the direction of human life and the incidence of the spiritual in the temporal: and one called *information*, in which would be brought forward, and only in which would be brought forward, questions of a properly temporal and cultural order—and how? In a way which would evade the difficulties pointed out above, and which, far from concealing, would show as fully as possible the diversity of standpoints natural to that order. In this section the reader should, by means of a review of the press, of inquiries, of correspondence, of an 'open forum', etc., be made aware of the whole span of the attitudes taken up by men to-day, and notably by Catholics, in the purely secular field, in political and social activities, national and international ones, as in those of aesthetics and literature, in painting or music, or the scientific activities of the hour.

To watch over the rigorous objectivity of this *information* section, to eliminate strictly everything with a more or less tendentious inspiration, and to keep it rigorously distinct from that of *catholic action*, will require—I am in no illusion on the point—a vigilance of a quality almost heroic. But a christian journalist is surely capable of it.

Nor let it be said that a paper of this type will find no readers! I am persuaded that there are numerous minds to-day who would, on the contrary, be glad to find a periodical able, on the one hand, to give them the doctrinal formation for which they feel the need, to explain and comment on the papal encyclicals and acts, to make known to them the great syntheses of christian political and social wisdom; and, on the other, to offer them exact and objective information on all the aspects of the temporal problems of our epoch, and so allow them to escape from an atmosphere poisoned with the lies for which party excitement is responsible.

Specifically 'temporal' periodicals catholic in inspiration

Periodicals of the second type belong to the temporal sphere as such, which implies that they have taken up concrete and determined standpoints on questions of this order, and that they have adopted not only a social and political philosophy, but a well-defined concrete political and social line—not only in function of religious interests and the good of the Church, but also in function of the temporal and earthly good of the commonwealth and of civilisation.

By this very fact it is obvious that they do not engage the Church—even if, as is to be desired, they draw their inspiration in the most courageous and intrepid manner from christian wisdom—and that they involve no other initiative than that of the particular persons or groups who have started them.

And doubtless, to the extent to which their inspiration is truly and integrally christian, they witness to the Gospel and serve in an effective way in the penetration of the world and men's lives by Christianity. But the proper aim they set before themselves is not the apostolate; it is the accomplishing of a temporal work, the service of a secular truth, the assuring of an earthly good.

The considerations set forth above make it clear that such temporal ends are normally diverse, indeed contrary. That Catholics should form different groups on the temporal plane, and even ones which are mutually opposed, is normal: what is demanded here is that they should keep among these diversities and oppositions those laws of truth, of loyalty, of justice and of charity to which they are bound to conform their actions, not only with regard to those who share their faith, but with regard to all men whatsoever.

[303]

We must choose one or the other formula

This second type of periodical, this press formally belonging to the temporal plane and christian by inspiration not denomination, appears to correspond to a vital necessity.

The first type of periodical, which corresponds to a formally and specifically religious press, a press of general or specialised catholic action, is no less necessary.

The one and the other type are already represented, both in France and abroad, by a great number of papers and reviews. It is the problem of their differentiation which I have here wished to put forward. To my mind it is highly important that this differentiation should be more and more clearly and explicitly marked. I am convinced that those Christians who wish to start and to direct periodicals should begin by choosing one or the other formula, and it would be very harmful to endeavour to fuse the two or produce some sort of hybrid: for essences claim to be respected.[1]

[1]Reprinted from *Sept*: 12th and 26th April, 1935.